Marketing Kit

FOR

DUMMIES®

2ND EDITION

Marketing Kit For Dummies, 2nd Edition

Cheat Sheet

Planning with the Five Ps

When in doubt about how to improve your sales and marketing performance, stop and think about whether you can take some action in one of the "P" areas:

- **Product:** Improve quality? Add new products or upgrades? Provide better service and support? Add a warrantee? Bundle products?

- **Price:** Cut costs? Reduce prices? Offer discounts for quantity? Offer discounts for loyalty? Offer discounts for timely purchases? Offer better terms? Guarantee a refund for dissatisfied customers?

- **Placement:** Increase the availability of your product(s) by adding more distributors, retailers, or salespeople? Expand your target market to new geographic areas? To new groups of customers? Sell product over the Internet?

- **Promotion:** Improve the quantity or quality of sales leads through direct-response ads, trade shows, a Web site or e-newsletter, direct mail, better brochures and letters, or a catalog? Polish your visual image by upgrading your business card, letterhead, Web brochure or other materials? Raise the stopping power of your ads or marketing materials? Write letters that create high involvement? Close more sales by diagnosing style issues behind tough customers? Use promotions more effectively?

- **People:** Improve service? Train sales or service people better? Replace the computer voice on your telephones with helpful people? Work on motivating employees or distributors?

Ways to Generate More Sales Leads

To get more people to ask about your offerings, make sure you have plenty of lead-generating communications out in the market at all times. Here are some of the best all-around options:

- Toll-free telephone numbers
- Directory listings
- Web site address (in all your materials and ads)
- Reader service cards (in trade magazines, along with your ad or insert)
- Fax numbers (on all your catalogs, brochures, and ads)
- Offers of free catalogs (through ads, brochures, directories, and Web site)
- Coupons
- Publicity (any media coverage tends to generate leads)

If you turn one in three leads into a sale, then all you need to do to get 50 more sales is generate 150 new leads. Not so hard when you look at it that way, is it?

Different Sales Closing Techniques to Try

If you're having trouble getting someone to sign on the dotted line, try using a different closing technique than your usual one. Here are some options:

- **Direct close:** Ask your prospect whether he's ready to place his order.

- **Trial close:** Ask him to make small decisions that may eventually add up to a completed order.

- **Wrap-up close:** Summarize your presentation and his needs to set the stage for order-taking.

- **Process close:** Take him to the next steps as if he were going to order (for example, write down specifics of what he needs).

- **Analytical close:** Examine the pros and cons of different options or otherwise analyze the prospect's decision, leading him to a logical purchase option.

- **Sales promotion close:** Offer a discount, time-sensitive extra, or other incentive to get him to make the purchase.

For Dummies: Bestselling Book Series for Beginners

Marketing Kit For Dummies, 2nd Edition

Cheat Sheet

Newsletter Do's and Don'ts

- Do lay out your newsletter with plenty of headers, subheads, boxes, figures, or illustrations.
- Don't invest in expensive four-color printing; desktop publishing, Web distribution, or photocopying are best unless you have a large, paid circulation.
- Do build and nurture your own in-house list of customers, leads, and referrals.
- Do understand the difference between an e-newsletter that annoys the recipient and a valuable e-newsletter people look forward to receiving.
- Do send your newsletter to a media list to generate publicity.
- Don't charge money for your newsletter unless you want to make it a serious product on its own rather than a publicity piece for your business.
- Do provide useful information, tips, and news about your industry in every issue.
- Don't go into your own products in too much detail, otherwise readers won't value the newsletter as an objective source of information.

Making Sure Your Business Card Brings You Business

- Print custom business cards for specific events (your local copy shop can do short runs for you on the cheap).
- Design a two-fold, triple-sized business card. Its face looks like a normal card, but when you open it up, you get a mini-catalog or brochure.
- Include customer quotes or testimonials on the back of your business card.
- Put a beautiful landscape photo on your card to make it appealing and memorable.
- Include a tagline emphasizing your benefits to customers or your mission statement.
- Use unusual, high-quality paper to give your card a unique feel in the hand.
- Always have a business card with you and don't be afraid to ask for referrals. People are usually more than happy to help.
- Update your logo and layout to make your card look more sophisticated than the competitors' cards.

Ways to Simplify Your Planning

- **Figure out what you do best and what your customers like most.** Let this strength form the foundation of your plan. Invest in making it even better, and in communicating it to customers and prospects.
- **Find out where new customers come from.** In your new plan, invest in these productive marketing activities and cut others.
- **Use a template!** There are templates and outlines you can use (see Chapter 2, the CD, or the supporting Web site for this book), so don't reinvent the wheel.
- **Write a paragraph for each line in your budget.** The text and spreadsheet parts of the plan should correspond closely.

Copyright © 2005 Wiley Publishing, Inc. All rights reserved.

Item 5999-0.

For more information about Wiley Publishing, call 1-800-762-2974.

For Dummies: Bestselling Book Series for Beginners

Marketing Kit
FOR
DUMMIES®
2ND EDITION

by Alexander Hiam

WILEY

Wiley Publishing, Inc.

Marketing Kit For Dummies®, 2nd Edition

Published by
Wiley Publishing, Inc.
111 River St.
Hoboken, NJ 07030-5774
www.wiley.com

For general information on our other products and services, please contact our Customer Care Department within the U.S. at 800-762-2974, outside the U.S. at 317-572-3993, or fax 317-572-4002.

For technical support, please visit www.wiley.com/techsupport.

Wiley also publishes its books in a variety of electronic formats. Some content that appears in print may not be available in electronic books.

Library of Congress Control Number: 2004113122

ISBN: 0-7645-5999-0

Manufactured in the United States of America

10 9 8 7 6 5 4

2B/RQ/RR/QU/IN

WILEY

About the Author

Alex Hiam is the best-selling author of *Marketing For Dummies* and *The Portable MBA in Marketing*, as well as numerous books on management and leadership. He is the founder of INSIGHTS for Training & Development, which provides management, customer service, and sales force training to client companies throughout the world. He also designs and publishes training materials and curricula used by the in-house training departments of many companies and government agencies. You can find descriptions of his firm's marketing and sales products and services at www.insightsformarketing.com.

Alex gives keynote addresses on topics ranging from marketing for breakthrough performance to effective leadership in business to how to negotiate with sharks. He received his AB from Harvard, his MBA from U.C. Berkeley, and was a full-time faculty member of the U Mass Amherst business school when his children were younger. Now he devotes his time to consulting, speaking, and running his own firm, where he often gets the chance to apply the principles of "streetwise" marketing himself as well as write about them for his many readers.

Alex's marketing-related consulting and training work includes leading product and branding brainstorm sessions, consulting on business and marketing planning, helping to motivate salespeople, and performing communications audits for clients. When not at work, Alex sails his ketch, the Blue Moon, throughout the waters off the East Coast of the United States.

Dedication

There are so many wonderful people in my life, it is hard not to overflow the dedication page with their names. But as I worked on this book, my mind kept returning to my Dad, who passed away about the same time we were negotiating the contract to do this second edition. A quiet leader and generous-hearted grandfather, friend, and philanthropist, he set an example for business and personal success that inspired his family and friends. He never boasted about his many accomplishments, so I won't here. Suffice it to say that his warm support and fine example are with us still.

Author's Acknowledgments

Thanks to my able staff and associates for all their contributions to this book and the Web site that supports it, especially to Stephanie Sousbies, Eric Riess, and Angela Pablo. (Check out Eric and Angela's great work at www. insightsformarketing.com — they did a bang-up job on the new Web site!)

Also thanks to Chrissy Guthrie, Project Editor for this book at Wiley, and to the able editorial and media staff working with her.

And a very special thanks to Celia Rocks, marketing maven extraordinaire, founder of the Rocks DeHarte agency, advisor and friend, who is the brains behind the publicity chapter in this book (those are her clients whose press releases are on the CD, by the way), and who served as technical editor on the new edition of this book and also *Marketing For Dummies,* 2nd Edition. Celia doesn't just talk or write about brilliant marketing, she does it and makes it look effortless in the process. Check out her brilliance marketing audit and related services if you need breakthrough results (click on the lighthouse at www.insightsformarketing.com for a quick link to her special brand of marketing magic).

Publisher's Acknowledgments

We're proud of this book; please send us your comments through our Dummies online registration form located at www.dummies.com/register/.

Some of the people who helped bring this book to market include the following:

Acquisitions, Editorial, and Media Development

Project Editor: Christina Guthrie

Acquisitions Editor: Stacy Kennedy

Copy Editor: Michelle Dzurny

Technical Editor: Celia Rocks

Permissions Editor: Laura Moss

Media Development Specialist: Kit Malone

Editorial Manager: Christine Meloy Beck

Media Development Manager: Laura VanWinkle

Editorial Assistants: Courtney Allen, Melissa Bennett, Nadine Bell

Cover Photos:

Cartoons: Rich Tennant, www.the5thwave.com

Composition

Project Coordinator: Maridee Ennis

Layout and Graphics: Jonelle Burns, Andrea Dahl, Lauren Goddard, Joyce Haughey, Jacque Roth, Heather Ryan

Proofreaders: John Greenough, Joe Niesen, Carl William Pierce, Brian H. Walls, TECHBOOKS Production Services

Indexer: TECHBOOKS Production Services

Publishing and Editorial for Consumer Dummies

    Diane Graves Steele, Vice President and Publisher, Consumer Dummies

    Joyce Pepple, Acquisitions Director, Consumer Dummies

    Kristin A. Cocks, Product Development Director, Consumer Dummies

    Michael Spring, Vice President and Publisher, Travel

    Brice Gosnell, Associate Publisher, Travel

    Kelly Regan, Editorial Director, Travel

Publishing for Technology Dummies

    Andy Cummings, Vice President and Publisher, Dummies Technology/General User

Composition Services

    Gerry Fahey, Vice President of Production Services

    Debbie Stailey, Director of Composition Services

Contents at a Glance

Table of Contents

Introduction

● ●

*E*veryone in business wants one thing: profitable sales! In this book, I share a host of techniques and tools to help you grow the quality and quantity of your sales. In fact, I designed this book to help you develop and implement a full-blown marketing plan, including advertising, personal selling, publicity, brochures, networking, and many more elements that add up to sales success.

What can you do today to boost sales, attract new customers, and retain old customers? Well, for starters, you can read this book and make a commitment to work on your marketing program! In *Marketing Kit For Dummies,* 2nd Edition, I provide information, resources, and tools for the active marketer, salesperson, or manager. Furthermore, you get the benefit of an accompanying CD-ROM that's chock-full of templates for making plans, sales projections, surveys, and coupon profitability analysis, to name just a few of the goodies I put on there for you.

About This Book

Marketing Kit For Dummies, 2nd Edition, covers a wide range of subjects and offers a lot of help to anyone in business, including:

- ✔ Insights on how to successfully close the sale through improved sales or marketing techniques

- ✔ Lots and lots and lots of tools you can use — right on your computer or in the pages of the book! — to perform useful sales and marketing activities with greater ease

- ✔ Plenty of ideas, examples, tips, and templates to make your sales and marketing materials look great — and function well, too

- ✔ Neat marketing software I created to help you do the chores of good marketing quickly *and* well

- ✔ A collection of advertising templates, brochure templates, and even templates for letterhead and business cards

- ✔ Marketing plans and audits — with templates and forms as well as instructions

- ✔ Plenty of hands-on tools and activities — many of which I borrowed from high-level corporate training events and workshops — to help you boost your own performance in sales and marketing

I wrote *Marketing Kit For Dummies,* 2nd Edition, for all of you who want to take responsibility for any aspect of sales or marketing in your organization — whether that organization is a small one-person operation or a large multinational corporation.

This book is certainly for the hundreds of thousands of readers of my earlier marketing books, many of whom have called, e-mailed, or written to share their interesting challenges and achievements in the past. You'll find exciting new resources in this book to take you farther than ever before. But this book is also for a new generation of marketers — from dot-com entrepreneurs to newly appointed marketing managers, from big-company executives to owners of family businesses, from front-line service and salespeople to managers of customer-oriented functions.

Marketing Kit For Dummies, 2nd Edition, focuses on helping readers communicate better with customers. Whether person-to-person, through a letter, the telephone, a brochure, a Web site, or any other medium, your customer communications play a vital role in the success of your business. I've cued up an immense amount of information, resources, and templates to help you improve your customer communications and your overall business image. Have a peek at the contents of the CD to see what I mean! (But be sure to use this valuable CD — just a peek won't do — using it correctly can make the difference between a profitable business and no business.)

Conventions Used in This Book

When reading this book, be aware of the following conventions:

- ✔ Web sites and e-mail addresses appear in `monofont` to help them stand out.
- ✔ Any information that's helpful or interesting but not essential appears in sidebars, which are the gray-shaded boxes sprinkled throughout the book.
- ✔ Whenever I introduce a new term, I *italicize* it.
- ✔ CD files are numbered, with the first two digits designating the chapter they support and the next two digits indicating the order in which I refer to them in the chapter.

What You're Not to Read

For those among you who just want to get down to business, you can safely skip the sidebars and still get all the info you need.

Foolish Assumptions

I hate to make assumptions about people I don't know, but, dear reader, I did have to assume a few things about you when writing this book. Hopefully at least one of these assumptions applies to you:

- ✔ You're a marketer, salesperson, or at least are interested in marketing.

- ✔ Your business isn't as successful as you'd like it to be, and you want to know how you can fix that.

- ✔ You know what you need to do to improve your marketing program, but you want someone to walk you through the necessary planning and actions.

- ✔ Or maybe you aren't sure what to do; you need to do some planning or develop a winning strategy.

How This Book Is Organized

Marketing Kit For Dummies, 2nd Edition, consists of 22 chapters and a CD-ROM that has examples, templates, forms, and software organized to support and extend each chapter's coverage. Here's how I organized all this great information.

Part I: Tools for Designing Great Marketing Programs

Things go better when you have a plan in mind. In marketing, this plan can be as simple as a back-of-the-envelope program using the Five Ps (product, pricing, placement, promotions, and people), which I cover in Chapter 1. Or it can be as complex as a detailed, systematic audit of all marketing activities, followed by a carefully written plan and a spreadsheet-based budget to go with it. I cover all these options in Part I, and I include the templates needed to take the sting out of designing a good program that boosts sales and profits.

Part II: Boosting Your Marketing Skills

Some important skills are involved in doing good marketing. For example, you need to do market research to find out what customers want and how to sell better than your competitors do. And communicating well is obviously important in marketing, so I cover writing in this part as well. I also include a topic close to my heart: how to solicit and use customer quotes and testimonials, because this strategy is one of the least-used but most powerful skills in all of marketing. The star of this section, however, is that secret ingredient that transforms ordinary marketing into the stuff of brilliant breakthroughs: creativity. I include a chapter that shares many of the techniques and tools from my firm's corporate creativity workshops to help you make sure you get that special leverage that only creativity can provide.

Part III: Advertising Management and Design

Ads are always an important element of any marketing program, and in this part, I share insights, how-to tips, and tools to help you design winning ads for your campaign. Advertising has many aspects, including planning and budgeting and also creativity and great writing, so I include something helpful in each of these areas for you.

Part IV: Power Alternatives to Advertising

You have so many ways to make an impact on business. Sometimes something as simple as a really well-designed business card is the secret to winning business and boosting sales. I cover this idea along with dozens of other alternatives to expensive advertising in this part, paying special attention to newsletters, publicity, catalogs, logos and letterhead, and other essentials of marketing success. Check out this part if you want to save money on expensive advertising or just to make sure that you're doing these essentials as well as you can.

Part V: Sales and Service Success

Sales and marketing: That's what people usually say, separating these two intertwined activities in an artificial way. I don't really know where selling stops and marketing begins. In every successful business I've seen, the two activities work hand in glove to signal new customers to the door, serve current customers, and thank past customers for their business in such a way that they feel good about coming back again. So this part on how to do great sales is an important complement to the other parts of the book. Use it to make sure you're finding and closing as many good leads as you possibly can. Or use it to diagnose or improve any sales process, because there's often room for improved performance. (By the way, I'm especially excited to share some of the popular techniques on customer service and dealing with difficult customers that my company offers clients through our sales-force training programs.)

Part VI: The Part of Tens

With this part's useful information on how to be a more creative marketer (creativity does drive marketing success, after all) and a collection of hot marketing ideas you can try, some readers may want to start here. Also, here you'll find ideas for saving money with your marketing and tips for boosting sales through good creative use of your Web site.

And don't overlook the appendix on how to use the CD or the CD itself. It's attached to the inside back cover of this book.

Icons Used in This Book

I occasionally use icons to flag certain passages. Here's what the icons mean:

This icon points out good ideas and shortcuts to make your life as a marketer easier.

Any information that's especially important and worth remembering gets this icon.

This icon points out mistakes and pitfalls to avoid. Whatever you do, don't skip these paragraphs!

This icon highlights a method or approach that has been used successfully in real life.

When you see this icon, you know that an accompanying example, form, or spreadsheet is available on the CD that comes with this book.

Where to Go from Here

The beauty of this book is that you can skip to any section or chapter as you desire. You can certainly read the book from cover to cover, but you don't have to. Start with whatever topic is most important to you, and don't forget to use the accompanying tools on the CD.

I encourage you to start using the ideas and tools from this book right away to improve your marketing and boost your sales. I also encourage you to tap into the supporting Web site, www.insightsformarketing.com, to take full advantage of all your resources as a reader of one of my books.

And if you want even more information and advice about marketing principles, check out my other book *Marketing For Dummies,* 2nd Edition (Wiley). You certainly don't *need* both books, but they do complement one another nicely, if I do say so myself.

Part I

Tools for Designing Great Marketing Programs

The 5th Wave   By Rich Tennant

"I opened with a big sale on 'CLOSED' signs, and no one came in. I decided to add some 'KEEP OUT' signs but still no one came in. But now I'm gonna invest in some 'BIO-HAZARD' signs—throw 'em in the window and see what happens."

In this part . . .

I equip you with ideas for improving your marketing and boosting your sales through my patented Five-Minute Marketing Plan (see Chapter 1) and a powerful marketing audit (see Chapter 2) that some of the most expensive marketing consultants use. You'll be amazed at how many activities fall under the marketing umbrella and how many you can use to attract and retain paying customers! I guarantee at least an "aha!" every few pages as you find out how to use these powerful marketing tools.

Need a marketing plan? Honestly, everybody does, but most people dread the challenge of creating one. Perhaps the best feature in this part is the template and instructions for preparing your own marketing plan in Chapter 3. I include a really cool set of templates: a Word file that you can customize for the text portion of your plan and Excel spreadsheet templates that you use for your sales projections and marketing budget. I must be out of my mind to give these away (my competitors charge hundreds of dollars for template software like this), so take advantage of it before I come to my senses!

Chapter 1

Boosting Your Business with Great Marketing

My goal in writing the second edition of this book is to help you develop and execute great marketing ideas and programs that boost sales and lead to business success. In this edition, I revamped the book so that you can use it as a planning tool when you need to do a marketing plan — with all new planning templates and spreadsheets to simplify this important task and keep it from getting too complex and time consuming. If you need to write a marketing plan, you'll find this book and its CD files are — not to be bashful about it — the best single aid you can get to make that job easier.

But you certainly don't have to write a plan to boost your business and achieve greater success through marketing. In this chapter, I help you zero in on some good actions and strategies that you can use right away or build into a larger plan of action. You'll find plenty of tactics to try out as you read this chapter.

Understanding the Benefits of Marketing

Why marketing? Why not just more accounting, financial management, or something else? Because marketing is essential to attracting customers and making sales, and that makes all the rest of the things a business does possible. Every hour you spend thinking about and working on marketing usually yields a bigger bottom-line return than the time you spend on other aspects of business.

Here are some great things marketing can do for you and your business:

✔ Increase customer loyalty and commitment, which benefits you by boosting profit margins, reducing customer turnover, and also generating positive word of mouth — which means those customers boast about you to others and bring you new customers

✔ Attract new customers by raising awareness and interest in your offerings among prospective customers who'd like you if they only knew enough about you to realize your offer is appealing to them.

✔ Help you expand your market to achieve sales levels that you deem necessary for financial or strategic reasons (because often a business has to achieve a certain scale to be profitable and stable in the long run).

✔ Fend off a rival whose marketing is aggressively targeting and stealing your customers

✔ Help you roll out a new product or service or bring an existing one to a new territory, as part of a growth plan for your business

✔ Solve a problem, such as poor sales for a product or service that you feel ought to be better received than it has been

These are the kinds of things marketing can and should be doing for you, no matter the type or size of your business. In *Marketing For Dummies,* 2nd Edition (Wiley), I cover hundreds of strategic and practical marketing methods to help readers accomplish fundamental business objectives, such as the ones in the preceding list. In this book, I still focus hard on these same vital marketing benefits, but I use a more hands-on approach that uses worksheets and templates from the CD so you can roll up your sleeves and do it! (The two books complement each other, but this one can also stand alone. So don't worry — you don't have to rush back to the bookstore!)

Where should you start your efforts? Marketing is a complex field, but at heart, it's very, very simple. Marketing comes down to you, your customer, and the relationship (or lack thereof) between you. I don't care if you never meet your customers face to face or if you spend days with them; marketing is still all about that relationship. You achieve all the objectives I listed previously (and more) by, first and always, making sure you're building that relationship so you have committed customers who care about you or your product or service.

Without a strong relationship and a committed customer, you're just peddling a commodity. You may as well be selling pork bellies because you won't have any more control over your pricing or customers than if you were offering any traded commodity on the open market. And when you lose control — when no customers are committed to you, your product, service, or brand name — then you've lost the marketing game before you've even gotten started. So, start working on this vital relationship with your customers right away!

The Heart of the Matter: Knowing What Your Business Needs

The heart of successful marketing — and of success in business in general — is customer commitment. Customers who really, really like what you're selling are going to buy it at a fair price rather than the competing options. Your committed customers will make your business a success. So marketing, at its heart, should always be building customer commitment, which is the means to any and all marketing ends. That's why I want you to do a simple, quick exercise to evaluate your level of customer commitment right now.

Evaluating customer commitment

How strong are you on each of the ten components of customer commitment listed here? Why don't you quickly rate yourself (or your company, product, service, or brand — whatever you're marketing right now) on each of these components by using a 1 to 10 scale? (Or, if you're near a computer, open the worksheet on your CD called CD0101 and use the more detailed questionnaire with automatic scoring that I've provided.)

How well would customers rate your product on

- ✔ Practical benefits (what your product does and how well it works)

- ✔ Quality (how your product compares to customer expectations and competitors)

- ✔ Uniqueness (how special your product is and whether it stands out from the competition)

- ✔ Customer loyalty (how dedicated customers are to your particular product or brand)

- ✔ Customer pride (whether customers feel good about the product and are proud to use it)

- ✔ Appealing personality (how likeable and appealing your product's image is)

- ✔ Emotional ties (whether customers feel emotionally bonded to and good about your product)

- ✔ Shared values (what values your product expresses or symbolizes that the customer also believes in)

- ✔ Perceived value (good price compared to similar alternatives)

- ✔ Active commitment (whether customers are willing to go out of the way to buy your product)

For example, if your customers generally feel that your product or service works exceptionally well and is highly functional, you can give yourself a 9 or 10 on the first item, practical benefits. If your product or service is seen as having exceptional quality (no flaws, errors, or breakdowns), you score high on the second category, quality. And so on, right down the list.

Do you have to be great on all ten of these dimensions? No. Sometimes customers are strongly committed to a product, service, or company because it has just one or a few exceptional points. For example, customers may feel sentimental about a brand they grew up with, and this factor makes them loyal to it no matter what. But you have to either be fairly high (average of 7.5 or more or total of 75 or higher) across the board or exceptional (9 or 10) on a few key dimensions. And I always prefer seeing at least one really strong dimension that helps you stand out and be noticed.

You have to have a strong profile on this customer-commitment rating in order to achieve any lasting or significant success in business. You can use this rating system as your ultimate yardstick to measure how you're doing and, more important, to tell you where your weaknesses and strengths may be.

And this customer-commitment indicator gives you the best way to focus and design your marketing programs. You want to use your customer-commitment profile to help you focus your message and the ways you deliver that message (plus everything else in marketing; see coverage of the Five Ps later in this chapter). Your goal is to strengthen this profile, either by improving upon weak scores, investing in high scores to make them even higher, or both. I help you dig into the hows and whys behind that profile in a minute.

Are you accurate in rating customer commitment? I don't know whether you, as the marketer, are the best person to rate your customer commitment. If you have the opportunity, consider asking customers or anyone else who's familiar with your business, service, or product to fill in the survey called CD0102 on your CD, which gives you a way to compare your self-scores with scores from the market. The survey is in a Word document, so you can print and copy (and if you want, edit it to customize to your company's name, product name, or brand). Collect as many ratings as you can, and then average the results to get your customer rating score. (Send out your surveys with a nice cover note by e-mail or mail it to your customer list; you can also ask people to fill them out face to face so you can hand it to them and hover over them until they hand it back. Filling out a survey takes them only a few minutes to do.)

When marketers compare their self-ratings with ratings from participants in a survey, they often find they've rated themselves about 10 percent higher. So an alternative is to adjust your self-rating scores down one point on each 1 to 10 scale, or 10 points on the overall 10 to 100 scale, to accommodate for this bias. Do this if you don't have the time or opportunity to do a customer survey right now.

Knowing your customers

To create a durable and profitable relationship with as many customers as possible, you need to understand your customers. I know that sounds obvious, but how much do you really know about your customers and would-be customers? And how much of what you think you know isn't true? Customers are harder to understand than most people think.

In mega-companies that have many millions to spend on marketing, the marketing director usually commissions an attribute analysis from time to time. An *attribute analysis* is a survey of lots of customers to find out what things they think are important when deciding whether to buy or whether they like what they bought. For instance, the attributes customers evaluate a mattress on are issues like comfort, firmness, and appearance. Attributes for a bookkeeping service may include accuracy, expertise, cost, and speed. Your customers care about certain attributes, too — but which are they, and which are most important to them? Keep reading to find out.

To explore your customers' perspectives, make a list of a dozen *attributes,* or specific factors they look at in deciding whether they like a product or service like yours. (You can use file CD0103 on your CD to make your list of attributes.) Take some time to brainstorm a good, long list. I ask for a dozen attributes to make sure you consider lots of options and explore customer thinking in detail. Then after you have your list, rate each attribute by how important it is to customers.

Some attributes matter more to your customer than others. For instance, some people care about firmness in a mattress above everything else; others care about softness; and still others care about length (because they're too tall for ordinary mattresses). Overall, however, most people care about comfort, so you'd rate that attribute very high, which suggests that you should focus your mattress marketing on comfort.

My goal in asking you to do this exercise is to make sure you know which attributes matter most to the customers you care about and want to do business with. Now hold these attributes in mind in all your future marketing efforts. You'll want to talk about these attributes when you communicate with your customers. And you'll be looking for ways to be even better on these key attributes of your product or service whenever you can. They're going to be important as you build stronger connections with customers and increase customer commitment to you and your offerings.

Knowing your product

Knowing what customers like is one thing, but succeeding in the market is quite another. It just isn't as simple as running an ad that says your product is less expensive, faster, nicer, more reliable, and anything and everything else any customer may want. You have to be clearly different and better — at least in one or a few key areas. And that can be a challenge. But I know something that, perhaps, you don't: You or your product has certain qualities and strengths that have helped you achieve some success in business already, and you can amplify and communicate those strengths through your marketing to achieve considerably more success. I want to make sure you're fully aware of your product's strongest qualities and are ready to leverage them in every aspect of your marketing.

To explore your greatest strengths and find out what will give your marketing the greatest power to pull customers to you, take another minute to make a list of your strengths and any special qualities you may have (apply this exercise to your business, product, service, brand, or whatever specifically it is that you're marketing). You can use Form CD0104 from the CD to help you do this exercise. After you've made a good long list of strengths, rate yourself on each one to help you figure out which ones are strongest and make you (and your offering to customers) stand out as special and unique. And if any of your strongest qualities overlap with high-priority attributes that customers want, then you should emphasize those desirable qualities above the others.

Celia Rocks, the author of *Brilliance Marketing Management* (Facts on Demand Press) and a long-time associate of mine who performed the technical review of this book, champions the view that you're going to succeed in marketing (and in business and life in general) on the strength of your best qualities and your special brilliance, not by just trying to match competitors or being as good as the average. The exercise in which you explore your strongest qualities is based on this notion that great marketing needs to be in touch with your special brilliance.

The word "brilliance" suggests light, and as a marketer, you want to think of your marketing as a lighthouse casting its beam far out into the darkness to guide ships into its safe harbor. When you're clear about what makes your product special and appealing to customers, you can focus your marketing light on this one or these few best qualities and project them far into the murk of the competitive market. (Because this is marketing, we're going to work frequently with imagery and metaphor. I think they're the best ways to express ideas powerfully and memorably. I bet you're going to remember the image of a lighthouse and the idea that your marketing should be that powerful, right? Good! And by the end of this book, if not sooner, you'll have some equally powerful messages and metaphors to offer to your customers.)

If you aren't yet completely clear on what your strongest quality is, take a look at your lists of your own strengths and your customers' priorities side by side. In doing so, you'll find overlap in your lists. Find the best match possible (given what assets you have to work with) between your strengths on the one hand and the customers' priorities on the other, and then work with those as best you can in your marketing efforts in the future.

For example, if you're in the mattress business and your factory can make extra long and oversized mattresses, and you know most people rate comfort as their top priority for mattresses, then your brilliant strategy may be to offer comfort to people who have special needs like an extra long or wide mattress.

Another common example is a business service firm of some kind (consulting, for example) that's strong on service as well as friendly and supportive to its customers. If its customers value good service, obviously the firm needs to build a marketing program (and perhaps an entire business plan) around customer service. That strategy sounds obvious, but I too often see a company that ought to compete on service getting distracted by discounts, high-tech product upgrades, expensive brand advertising, and other things that sap their resources and take attention away from focusing on their service excellence.

Focus! Focus on what makes your product special and on what your customers consider important. When you do, you're building the elements of customer commitment and strengthening your bonds with your customers — not to mention making your marketing a success. Otherwise, your marketing is just a lot of heat and noise and very little light — which is what most marketing programs are like, to be honest.

Designing Your Marketing Program

A *marketing program* is a coordinated, thoughtfully designed set of activities that help you achieve your marketing objectives. Your *marketing objectives* are strategic sales goals that fit your strengths and are a good way to stretch your business in its current situation (see Chapter 3 for how to create marketing objectives that are anchored in practical strategies). In order to build strong customer relationships and maximize your sales, you need to put every possible marketing tool to work for you. Marketing is a broad field, encompassing elements as diverse as advertising, brand and logo design, sales calls, Web sites, brochures, packaging, shows, conferences and other events, and so on. The more tools, the better. But the variety and complexity of choices makes getting organized and focused hard. In this section, I share a basic method for organizing your marketing, deciding what to do, and documenting and budgeting your program.

The *Five Ps* stand for the five broad areas (product, price, placement, promotion, and people) you can look to find ways to boost sales or accomplish other marketing goals as you build customer commitment to your brilliant products, services, or brands. The following sections cover the Five Ps in detail.

Product

To marketers, *product* is what you sell, whether it's a physical product or a service, idea, or even another person (like in politics) or yourself (like when you search for a new job). When you think about ways of changing your product offering to boost sales, you can look at anything from new or upgraded products to different packaging to added extras like services or warranties. And you can also think about ways to improve the quality of your product. After all, people want the best quality they can get, so any improvements in quality usually translate into gains in sales as well.

Price

To marketers, *price* is not only the list price or sticker price of a product, but it's also any adjustments to that price, such as discounts and any price-oriented inducements to buy, including coupons, frequency rewards, quantity discounts, and free samples. Any such offers adjust the price the customer pays, with the goal of boosting sales. Price-based inducements to buy are generally termed *sales promotions* by marketers, just to confuse the issue hopelessly. As I delve further into this subject, you'll also find out how pricing your product too high or too low can be bad marketing.

Placement

Placement is where and when you present your product to customers. You have many options as to how you place the product in both time and space. Whether you're dealing with retail stores, catalogs, sales calls, Web pages, or 24-hour-a-day telephone services that can process customer orders, you're dealing with that placement P.

If you want a feel as to how valuable this P is to the marketing mix, just think about how valuable shelf placement at your local grocery store is to, say, Coke or Pepsi. Imagine what that placement is worth to the marketing of those products! Oh, by the way, marketers stretch a point by calling this third P "placement" because it's more conventional to call it "distribution." But that starts with a *d,* so it doesn't sound as good. However, just remember that when people talk about distribution, they're talking about placement, and vice versa.

You'll hear one more term that relates to placement: logistics. *Logistics* is the physical distribution of products — shipping and taking inventory, and all the fancy transportation and information technologies that can be harnessed to improve the efficiency and effectiveness of your distribution processes. So logistics is another useful path to go down when you want to think about where products should be placed for easy purchase.

Distribution concerns where and when products are offered for sale, whereas logistics addresses how they get there. These are related concerns, of course, and so they both fall under the list of options when you want to think hard about placement. You can play around with either or both in your efforts to build stronger customer commitment. For example, if you add distributors and enhance your Web site to offer online ordering, you're boosting placement by enhancing both distribution and logistics to create more ways to get the product to customers.

Promotion

Promotion is all the sales activities, advertising, publicity, special events, displays, signs, Web pages, and other communications designed to inform and persuade people about your product. (Remember, please, that "product" simply means whatever you have to sell, be it an actual product, service, idea, or candidate.) I like to think of promotion as the face of marketing because it's the part that reaches out to ask customers for their business. It ought to be a visible and friendly face because you can't just tell people what to do and expect them to obey. Instead, promotion must find ways to attract prospective customers' attention long enough to communicate something appealing about the product.

The goal of all promotions is to stimulate people to want to buy. Promotions need to be motivational. They also need to move people closer to purchase.

Sometimes a promotion's goal is to move people all the way to purchase. That's what a so-called direct-response ad is supposed to do. *A direct-response ad* invites people to call, e-mail, fax, or mail in their orders right away. Many catalogs use this strategy. Readers are supposed to select some items, fill in their order forms, and mail them in with their credit card numbers, for example.

Other promotions do less. For instance, a 30-second television spot may be designed only to make people remember and like a brand so that they'll be a little more likely to buy it the next time they're in a store where it's sold. But all promotions work toward that ultimate sale in some way, and when you think about all the creative options for communicating with prospective customers, you should always be clear about what part of the customer's movement toward purchase your promotion is supposed to accomplish.

People

In most businesses, people are responsible for many aspects of product or service quality. Help them work better, and you improve the product. In fact, the personal connection between your people and your customers and clients may do the most for *referral marketing* — a powerful marketing force where your customers serve as a sort of "mini" sales force for you. They refer others to you because they've had a positive relationship with your people. In many businesses, people are directly responsible for the customer contacts through personal sales and service.

And in all businesses, people are responsible for performing the many behind-the-scenes tasks and jobs that make offering products to customers possible. Businesses and other organizations are simply groups of people. Sure, sometimes they use lots of fancy machinery or computer equipment, but no organizations exist without people. Not a one. And so when you're looking for ways to improve your offerings or otherwise boost your sales, turning your attention to your own people is often profitable.

There are many and, often surprising, connections between how employees feel and how customers feel. For example, I often work with companies where the salespeople or service people say that they're frustrated because they have to deal with angry, uninformed, or otherwise difficult customers. If the employees feel this way about the customers; then of course they tend to be negative (impatient, curt) with customers, which makes the customers even more difficult. In my training and consulting work, I explore a variety of interesting techniques based on building the motivation of salespeople and other employees, improving communications with customers, and handling service problems and customer frustrations (see Chapters 15 and 18 in this book for some of the most important ways of improving customer service).

The people side of marketing is certainly the least visible — that's why people aren't traditionally included in the list of marketing Ps. But adding people to the list offers you another powerful lever for achieving your sales and marketing goals. In this book, I include a bunch of people-oriented tools along with the many tools that help you apply your marketing imagination to successful experiments in the areas of product, pricing, placement, and promotions.

Profiting from the Five Ps

I should tell you that the "Four Ps" is the first thing taught to students in a formal marketing class. It's just like my list, except it leaves out the people (a big mistake in real-world marketing, if not at business schools). To profit from the Five Ps, use the list as a mental tool to think about these five broad ways of growing your business and boosting your sales. The Five Ps are just a starting point — the street signs at an intersection — and to benefit from them, you have to explore the paths they mark.

One way you can profit from the Five Ps is to systematically look for weaknesses and strengths in each of the five areas: your product, pricing, placement, promotions, and personal connections with customers. Notable weaknesses can hurt you by reducing customer commitment, so you may want to work on eliminating them. Notable strengths in any areas can be the basis of strong customer commitment, so you want to invest in your strengths to make them even stronger and let the market know about them. You can do a very detailed and careful analysis by using CD0105, a form for analyzing customer commitment that lists many of the most important contributors to marketing success. Rate yourself as you think customers would or photocopy it and hand it out to customers and others who have knowledge of your market; then combine their results and apply them to your marketing.

Form CD0105 divides each list into facts and feelings because customer commitment can arise for both rational and emotional reasons. Look for strong scores in any of the Ps and work with them in your marketing, whether they're more fact- or more feelings-based. What the basis is for customer commitment doesn't really matter, as long as there is one. Build on the strongest scores in each of the Five Ps. For instance, if you market a restaurant, you may find that you score high on some of the product feelings like "nostalgic, traditional" and "attractive; aesthetically appealing." These scores mean that customers have a strong emotional bond with the restaurant, and their feedback indicates that you should emphasize traditions and long-term relationships when you design your ads. The feedback also tells you to avoid doing things that can weaken this source of commitment, like redecorating to make the restaurant trendy.

By the way, when you use a worksheet such as the detailed customer-commitment worksheet in CD0105, remember that I designed it for a wide range of marketers. You may want to take the analysis a step further for your own business by making the worksheet more specific. For example, if you market a restaurant that's loved for its traditional, friendly atmosphere, you may want to do some research to come up with a menu of traditional, comfort-food-oriented dishes because they'll help strengthen the nostalgic appeal behind your customer commitment. But the implications of nostalgic appeal would be very different for a greeting-card company and still different for a radio station. The tactical elements of marketing vary much more than the basic strategies.

Another good way to profit from your knowledge of the Five Ps is to do some creative thinking about each of the Five Ps every day. Stop and ask yourself these five simple, powerful questions and see whether you can find ways to build your sales by doing something new and creative in at least one of these vital marketing areas:

- ✔ What can you do to make your product more appealing?
- ✔ What can you do to make your product more accessible?
- ✔ What can you do to make your prices more appealing?
- ✔ What can you do to make your promotions more visible and persuasive?
- ✔ What can you do make your human interactions with customers more friendly and helpful?

Notice that these questions are open ended. They don't have right answers. Instead, they invite exploration and experimentation. They're the kind of questions you can even ask your employees — and offer incentives for new ideas. These questions tease the imagination. That's because a considerable amount of imagination is necessary to grow any business or boost the sales of any product. You won't find any pat formulas that are guaranteed to work.

Marketing isn't like chemistry or algebra or bookkeeping: Marketing has no right answers — only the answers you invent, test, and develop. After much thinking and trying, you develop new and better formulas for yourself and your business; formulas that'll give you pretty good results, at least for a time, and then you'll have to update or replace them in order to keep sales flowing and growing.

Exercising Your Marketing Imagination

What's marketing imagination? It's the one term I wish everyone would associate with marketing if they remembered only one thing, because it's a great deal more important than the Five Ps. In fact, it's the most important factor in marketing. *Marketing imagination* is creative questioning about everything and anything that may help boost sales and make for more satisfied customers. And marketing imagination is what drives growth and development in your business.

Look at any successful business and you find that it's done innovative things and tried many new ideas. Business leaders are imaginative and willing, even eager, to try out new ideas and approaches. They have active marketing imaginations. And good marketing is creative marketing. Having marketing imagination is always seeking new and better ways, always looking to perfect all five Ps.

Oddly, creativity is often left out of books and courses on marketing. People tend to think of advertising as creative, but they overlook the importance of creativity in the aspects of marketing. Yet a creative approach to your basic marketing strategy can also be very powerful. Think about the success of Ebay.com, the first company to offer virtual auctions that you can participate in from any computer in the world. I guarantee that you can innovate in your distribution and logistics in order to win more sales through placement, if you're willing to be open-minded and inquisitive about your options (for more on marketing strategies, see Chapter 3, and for more on using the Web in your marketing, see Chapter 21).

Similarly, plenty of examples of creativity exist in pricing and product offerings. How many times does a business succeed by offering a new or different product selection? Here's a simple example from the town where my offices are located. Quite a few gyms in the area compete for customers, and one of them recently made two simple changes:

- ✔ **Product innovation:** They introduced a new class on kickboxing — something that hadn't been offered locally before — featuring a high-energy workout that appeals to people who are looking for something new and exciting to do.

- ✔ **Pricing:** They advertised a first-class-free policy for the new kickboxing class because they felt that people would really like it if they just tried it. The price promotion worked. It attracted a whole bunch of curious people, many who liked the free course so much that they signed up for ten more courses at full price. And some of them went on to become full members of the athletic club, using the weight machines and other services, too.

This example illustrates two important points about the exercise of marketing imagination. The first point is that you don't have to come up with something dramatically new. Sure, a patentable new invention might be a great product innovation. But in general, you can make plenty of progress simply by coming up with many small ideas. We're not talking rocket science here. Anyone in business has enough intelligence, imagination, and funding to be a great marketer. And the second point is that you have to go out and try your ideas; try them in simple, easy ways that don't expose you to excessive risks of failure.

Great marketing arises from frequent cycles of thinking (or intuiting) and trying. You have an insight or idea. You think of ways to try it out. You test it in the real world and see what happens. You learn from how customers respond. Their responses fuel more imagining and planning, which then leads to more testing and trying. And so the process goes on in an endless loop driven by your marketing imagination but firmly rooted in the real world of customer opinion and action.

Breaking the rules in car sales

What can you do to increase the number of shoppers visiting a car dealership? This simple marketing question gets a lot of attention every day because so many dealerships are competing for business. In the United States, the usual answer involves local television commercials featuring attractive shots of the latest car models. Sometimes human models are added to the scene. An attractive woman may smile or wink from the driver's seat of a sports car. Or perhaps the owner of the dealership (usually a balding fast-talker) stands stiffly on his car lot and delivers some wooden lines to the camera. Sounds like an opportunity for marketing imagination.

C&S Motor Cars (now Lia Nissan Pontiac), a Connecticut-based marketer of new Pontiac and Nissan automobiles and used vehicles of all makes, wanted to try something different. Those at its helm wanted to get away from the slick salesman image that characterizes so many companies in their industry. They wanted to emphasize customer relationships. And they wanted to be seen as friendly and helpful, not pushy and sneaky. But how?

First, they decided not to hire experienced automobile salespeople. They decided to hire nice people from other professions (like teaching) instead — people who are polite, friendly, and good listeners. People who naturally want to help customers find what they're looking for. People who don't have a preconceived notion of how a car sales transaction should work.

So they hired a woman who'd raised four children and another woman who'd worked in ski resorts. You get the idea. Not the sort of people who have "super salesperson" written all over them. In fact, they hired the sort of people you'd feel comfortable dropping by to chat with.

And then they hired a regional ad agency, Darby O'Brien, to help them communicate their unique point of difference to prospective customers.

Their goal was to come up with an inexpensive ad campaign that would quickly let the community know that a new, friendlier, more helpful option was in town when it came time to shop for cars.

Now, this is a dream assignment for a good creative agency, because the dealership really had a point of difference to talk about. The client didn't leave the creativity entirely to the advertising stage. C&S Motor Cars had already done some imagineering of its own. All it needed was a great ad or two — and maybe a fly swatter, although they didn't know they needed that until Darby O'Brien had done some imagineering of its own. Here's what they came up with: an ad featuring a stereotypical car salesman along with "other pests," such as a mosquito, tick, and fly. The headline was definitely designed to get a laugh — but also to make the key point clearly and memorably.

Then the small print of the ad (the *body copy,* as it's called in marketing) told the story of what made this dealership different — a less-pressured environment where it's comfortable to shop, along with good selection and service. As the tag line at the end summed it up, "Same cars. Different people."

Oh, and then there was that fly swatter. They bought a bunch of them and had a local screen printer put the company's name and tag line on the handles. And in their print ad, the company promised to give anyone who stopped by the dealership a fly swatter, so "If you do want to shop around someplace else, you'll be able to defend yourself." Point made. And they made a good case for the power of marketing imagination, too.

By the way, did I mention that this campaign was not only inexpensive — ads ran just a few times in local newspapers — but also highly effective? The dealership's store traffic increased dramatically as a result, boosting sales significantly and making a lot of customers and marketers very happy.

So what you want to remember about marketing imagination is that it's not only creative but it's also experimental. Great marketers wear two hats — the hat of the artist and the hat of the scientist. A great marketer may have an "Ah ha!" experience in the shower one morning and show up at work thinking, "Wouldn't it be cool to do such and such?" By lunchtime, she's changed hats and is carefully reviewing her options for trying the idea out. By the time she goes home, she's already said to herself, "I think I've figured out how to safely test my cool new idea."

The Five-Minute Marketing Plan

Here's a simple five-minute marketing plan you can prepare once a week to help you apply your marketing imagination and boost your sales. Or you can use it as the starting point for a longer, more careful annual planning process (see Chapter 3 for how to do that).

To use this plan, ask yourself each of the questions and jot down quick answers to each. Then revisit your answers at least once a week to make sure you're pursuing any ideas they brought up.

And yes, I really want you to time yourself and give each of the five sections just one minute. Because each section has two questions, you can spend only 30 seconds on each question, including both thinking and writing time. So this exercise requires almost instantaneous responses. You'll have to scribble frantically to complete it in five minutes. And I want you to. As you'll see when you try it, attacking these questions at very high speed loosens up the marketing imagination. Fresh ideas may pop up or you may find yourself bringing a long-standing assumption into question for the first time. So limber up that wrist, clear your head, take a deep breath of fresh air, and then glance at the clock and get started!

Come up with any useful ideas? Have a look at what you wrote and see whether any of the ideas are worth pursuing. In the majority of cases, people come up with at least one good idea in the five minutes it takes to do this creative planning exercise.

And one good idea can be worth a lot of sales some day. That's the nice thing about using your marketing imagination.

You'll find a template for Five-Minute Marketing Plans on the CD (filename CD0106) so you can do this exercise regularly. Here is the heart of it, the questions you need to ask yourself:

1. **First Minute: Product**

   What can you do right now to improve the quality of your product(s)/service(s) in the eyes of your customers?

What additional product or service would your customers most like your company to offer?

2. **Second Minute: Price**

   What can you do right away to cut costs without hurting your quality?

   What offers can your company afford to make to encourage new customers to try your product/service or encourage current customers to be more loyal?

3. **Third Minute: Placement**

   What can your company do right now to make your current distribution process work more efficiently or effectively for your customers?

   What new approach can you try to reach different customers or reach current customers in a different way?

4. **Fourth Minute: Promotion**

   What can you do right now to make your customer communications clearer and more compelling?

   What new ways of communicating with customers can you try right away?

5. **Fifth Minute: People**

   What can your company do to increase its motivation and enthusiasm?

   What can you do to make your customers feel more enthusiastic and thankful toward your company?

Stop! Your time is up. Good job!

On the CD

Check out the following items on the CD-ROM:

- ✔ Customer Commitment Worksheet (CD0101)
- ✔ Customer Survey (CD0102)
- ✔ Know Your Customer Worksheet (CD0103)
- ✔ Know Yourself Worksheet (CD0104)
- ✔ Detailed Customer Commitment Worksheet (CD0105)
- ✔ Five-Minute Marketing Plan (CD0106)

Chapter 2

Auditing Your Marketing to Achieve Your Business Goals

In This Chapter

▶ Evaluating the effectiveness of your marketing process

▶ Identifying priorities for marketing improvements

▶ Developing agenda items and putting them into action

A marketing audit often identifies problems that are holding you back, and an audit is a great way to quickly find and work on weak areas in your marketing process. A marketing audit can also form the basis of your marketing plan (see Chapter 3). How? Well, if you take the audit, which you'll find on the CD, and then make a list of the items that you scored a "no" on, this information can become a starting agenda for what to do in your next plan to improve your marketing performance and results.

In this chapter, I discuss the various elements of the marketing audit and show you how to use the results of this audit to analyze and improve your marketing approach.

Keep in mind that this audit is a serious tool. You may be surprised at how many details it asks for. Many people's first reaction is something like, "I had no idea marketing could involve all of that!" Well, it can. Marketing's a big topic, but this audit gives you a relatively simple and quick way to wade right into the depths of it and begin identifying opportunities for improving what you do.

Performing a Marketing Audit

A *marketing audit* is a systematic examination of every aspect of sales, marketing, customer service, and all other operations that affect sales and marketing. It provides you with the quickest, easiest way to take a hard, strategic look at your entire marketing process. The audit often reveals the hidden weak spots so you can focus on strengthening them. I like to think of audits as revealing the weak links in the marketing chain.

You can perform a simple audit yourself in a relatively short period of time with the audit form I include on the CD. Many consultants have found this audit form so useful that they've turned it into a service for their clients (they licensed it from the first edition of this book), so I'm pretty sure it'll do you some good, if you work through it carefully.

The marketing audit on your CD (filename CD0201) is a simple Word document that you can edit to include more or different items, if you want. Or you can simply print it out as is and use it like a questionnaire to evaluate your organization. I divided the audit form into nine areas, each with a list of a dozen or more specific questions. The questions have yes/no answers, which makes the audit quick and easy to complete. When you complete it, simply count the number of "yes" answers in each section and enter them into Table 2-1. This table also appears on the CD (filename CD0202). (Don't bother counting the "no" answers — that result is the inverse of the number of "yes" answers and doesn't tell you anything new!)

Table 2-1	Marketing Audit Worksheet	
Activity Area	*Formula*	*Profile Score*
A. Marketing focus	# of yeses_____ ÷ 12 =	_____ %
B. Marketing scope	# of yeses_____ ÷ 10 =	_____ %
C. Customer acquisition activities	# of yeses_____ ÷ 17 =	_____ %
D. Information-gathering activities	# of yeses_____ ÷ 16 =	_____ %
E. Marketing planning activities	# of yeses_____ ÷ 18 =	_____ %
F. Communications activities	# of yeses_____ ÷ 37 =	_____ %
G. Customer service activities	# of yeses_____ ÷ 15 =	_____ %
H. Management and control	# of yeses_____ ÷ 12 =	_____ %
I. Creativity	# of yeses_____ ÷ 13 =	_____ %
Overall Score Calculation	Total # of yeses_____ ÷ 150 =	_____ %

Audits reveal strengths, too

Don't ignore your strengths while you're working on your weaknesses. If you score relatively high on one or two of the sections of the marketing audit, these activity areas are probably the ones that are working the best for you right now. Activities in these areas no doubt contribute disproportionately to any successes you now have, which means you'd better take good care of them! Don't divert resources from areas of strength to areas of weakness, unless you're sure that you'll get improvements in efficiency and effectiveness as a result. Sometimes strengthening your best area first makes the most sense because you can generate more surplus profits before you try to do too much to improve a weak area.

Precisely how you should invest in improving your marketing is a complex strategic decision, and no audit — and certainly no book — can give you an absolute answer. Spend some time with the results from your marketing audit and with any other inputs you can gather, thinking about your options and weighing different possibilities. And then proceed with caution — a step at a time, testing as you go to see what kind of results you get. Great marketing is the result of creative learning, not the output of any formulaic audit or plan. So when the dust settles, this audit should simply help you initiate a thoughtful, creative, and intelligent learning process. In other words, don't forget to think.

As you can see, Table 2-1 guides you through the process of calculating your audit scores, which are represented as percentages for each of the nine sections of the audit. Obviously, a 100 percent score is the best. Any score less than 85 percent for a section indicates a weakness in that area that probably deserves close attention.

After you convert all your section scores into percents, you can easily compare them and see which areas are lacking and deserve more immediate attention. Working on the one or two areas where your scores are lowest is a good idea because it gives you a helpful focus in your future sales and marketing efforts.

You may find giving copies of the audit form to multiple people — such as the senior managers, a couple of especially good customers, some of the salespeople or service employees — helpful. Capture multiple perspectives, and then average the results to get a more accurate picture of your marketing program. Customers often rank firms lower on marketing audit items than employees of the firm do. Why? Because customers may not be aware of initiatives or programs that are supposed to reach them but don't. So when in doubt, as always, ask the customer — and trust his judgment above your own. When you're trying to make a sale, only the customer's opinion counts!

Examining the Parts of the Audit

I assume that you've taken the marketing audit and are now ready to analyze your results in each of the nine areas.

Evaluating your marketing focus

Part A of the marketing audit helps you evaluate your *focus,* which means how clearly and how well your marketing takes aim based on your strengths and opportunities. One of the questions is: Do you have specific growth goals to motivate and focus your marketing efforts? Another is: Do you have a clear strategy to help you achieve those growth goals? These questions are just about the most important questions you can ask, and they need to have good, clear answers before you worry about any of the hundreds of details of your marketing program. Don't take action until you have a clear strategic focus to give your actions purpose and direction. You want your marketing program to be a wolf leaping forward, not a hundred scared rabbits hopping in all directions at once.

Your answers in Part A of the audit give you a good idea of how clearly and how well you focus your marketing and whether or not you need to do more thinking and focus your marketing more. If you had a difficult time answering any questions with a "yes," take some time to work on the basics of getting focused.

Although 85 percent is a minimum score for the audit, you really want to get as close to 100 percent as possible on the focus section. Consider going back to the exercises and customer commitment worksheets from Chapter 1 to explore your strengths and weaknesses and to see how you can best build greater customer commitment in general and, more specifically, in each of the Five Ps (product, price, placement, promotion, and people).

Evaluating your marketing scope

I think of the *scope* of marketing as how broadly and aggressively you pursue customers and try to make sales. To win the great game of marketing, you have to first show up. Auditing your scope helps you figure out whether you're showing up and pursuing sales in the markets and with the customers who matter to your success and on a large enough scale to achieve your goals and realize your potential.

Don't even think of skipping this section of the marketing audit. Saying that your marketing has to have enough scope to achieve the impact you want may sound simplistic or obvious, but in almost every company I visit that's having problems with sales or marketing, I can trace at least some of the problems to the issue of scope. Thinking big isn't enough — you have to act big, too.

For example, many companies provide just one or a few products or services to their customers when offering a broader range would be easy — and helpful to the customers. Don't limit your potential by offering just one product or service or in any of the other ways covered in Part B of the marketing audit. So take a look at the questions in this section of CD0201 and, if you answer "no" more than once or twice, rethink the way you're approaching marketing. Ask yourself what you can do to think bigger and expand the scope of your marketing efforts. Maybe the solution is as simple as advertising to a larger geographic area or seeking new, larger, and more professional sales representatives or distributors. Aiming for the best customers in your market — the biggest purchasers or the ones who set the lead in buying trends and fashions — is important, too.

Thinking big is an important part of marketing success.

Auditing your marketing activities

Parts C through G of the marketing audit look at many of the specific activities that you ought to be doing or having competent people do in order to have a really good marketing program. Depending on your business's size and type, some of these activities may not be relevant for you, but most, if not all, of them are important. Take a good hard look at any "no" answers in these parts and try to introduce activities to fill in the gaps. (You can find lots of specifics about your marketing activities in Parts III, IV and V of this book.)

I divided the audit of marketing activities into multiple sections to reflect the reality that, in effective marketing programs, a variety of activities are in each of the following areas:

- ✔ **Customer acquisition:** Actively reaching out to attract and retain good customers
- ✔ **Information gathering:** Studying and tracking trends, listening to customer input, and other activities that make marketing intelligent
- ✔ **Planning:** Organizing and coordinating the activities to give them a coordinated focus

> ✔ **Communications:** Sending clear, well-targeted messages out through
> multiple channels and media
>
> ✔ **Customer service:** Interacting with customers to make sure their experi-
> ence is rewarding and to encourage them to become ambassadors for
> your company, product, or service

I'm a big believer in taking an activity-based approach to planning and managing your marketing. You can't just plan or talk about marketing, you have
to *do* specific things to get any desirable results. All a marketing program or
plan really comes down to is a set of actions that (hopefully) has a positive
influence on sales and profits. So the section of the audit where you evaluate
your marketing activities strikes at the very heart of your marketing and can
quickly tell you whether your program is coming up short.

You should make marketing decisions according to the Five Ps (by deciding
what your product, pricing, placement, promotions, and people should be), as
I show in Chapter 1. But you should also monitor ongoing actions across all
these areas by looking at activities in the sorts of generic business processes
that I list earlier in this section. You'll probably notice that most of the sections of the marketing audit have questions about the Five Ps. The reason is
because you really need to take actions to help implement your marketing
program across all the Ps. For example, your workers in information gathering need to keep you informed about competitor product development, customer reactions to your pricing and promotions, and so on. If you like having
everything integrated into one big model, you can think of the audit as cutting across the Five Ps, and you can even build a big grid out of the two lists,
if you want to.

Analyzing your management and control

Control is sometimes hard to achieve in marketing. Some businesses don't
really know what's going on in their marketing because so many marketing
activities can occur and customers can be so widespread and difficult to
track. For these reasons, many companies waste time and money on their
marketing and don't even realize it.

Writing everything down

One of the first things you should do to control your marketing is make
sure that you document and record every action and expense. Keep good
records and make careful lists. This concept may sound obvious, but keeping track of your marketing can be difficult to do. For example, my firm sells

training materials and publications to companies directly for use in their training programs. We track our direct contacts with clients and know who buys and uses what. Or do we? We also work with multiple distributors and publishers who may sell our publications to companies, sometimes without our knowledge. And to make the situation more complicated, we also sell publications to consultants who then sell trainings based on our publications to companies. So a company can purchase one of our products in many ways.

What all this means is that we don't always know who's using our products or which products they've tried and which they haven't. That lack of control gets to be a problem when we want to send out a letter promoting a specific product. We may send the letter to some companies that already use that product without our knowledge, which is a waste and makes us look disorganized. Even worse, we don't have the names of all the companies that have used one of our products, and thus would be especially receptive to a promotional letter. I'm gradually working on my firm's business partners to get them to trade customer lists with me, but not all of them are willing to. Controlling something as simple as our own customer lists isn't as easy as it sounds.

Keeping the communication lines open

Another foundation of marketing control is what I think of as the human element, which encompasses how people are organized and how they divide the work and communicate about it. Make sure that you've clearly defined roles and goals — this element is fundamental to good marketing management.

And ask lots of questions and share lots of information to keep the communications flowing. I bet you haven't heard about all customer complaints or concerns — most marketing teams don't. I also bet your company offers products that some of your customers don't yet know about; this issue is also a common communication problem in marketing. Management and control is all about making sure that your company has an efficient, effective connection to your market.

Checking your creativity

The very idea of auditing your creativity may sound strange because audits and creativity sound like opposites. But because creativity is an essential component of your marketing success, you do need to manage it, just like any other important business activity or asset.

How do you know whether you're being creative? Consider the following:

- ✓ **Creativity means doing things differently and doing new things.** If your marketing seems routine, tame, and overly familiar, it doesn't pass the first creativity test: freshness. You really ought to try something new.

- ✓ **Creativity equals originality.** If you're not leading the way with a new idea, method, or approach this year in your industry or market, then you're not being very original. Yet you *are* a unique individual: Your company is like no other, your products have many minor differences, your employees have unique cultural and geographic roots, and so on. Tap into these differences to come up with original ideas and approaches. Try to make your marketing distinctive and special, not me-too and imitative. Why? Because the first person or company to try something new usually gets more money and success out of it than any imitators.

When you weave creativity into your marketing, it gives your marketing activities more impact and helps your business grow. A dollar spent on a dull, typical ad, mailing, brochure, or Web site doesn't have much impact. Any company, big or small, in today's competitive market and unsure economy has to figure out how to maximize every dollar. However, if you have limited funds, then you really do care how much impact your marketing has. A creative approach can increase your marketing's impact by ten or more. That's how powerful creativity is, so please give this last section of the audit (on CD0201) careful attention.

If you need help making your marketing more creative, take a look at Chapter 5. I also posted some additional creative tools and techniques at `www.insights formarketing.com` in Portable Document Format (pdf) files that you can download and use for free.

Using Your Results to Plan Your Attack

When you look at your scores on all nine sections of the marketing audit, you're able to see your *audit profile,* defined as the overall strengths and weaknesses from your audit. (You can graph this profile using the audit template on your CD, by the way.) This profile is a useful planning tool. Use it to identify areas where you need to improve and areas where you have strengths you want to maintain and take advantage of.

One of my associates, Professor Charles Schewe of University of Massachusetts Amherst, used a version of this marketing audit to help executives from electric utilities look at their marketing functions. They all faced the challenge that their markets were opening up to competition for the first time due to deregulation. This challenge meant that these utilities could no longer take their customer base for granted.

Of course, you probably haven't been able to take your customers for granted. But wouldn't having regulatory protection of your market area be nice? Ah, well, the days of regulated monopolies are ending, and even utility companies have to find out how to recruit and retain customers.

The loss of regulatory protection of their customer base made the marketing audit a very powerful marketing tool for these electric utilities. The marketing audit was a real eye opener, to say the least: It revealed large areas of marketing in which they simply weren't active. In some of these organizations, the audit led to an agenda that required several years or more to complete.

Developing your marketing agenda

In your business, the results may be less radical than in the case of the electric companies, but I'm sure that your marketing audit can lead to an agenda of some sort. If it doesn't, then it hasn't done you any good. After all, you have to act on insights to profit from them.

Marketing audits always seem to reveal some needs and generate a few ideas for positive action. Being fully customer-oriented is hard, and creating and integrating effective marketing actions in all areas of your business is very hard to accomplish, too. So a great next step is to follow up on your audit to review the findings again — especially in areas of particular weakness or strength — and to develop some agenda items that'll help you to better attract and retain customers.

I recommend doing that thinking right now while the experience of the audit is still fresh in your mind. If you can't come up with at least five high-priority actions for your agenda as a result of the audit, I'll eat my marketing hat. But do put a good effort into it, because I'm rather attached to my marketing hat. I wear that hat quite often when running my own business!

You'll find a set of templates on your CD (filename CD0203 and CD0204) for developing your marketing agenda based on the marketing audit you performed. Figure 2-1 shows you what a sample planning form looks like (although four more sample forms are on the CD, so you can develop a five-item agenda if you want).

Agenda item #1 is to: _____

Mini-plan for agenda item #1:

Who should spearhead this action? _____

By **when** should it be completed? _____/_____/_____

What special **resources** might be needed?

    Other people?

    _____
    _____
    _____
    _____

    Money? $_____

    Special Expertise? _____

    Special supplies/equipment? _____

What should this action **accomplish?**

    Key objective: _____

Figure 2-1:
A sample
planning
form.

Reality check

Okay, now that you've developed five good action items for your marketing agenda (and saved me from having to eat my marketing hat!), I want you to do a quick reality check.

Specifically, I want you to look at the resources those agenda items require; namely, the people, money, special expertise, supplies, and equipment you need to complete those agenda items. When you add up all those requirements, you have a pretty big investment — perhaps too big. Your marketing capacities need to expand with your capabilities; otherwise, you'll run into time pressures, cash-flow issues, or other practical constraints.

So stop and think about the combined impact of all those nice agenda items. If the agenda items require more resources than your organization can reasonably bear right now, then prioritize. Pick the one or few actions that you think need attention first. Or perhaps the ones that you can *afford* to do first. I'm talking about real-world marketing, after all, so your action has to be doable or it won't get done.

And if the agenda items you put into action first are as good as you think they are, then they should increase your revenues and hopefully even increase your profits — which means they'll help create the resources you need to move on to additional improvements and agenda items. So the actions you take to enhance your sales and marketing as a result of the audit process should increase your resources, not reduce them.

Your goal is to invest in actions that bring in new business and/or retain or increase business from existing customers. Growth is the goal. And no matter how small the first steps you take are, after you start pursuing growth through improvements in your sales and marketing, you'll find that the resulting growth makes more improvements and additional growth possible.

On the CD

Check out the following items on the CD-ROM:

- ✔ Hiam's Marketing Audit (CD0201)
- ✔ Hiam's Marketing Audit Score Form (CD0202)
- ✔ Analyzing and Interpreting Your Marketing Audit (CD0203)
- ✔ Marketing Agenda: Actions Suggested by the Marketing Audit (CD0204)

Chapter 3

Marketing Plans

In This Chapter

▶ Deciding whether you need a marketing plan

▶ Designing your plan using a standard outline or the CD template

▶ Choosing your marketing strategies

▶ Creating a formal marketing plan

▶ Knowing how much to spend on marketing

A *marketing plan* lays out your analysis of the situation in your market along with your strategies and how you'll use the various elements of your marketing mix (such as advertising, your Web site, and pricing) to execute the strategy. It also has sales projections and a budget for your marketing spending.

You do need to write a marketing plan, but you may not know it. Some companies get along pretty well with little more than a simple spreadsheet budget, a set of traditions, and general rules — at least for a while. But to really succeed and be ready for changes and challenges in the world around you, you need to write a thoughtful plan each year. Use this planning process as an opportunity to gather new information, re-examine your strategies, and refine your tactical marketing and sales efforts. (If you're not sure whether you believe me, write a good plan now and see how much better your company performs in the next year. I'll bet you'll become as big an advocate of planning as I am!)

In this chapter, I show you how to create a relatively simple and easy marketing plan in a hurry using the templates on your CD.

I've written a lot of marketing plans using a wide variety of formats and approaches. I've also designed an elaborate marketing plan software program, which is marketed with great success and ongoing improvements and additions by JIAN under the name *MarketingPlan Builder*. If you're writing a detailed plan for a relatively large or complex marketing program, I recommend supplementing this chapter with a copy of that software program (I provide a link to JIAN's information, plus any other planning information I find, on www.insightsfor marketing.com).

Considering Marketing Plan Designs

You can design a marketing plan in many ways. No two plans are identical in their formats and structures because no two organizations are identical in their needs. So don't be afraid to adapt planning outlines and templates to your own needs.

To help you begin thinking about your marketing plan's design, here's an example of a plan outline used by a divisional manager at a large industrial chemicals company.

A Sample Marketing Plan

Situation Analysis

    Sales history

    Market profile

    Sales versus objective

    Factors influencing sales

    Profitability

    Factors affecting profitability

Market Environment

    Growth rate

    Trends

    Changes in customer attitude

    Recent or anticipated competitor actions

    Government activity

Problems and Opportunities

    Problem areas

    Opportunities

Marketing and Profitability Objectives

    Sales

    Market profile

    Gross margin

Marketing Strategy

Marketing Programs

Product Assumptions

This outline is one way to set up your marketing plan, but it may not be the right way for you. A different — and simpler — way to outline your plan is as follows:

The Simplest Marketing Plan

Situation Analysis (reporting on your customers, competitors, products, and results from the past period)

Strategies and Actions (with Budgets and Timelines) for the Five Ps

Products

Placement

Pricing

Promotion

People

Budget Analysis

Writing Your Marketing Plan the Easy Way

A good way to begin writing your marketing plan is to convert one question into many. The question you have is, "What is my marketing plan for next year?" I can't tell you the answer because I'm not sitting next to you analyzing your business. What I can do is break down your rather difficult question into a bunch of easy questions that you can answer on your own. Questions like "Do you think a newsletter would be useful and interesting to your customers?" That question is very specific, and it's one you can probably answer with a little thought.

If you decide that, yes, a newsletter may be appealing to your customers, then you can think about a bunch of even more specific questions, like "How many people are on your mailing and e-mail lists?" and "Will you write the articles yourself, or do you need to hire a writer or perhaps purchase the rights to reprint content?" By drilling down to specifics, you can turn a big, hard-to-answer question into a series of fairly easy, detail-oriented questions.

Lucky for you, the planning template in CD0103 helps you do just that. If you pull up the template and take a look at it, you'll probably notice right away how detailed and lengthy the table of contents is. That's because the table of contents reflects the specificity of the questions that the template raises for you to think about. I divided the plan into lots of very specific, small sections, so you never have to wing it and make up a lot of structure on your own. Instead, you always have specific, small chunks of thinking and writing to do — which is much more manageable.

A marketing plan is really a collection of multiple smaller plans that have synergy between them. Each small plan is easier to write compared to a big plan, so I want you to take this one building block at a time.

For example, if you look at the table of contents of the plan template in CD0301, you'll see that the following subsection covers a plan for publishing a newsletter:

Harnessing the Power of Newsletters

Plans for Writing Our Newsletter

Plans for Designing Our Newsletter

Plans for Distributing Our Newsletter

Schedule and Budget for Our Newsletter

Expected Benefits

This is, obviously, a plan for a newsletter, with places to describe how you'll produce and distribute it, a place to summarize the costs and timing of the project, and an end section to describe the benefits or returns from this newsletter plan (in terms of additional customer loyalty and orders, referrals from pass-along of the newsletter to new customers, and so on; the template guides you on how to fill in each section). Filling in a paragraph or two under each of these headings and working up some estimates for costs and benefits isn't that difficult because a newsletter is a specific, discrete thing to think about and plan.

At the end of the section on newsletters in CD0301, you'll have bottom-line costs, the timing of those costs for your newsletter, and also a sense of when you may get what kinds of returns from those investments. You can use these numbers as a basis for entering some numbers in the summary row in your overall marketing budget for your plan (using the Excel spreadsheet on CD0302). And with the detail section of the plan to support that row of your budget, you can feel pretty good about the numbers you enter there. Build up your budget this way — one line at a time — as you do each of the smaller, easier-to-think-about mini-plans in each subsection of CD0301. From the details, the big picture emerges, and you'll be pleasantly surprised to find that the budget almost writes itself as you work through the plan. Similarly, the returns you predict from the newsletter can support a row in the Sales Projection Worksheet on CD0303.

Using the Marketing Plan Template

The best idea I've had in a long while was to make the marketing plan template (CD0301) follow the structure of this book so that you can draw on each chapter of this book as you write a corresponding section of your plan. In other words, this book becomes your master reference guide as you write your marketing plan.

Because this book focuses on the kinds of marketing activities you're most likely to include in a simple marketing plan, I think you'll find that a marketing plan template based on this book is quite helpful and practical. If you need to add more topics to the template, I suggest getting a copy of the companion book to this one, *Marketing For Dummies*, written by yours truly, to provide you with the support you need to cover subjects beyond the ones that I cover here. (I mention some sections of *Marketing For Dummies* as optional reference aids in parts of the marketing plan template.) But if your plan is like most of the ones that I've worked on over the years, you'll probably find more than enough information in this book and the template to get you through a planning process and produce a serviceable draft of your plan.

By the way, I walk you through the Excel spreadsheets that are also on your CD for doing sales projections and marketing budgets later in this chapter. Combining the spreadsheets with the Word file of CD0301 gives you a complete and detailed marketing plan.

Gathering information before you start

Before you even start customizing the template in CD0301, I recommend taking a little time to assemble your marketing information. Make sure that you have records of last year's marketing activities, including expenses, and dig out all the sales records you can find. Also, if you have a little more time, use the audit and survey forms in Chapters 1 and 2 because they provide good ideas and information that you can use as you work on your plan.

In addition, you may want to do a little extra research to gather more information about your market. For example, you may want to do one or more of the following:

✔ Ask salespeople or distributors their views of quality, trends, competition, and so on.

✔ Gather details of sales for the last year or more.

✔ Get breakdowns of sales by product, region, or other category.

✔ Get some general statistics on sales in your market or product category so you can see what your market share is and whether you're gaining or losing share.

✔ Collect any information you can on where sales came from and which sales and marketing practices worked best in the last year or two.

✔ Get prices on printing, ad purchases, design services, or other costs you know you'll need to include in your budget.

✔ Quiz some customers for input about the quality of your service or product and get their ideas and suggestions on how to improve it.

✔ Plan some sales promotions and work out projected costs and returns. Special offers are a great way to get customer attention and stimulate new customers to try your service or product.

✔ Collect cost and price information to use in budgets and projections. For example, what is the total cost for your company to deliver one unit of your product to a customer? What net price does the average customer pay after any discounts or special offers? And how do your prices and discounts compare to your competitors'?

✔ Get information on any new products that you'll be introducing during the plan's period.

✔ Decide whether you want to or whether you can afford to hire a marketing consultant to coach you through the planning process. Or, if hiring a consultant is out of your reach, you can hire one to spend a day with you clarifying your strategy before you start writing.

Researching this shopping list of questions may occupy you for several days or more. Simply gathering the information needed to do a good plan is a serious undertaking. And you haven't even begun to write your marketing plan yet! But hang on. All this upfront work helps make the writing part as easy as possible.

Eventually, you have to roll up your sleeves and start writing. But don't just stare at a blank page or screen. Months could pass before you have anything competent written. (I'm reminded of a quote from author Gene Fowler: "Writing is easy. All you do is sit staring at a blank sheet of paper until the drops of blood form on your forehead.") I want you to avoid writer's block, anxiety, and the lack of structure that the blank-sheet-of-paper method provides! And I also want you to avoid the common mistake of making minor edits to last year's plan (if you have one). That method doesn't force you to rethink your marketing; it just creates something that fools you and others into believing that you've done real planning.

Instead, I want you to really write a plan because the writing process is also a thinking process, and coming up with good strategies and tactics takes a lot of thinking. But to make the writing process easier, I recommend following my template in CD0301 religiously. It includes detailed instructions for each section of your plan.

Checking out the format of the marketing plan template

Your CD contains a Word file that I wrote as if I were laying out a professional marketing plan, with a title page, table of contents, headings for each section, and body copy. But instead of writing a specific plan for a client, I used the body copy to give you suggestions, examples, and tips for how to fill in your own details. The outline of this planning template is as follows:

Introduction

Part 1: Program Overview and Marketing Strategies

Overview of Last Year's Marketing Program

Long-term Investments and Administrative and Overhead Costs

Audit Results and Agenda Items

Marketing Strategies

Part 2: Information and Skills Required for the Plan

    Market Research

    Creative Concepts and Plans

    Guidelines for Written Marketing Communications

    Testimonials and Customer Stories

Part 3: Advertising Management and Design

    Planning and Budgeting Our Ad Campaign

    Advertising Designs and Programs

Part 4: Other Elements of Our Marketing Program

    Branding through Business Cards, Letterhead, and So On

    Pricing, Coupons, and Other Promotions

    Brochures, Catalogs, and Spec Sheets

Harnessing the Power of Newsletters

Media Coverage through Publicity

Web Site Development and Promotion

Trade Shows and Special Events

Part 5: Sales and Service Success

Plans and Improvements for Our Sales Process

Improving the Way We Close Our Sales

Strategies for Dealing with Difficult Customers

Sales Projections

Part 6: Marketing Budget

Overview of the Marketing Budget

Marketing Budget and Spreadsheet Printouts

The outline is detailed to give you a lot of structure, which is helpful when writing a plan. The most you have to create on your own is a paragraph or two per topic.

Also, you'll find that there are many other forms on the CD (mostly Word and Excel files) described in other chapters of this book that you can incorporate directly into this planning template. Each time you use one of the other CD files, you're taking a shortcut to completing your plan. I want you to use all the resources in this book as fully as you can during your planning process so that it's as painless as possible! My philosophy is if you wanted to do it the hard way, you wouldn't have bought this book, so I want to make your planning as easy as I can.

Developing the Strategy Section of Your Plan

I don't need to guide you through every section of the planning template on CD0301 because most of the sections have a chapter devoted to them elsewhere in this book. But the section on your marketing strategies doesn't have its own chapter, so I discuss it here. Your marketing strategies are an important part of the plan — often the most important part, in my experience.

In the strategy section of your marketing plan, you describe the big-picture thinking behind your plan. The later parts of your plan get into all the specifics — the whats, whens, and hows. The strategy section is about the whys. Good thinking on the strategic level will make the rest of your plan much easier to write — and also much more profitable and effective!

In this section, I guide you through the process of selecting or refining your strategy and presenting it clearly in writing.

I have to tell you before you write the strategy section of your marketing plan that strategic planning is difficult. I think it's the most difficult thing any marketer, manager, or executive ever has to do. Even if you hire an expert consultant to do strategic planning with you, expect to spend many long meetings discussing it over a period of months. You probably don't have that kind of time today, however, so I show you all the shortcuts I know here. I can help you craft a rough-and-ready set of marketing strategies in as little as a couple of hours, if you're willing to focus hard on it for that long. If you have the time and funding to do a more formal planning process, by all means do, and use this section of your plan to summarize the results. But if you're in a hurry, don't skip this section. Just follow my pointers and choose one strategy from my list in this section, or perhaps (at the most) several strategies that seem to complement each other and fit your situation and opportunities well.

Basing your strategies on your core brilliance

Strategies have to be based on your product's genuine strengths: what I call "strategic assets." My technical reviewer on both my *For Dummies* books, Celia Rocks, calls this approach "brilliance marketing." The idea is simple and powerful: Get in touch with your best strengths — the thing(s) you can contribute to your market and to the world — and make sure you base your strategies and plans on them. I challenge in you in Chapter 1 to focus on and define your product's or company's core brilliance. Go to your results there, and make sure the strategy section of your marketing plan builds on and takes advantage of your core strengths. If it doesn't, then it's going to fail.

Think of your core brilliance as the foundation of a lighthouse. Your strategies are the ground-level section of the structure. Later parts of your plan build higher, until your promotions at the top provide a beacon to draw customers into your anchorage. Your marketing plan has to be an integral structure, based on a solid foundation of strategic assets. One person's or business's winning strategy is another's failure; the success of your strategy all depends on whether you have the right foundation for it or not!

Deciding whether to adopt a new strategy or perfect an old one

If you simply need to improve upon and continue using an already-successful strategy, say that clearly in this section of your plan and shape the plan to improve the efficiency of the marketing program you used last year. If, however, you really need to shop for a new and better strategic approach,then say so now and realize that you first need to figure out what your effective strategic plan is before you can expect to optimize any program based on it. In other words, pick one of these basic orientations for your plan:

- ✔ **Efficiency-oriented:** Say that your plan introduces a number of specific improvements on how you market your product but doesn't alter your basic strategy from last year.

- ✔ **Effectiveness-oriented:** Say that your plan identifies a major opportunity or problem and adopts a new strategy to respond to it.

Take a minute to think about the distinction between perfecting the implementation of last year's strategy and trying a new one. Which strategy you choose makes a big difference that will affect everything else about your plan! If you use last year's strategy and just try to do it more efficiently, then you can plan to do things on a fairly big scale. For example, you can plan to do one big mailing a quarter (assuming you do mailings — if not, imagine I'm talking about advertising, trade show booths, or whatever you do a lot of). But if you try some new strategy, don't plan to do a few big marketing activities because you could fail at one or more of them and blow your marketing budget in a hurry. Instead, plan to test a lot of smaller mailings and other kinds of marketing. Do a lot of marketing activities on a small scale and build in enough repetition to give yourself opportunities to experiment and learn as you go. If you're exploring a new strategy, your marketing program should be made up of a wider variety of smaller investments.

Improving your current marketing strategy

When designing your plan's strategy, the first choice you have to make is whether you have a pretty good overall strategy right now or not. If it *is* good and should continue to work for the next few years, then all you need to do in your plan is show how you'll pursue that strategy efficiently. The main point of your plan is to do marketing like you did last year, but better. In that case, your strategy section can be short and sweet. Just describe the strategy and why you think it's going to continue to work, and then say that the main contribution of your plan is to improve the efficiency of marketing by making certain improvements to last year's program.

The marketing audit (see Chapter 2) or your independent research can guide you to specific areas where improvements are likely to pay off. Mention those general areas briefly here, but save the details for later in the plan.

Scrapping the old strategy and creating a new one

If you feel that a new strategic direction or approach is needed or you want to try one because you see good opportunities, then your plan should be more effectiveness-oriented. What do I mean by effectiveness-oriented? I mean that you're going to try a new strategy that, if it works, will bring you exciting new opportunities for sales, profits, and overall business growth. So the critical issue for your plan and your next year's marketing program is: Can you effectively achieve some new strategic vision and accomplish the new objectives that you set for that strategy? If you even achieve this new strategic vision halfway, you'll probably be happy because doing something new isn't easy. So your plan should be about making your overall marketing approach more effective through a change of strategies. Don't worry about sweating every detail of your new strategy, just try to prove that it works without losing money doing it. Next year, you can switch gears and design an efficiency-oriented plan that perfects this year's more experimental one.

If you're trying a new strategy and don't have proven marketing formulas, you can't write an efficiency-oriented plan. For example, if you don't do mailings to purchased lists right now, then don't say that you're going to increase the response rate on mailings from 2.5 percent to 5.5 percent next year. Instead, plan on testing a variety of mailings and plan to have some of them fail (a less than 1 percent response rate) and hope to have one or two of them do pretty well (a 3 percent plus response rate). But you can't guess which ones will fail and which ones will succeed.

Choosing your strategy

If you're sticking with your existing strategy, you still need to clearly articulate it in this section of your plan and explain why it is so good that it can power your marketing for another year. If you're pretty sure you need a new strategy, then use this section of the plan to say why and to elaborate on your decision.

"Our strategy is a _____ strategy. Specifically, we are planning to _____." Can you easily fill in the blanks, or are you scratching your head?

Most people find completing those two simple sentences difficult, but I try to make it easier. First, I give you a master list of marketing strategies to choose from. Trust me, you're using or need to be using one (or possibly two or three, at the most) of these strategies in your marketing for the next year. Pick one strategy and you're ready to fill in the blank in the first sentence.

The second sentence requires a bit more thinking on your part because it says how that strategy applies to your own situation and market. See my notes about each strategy in the next section for clues on how to customize it to your own plan. By the way, I put the strategies in the order I want you to think about them; the easier ones are first. The farther you get into this list, the more difficult the implementation usually becomes. So all else being equal, I generally recommend using the easier ones.

Avoiding random activity

Planning exercises can easily turn into random listings of possibilities. The poor planners run out of insights, information, and time when they have to itemize the details of their marketing programs. Their thinking often goes like this:

> "What sorts of ads, mailings, or other marketing communications should we use? Hmm. Dunno. Maybe we should just list a bunch so we make sure that some advertising and mailings are included in the budget."

I guess that's a planning process, but not a very intelligent one! You can take many actions to promote your product or service. Often people just try one thing after another, hoping to see sales increase without any real idea of what may work, why, and how. I call this *random marketing*. It goes kind of like this:

> "Hey, we need to do something to get more sales. Let's do some advertising."

Or maybe it goes like this:

> "Our competitors are offering coupons. Should we do some coupons, too?"

And so on. What about trying some telemarketing? Or print advertising? Or even television or radio spots? Direct mail may be better. Hmm. Lots of choices. But which should you try? Is it entirely a matter of blind experimentation?

No. At least, it better not be unless you have a lot of time and money to waste groping around in the marketing dark. Random marketing is like the old philosophical theory that if you put enough apes at enough typewriters for long enough, they'd eventually type a Shakespearean play by chance. Same with random marketing. Eventually, you might produce a winning program by chance. But you better be very patient! The only difference between the old ape-at-the-typewriter theory and the typical approach to marketing is that nobody is silly enough to actually try the ape experiment, whereas the majority of businesses try random marketing. And then people wonder why their plans don't produce satisfactory results.

Reminder strategy

The reminder strategy is a very simple communications-oriented strategy that reaches out to loyal, regular customers to remind them to make a replacement purchase. If you have a solid base of loyal customers who ought to continue purchasing regularly, this strategy is for you. You can implement this strategy fairly easily: Just make sure you give your customers periodic reminders and perhaps small incentives or rewards so that they don't forget your product and wander off to some competitor.

Simplicity strategy

The simplicity strategy emphasizes ease and convenience for customers, and I recommend using it in markets where things have gotten too complicated. Can you simplify the purchase and use of your product or service to such an extent that simplicity alone can be a major selling point? If so, seriously consider this strategy, but be committed to keeping things simple — simpler than the competition —otherwise you won't have a durable advantage.

If you use the simplicity strategy, follow through with simplifying steps in all Five P's, not just in your promotional messages. Just saying that your company is easier and simpler to do business with isn't much good — you really have to be!

Quality strategy

If you can figure out how to make a better-quality product or offer better service, by all means do it! The most durable and profitable strategy in marketing is to be better than the competition — in your customers' eyes, not just your own. You can do this in many ways: by making fewer errors, by having better designs, by offering more reliable or rapid delivery, and so on. Pick one or two dimensions that your customers associate strongly with quality when they talk about your product category. Focus on these aspects and be prepared to redesign your business processes and your products to achieve noticeably better quality.

The fields of Total Quality Management and Process Re-engineering are dedicated to the technical challenges of redesigning businesses so that businesses can truly offer better-quality products and services without incurring high costs or raising prices above what customers can afford. I've written about the art and science of Total Quality Management and filled whole books on the topic, so I won't even try to cover it here. I just want you to recognize that you have to pursue this strategy seriously in every aspect of your business, not just in flashy advertisements or promotional claims!

Market share strategy

The market share strategy is a straightforward effort to get a bigger piece of the market than your competitors. Size often matters in competition, so gaining on your competitors by using aggressive sales and marketing to get more customers or more sales dollars than they do in the next year can be a good strategy.

You can be fairly careful and conservative when you use this strategy if you don't need to gain a lot of market share quickly; in which case, you may think of this strategy as being based on the basic efficiency-orientation I describe earlier in this chapter. Other times, your goal is to make significant progress in capturing market share compared to competitors, even if you have to overspend on marketing and reduce your profit margin for a year or two. You can use this new strategic effort to achieve greater effectiveness by changing your position in the market. The prize is that, if you succeed in becoming one of the leaders in your market, you can hope for high profits in subsequent years as your payoff for investing in competitive growth now.

Positioning strategy

This strategy is designed to create or maintain a specific image (or "position") in the customer's and potential customer's mind. This strategy is psychological, and it's all about how people think and feel. It uses words, stories, and imagery to reach out to customers so they form strong feelings or beliefs about your product. Often this strategy looks at how customers perceive the competition because communicating your own unique position in the marketplace — and not a confusingly similar position — is best.

To design a positioning strategy, you really need to find out what people think and what they care about. You can use the exercises (and surveys) in Chapter 1 to get a handle on how customers see the product category in general and what they specifically like most about your product, which is what you should build on when deciding how to position your product in their minds.

In Chapter 1, I talk about the importance of being brilliant at what you do and, in a positioning strategy, your goal is to communicate this brilliance in such a powerful way that you "own" that claim to brilliance and are strongly associated with it in customers' minds. Clearly, this strategy is going to need a lot of brand-building and marketing communications in the implementation parts of your plan.

Product life cycle strategy

The product life cycle strategy adjusts your marketing to the growth stage of an overall product category. Any product category goes through a broad life cycle, from early introduction through growth, to a slower-growing maturity and, eventually, to declining sales and death. Innovation drives this cycle:

New products are invented and introduced, and then they catch on, eventually getting replaced by even newer products. As the cycle goes on, competition grows because the once-new product gradually becomes commonplace and easy for many competitors to make and sell. The most fun period in this life cycle is the growth phase. During this phase, the market is beginning to embrace the new product and its sales take off. And during that phase, becoming a star by achieving high sales and profit growth is easiest.

You can use the life cycle strategy to refocus your efforts behind a rising star — a product or product line that you expect is going to experience fast growth in the next few years. Or you can use this strategy to adjust your expectations and refocus your efforts on competitive jockeying if you realize that your once-growing star is now fading and you don't have a replacement. Either way, knowing where you are in the life cycle of your product category is helpful so that you can adjust your efforts and expectations accordingly — and seek a new product with growth potential if your main product is getting too old.

Market segmentation strategy

A *segment* of a market is simply a subgroup of customers with needs that make them special in some way. For example, if you sell breakfast cereals for adults instead of children, you're targeting (that's what marketers say) the adult cereal market. When you specialize in just one segment of a broader market, you can be more specific and helpful to your customers.

A market segmentation strategy often requires a broader geographic area — perhaps even national or international — because your segment of people or businesses with special needs may be relatively rare.

You may be using this strategy already or you may decide to adopt it now as a way to compete more effectively in the market. Segmentation and specialization can be a great way to make yourself more valuable to certain customers, which allows you to outsell more generalized competitors within the target group or segment of customers.

Market expansion strategy

If you're currently selling in a three-state area, a straightforward way to grow is to add two more states to sell in. This strategy expands the size of your market. But to use this strategy, you need to make sure your new market area includes the right kinds of customers and that some new competitor won't undercut your pricing or make entering the market there difficult.

After assessing the new territory, decide what the main challenges of entering the market there will be. Then base your marketing plan on what you must do to succeed in the new, bigger market you want to pursue.

Setting specific objectives for your strategies

A *strategic objective* states something you hope that your business accomplishes in the next year as a result of pursuing a strategy. If you're pursuing an expansion strategy, for instance, you may set some goals for the number of new customers you want to acquire in each of the new territories.

If you're pursuing a positioning strategy, on the other hand, quantifying your success may be harder. You may have to do a survey at the end of the year to ask customers what they think and feel about your product. One objective may be to convince a significant percent of customers that your product is better, faster, more sophisticated — or whatever the positioning goal is — than your competition. A second objective may be to increase your sales by a certain percent as a result of communicating your special position in the market to prospective customers.

Set specific objectives that flow from your strategy and that also reflect your resources, like the number of salespeople or the amount of money you have to spend. Good objectives require you to stretch a bit but not too much. They should energize and give a purpose to the rest of your marketing plan. For instance, if your strategy is to gain market share and try to become one of the top three in your market, a good, energizing objective may be to increase your sales at twice the speed of the underlying growth rate in your market. (In other words, to grow twice as fast as the average competitor.) Trying to grow much faster than that may not be possible.

You'll also use your strategic marketing objectives again later in your sales projections (use CD0303 for that). One of your objectives must always be about sales, and this objective drives your sales projections. Pick a rough sales objective now, but expect to adjust it as you work on the tactical parts of your plan. Marketing activity is needed to generate sales, and marketing activity costs money and takes time and effort, so you have to make sure that the sales objective seems realistic before you finalize it.

What are good marketing objectives? Whatever objectives you need to help you achieve your mission or growth goals. Your marketing objectives may be to

✔ Boost the performance of salespeople or distributors

✔ Change the way customers think of your offering (reposition)

✔ Cross-sell more products to existing customers

✔ Develop new channels of distribution (such as the Web)

✔ Educate customers about a new technology or process

✔ Expand into new geographic markets

✔ Fend off a competitor's challenge

✔ Find new customers

✔ Generate more or better leads for the sales force

✔ Improve customer service

✔ Improve the distribution of existing products or services

✔ Increase the average order size

✔ Increase the perceived value of offerings to counter a trend toward price competition

✔ Introduce new products or services

✔ Recruit new distributors or retailers

✔ Reduce customer complaints

If you go through this list checking those objectives that apply to your situation, you'll probably come up with at least a few appropriate ones that you can use to guide your planning. If not, you can always make up some of your own. But make sure that you have clear objectives before you go into any planning process. Otherwise, you might as well design your program by picking options at random.

Goal-Oriented Marketing Experiments

There's always an important element of creative experimentation in any marketing or planning effort, but there's not random experimentation. When you experiment, you need to have *specific marketing goals* and a rough idea of the kinds of marketing activities that may achieve those goals. Then you can focus your creative experimentation on finding out how to better achieve those marketing goals by refining your ideas until you have a unique approach that produces a winning marketing program.

The formula you develop and continue refining through your marketing experiments is uniquely yours. No formula works for more than one organization. Yet your formula can and should rely on certain transferable elements — the certain fundamentals that hold up in all marketing programs. And the most easily transferable formulas have to do with marketing goals.

Specifically, you need to know that certain kinds of marketing initiatives tend to be appropriate for certain kinds of marketing goals and not for others. You can use that information to help you define the basic structure of any marketing plan or program — and narrow down those apparently random choices — simply by picking one or a few marketing objectives. Then, focus on the marketing techniques that are most likely to help you achieve those objectives.

Planning Benchmarks for Marketing Communications

How much should you spend on marketing communications (MarCom) like advertising, the Web, mailings, telemarketing, or whatever you plan to use? Communicating with your market takes many forms in your plan and will probably be a major part of it. If you want to truly achieve your strategic objectives, you need to have a plan that communicates well and often.

On the bottom of the spreadsheet in CD0302, I include a row that calculates your total MarCom spending by adding up any rows above it that involve spending on direct communications with your market. As you work on your plan, keep a close eye on this number and make sure it's a big enough percent of your projected sales to actually give you a good shot at achieving those sales projections.

What's a big enough percent to spend on marketing communications? As much as you can afford is one philosophy, but sometimes it's best to benchmark against industry norms rather than just maximize MarCom. If your company is an average size in your industry, then a spending level similar to the statistic from the industry closest to yours in Table 3-1 will probably keep you growing as fast as your competitors and the industry as a whole are. To grow faster than your industry or to make up for being smaller than average, you probably need to allocate more money, perhaps even two to three times the average amount.

Table 3-1	MarCom Spending as % of Sales
Product or Service	*Spending*
Services:	
Insurance	0.6%
Advertising	2.8%
Freight	1.2%
Cable/pay TV	1.0%
Nursing homes	3.4%
Hospitals	3.0%
Investment advice	6.8%
Personal services	4.0%
Services in general	2.5%

Product or Service	Spending
Products:	
Ice cream	5.4%
Furniture	5.0%
Clothing	5.1%
Auto parts/accessories	0.8%
Greeting cards	3.3%
Software	4.5%
Periodicals (newspapers/magazines/newsletters)	5.8%
Food products	9.4%
Toys	18%
Computer equipment	2.5%
Office supplies	4.2%
Building supplies	1.2%
Retail stores:	
Watch stores	15.7%
Department stores	4.3%
Furniture stores	9.0%
Clothing stores	3.2%
Hotels/motels	3.9%
Insurance agencies	1.6%
Banks	3.8%
Stockbrokers	2.0%
Consumer electronics stores	3.8%
Variety stores	2.0%
Gift shops	4.5%
Grocery stores	1.2%
Restaurants/bars	4.4%
Retailers in general	**3.4%**

For more information . . .

In this chapter, I queue up a number of tools, techniques, and benchmarks to help you with your marketing strategy and plan. Whether you need to just diagnose the situation or develop a full-blown plan, you should find plenty of guidelines in this chapter and its corresponding CD files. For more details on how to design and budget all the specifics of your plan, such as advertising campaigns, sales programs, and promotions, see the upcoming chapters that focus on each of these topics.

Often, a chapter in this book directly corresponds to a section on the market planning template and a section on the budget template, too. In addition, you can find complementary coverage of marketing plans in my other book in this series,

Marketing For Dummies, as well as in *The Portable MBA in Marketing* (Wiley), a book I co-authored with professor Charles Schewe of the business school at University of Massachusetts Amherst. And, of course, I'll continue posting helpful content and links on the Web site that supports my *For Dummies* books (www.insightsfor marketing.com).

I encourage you to seek additional resources as well. For instance, William Cohen's *The Marketing Plan* (Wiley), although written for classroom use, has a number of good examples of marketing plans that I recommend as benchmarks. In my experience, the more support and information you have on hand when undertaking a planning process, the better.

There's no harm in violating these norms, but I do recommend thinking about how your company's spending on marketing communications compares to others in your industry, and I want you to have a good reason in mind if you decide to be significantly different. For instance, if you want to gain market share or grow your company's sales, you probably have to outspend the averages. But if your plan produces numbers that are dramatically different than the norms and you don't know why, then you really ought to go back and look to make sure a good reason exists for the differences.

On the CD

Check out the following items on the CD-ROM:

✔ Marketing Plan Template (CD0301)

✔ Marketing Budget Worksheet (CD0302)

✔ Sales Projection Worksheet (CD0303)

Part II
Boosting Your Marketing Skills

The 5th Wave   By Rich Tennant

Sales &
Marketing
PICNIC

"Get names!"

In this part . . .

Sales and marketing always benefit from the dramatic boost that creativity can give your appeal, so in this part, you find lots of tips and techniques for harnessing the power of creative marketing. Writing is also essential to almost everything in marketing, from the lowly sales letter to the modern Web site, so I include a hands-on chapter on how you can make those marketing words and phrases ring out and draw in customers.

Because I'm a big believer in understanding and empathizing with your customers, I start this part with a chapter on what I think of as real-world research. By that I mean practical, affordable ways to find out what's happening in your industry and ways to stay ahead of the trends. If you want to be a leader in your market, you always need to be sniffing the wind!

I end this part with an essential skill that many marketers don't even know they need: How to secure customer stories and testimonials to use in marketing. The reason is simple: Nobody believes you if *you* say that your products or services are great. But if *your customers* say that your products or services are great, well, now we're talking credibility! I highly recommend spending some time with the chapters in this part to see what benefits you reap as you extend your marketing skills and apply them to growing your business.

Chapter 4

The Customer Research Workshop

. . . .

In This Chapter

▶ Using your customers as a resource

▶ Getting to know your customer

▶ Auditing your customer service

. . . .

*W*hat can you do to increase sales, reduce customer turnover, raise prices, increase profits — in short, make your sales and marketing more successful? Well, you can answer those questions in many ways. The most common way to tackle them in the world of marketing is to do a careful marketing audit (see Chapter 2) and/or marketing plan (see Chapter 3). Both exercises are worthwhile and can help you see ways to increase efficiency or effectiveness. If you read Chapters 2 and 3, you may notice that I often have you ask your customers what they think of your product. The customers' perception of your product is what matters, not yours. Do they think your product is better than the competition? What's the best and worst thing that customers say about your product? Do they even know your brand name and understand what it represents? These kinds of issues often determine success or failure in business, and you never know the answers regarding these issues for sure unless you do some customer research.

Asking for your customers' feedback is the single-most powerful technique for planning or improving your marketing activities. Somewhere in customers' heads or hearts lies the answer to every question, including how to grow your company tenfold in the next three years. You just have to get that information out of them in order to profit from it.

 Keep in mind that your customers probably don't know what they know, so the research process isn't as easy as just asking them what to do. You need a system, a method, and the willingness to sift through a lot of junk information for a few pearls of wisdom or a single startling insight. But doing customer research is definitely worth the effort. In this chapter, I cover the best ways to conduct customer research: interviews, customer service audits, and experimentation. I also point you to places on the CD that help you with these methods.

Talking to Your Customers

Industrial chemicals maker Cabot Corporation recently developed an informal marketing research technique that involved the use of in-depth customer interviews. The corporation designed the interviews to identify customer concerns and suggestions and to help Cabot find out how it was viewed in the marketplace. And here's the most original part of the project: Cabot's salespeople or distributors conducted all the interviews. No expensive survey research firms. No forms to send out by mail. No statistical analysis or boring bar charts. Just talking with customers.

Cabot implemented its plan as follows: People who normally made sales calls took a few days off from selling and spent the time conducting informational interviews with key customers instead.

To make sure that their salespeople and distributors knew how to conduct polite, research-oriented interviews, Cabot first ran them through a short training course. In the course, they received a printed guide with step-by-step instructions and questions to ask. The training also taught them *how to ask* by having them practice in role-playing exercises. The main point that a training session like this needs to convey is that the interviews are informational only and can't be turned into disguised sales pitches. Customers will be angry if they feel deceived about the purpose of the meeting or phone call. (I've conducted some training in informal, qualitative survey techniques like this and can tell you that it takes a little practice to become a good listener and a non-judgmental interviewer.)

The reason Cabot Corporation trained its people before letting them do customer interviews is because it really needed them to change their behavior to get good results. They couldn't act like an interested party. They needed to play the role of researchers if they wanted customers to play the role of "researchees."

Just remember when you're doing research, no matter what your customers say, don't argue with them. Got that? I don't care if their views are based on incorrect information or a false interpretation. You're doing research, not debating. For customer interviews to work, you need to avoid defensive reactions. Act like a dispassionate third party who just wants to clarify exactly what the customer thinks. Then study their reactions later and try to figure out why they think the way they do.

All you have to do is ask

Whenever you have questions, concerns, or a desire to boost performance, the first action you take is to talk to your customers. Customers usually know how to talk, after all, and getting them talking about your product or service isn't too hard. Often they're flattered that you value their opinions.

Here's an example from my own business of how willing customers are to answer questions. I recently went to a conference in Las Vegas (no, I didn't gamble wildly . . . just a little) where I gave a talk on how to train managers to be more effective leaders in the workplace. A lot of experts on employee training — who also happen to be my prospective customers — were in the audience. These people often spend their companies' money on course materials and books for their employees — and I write and sell that sort of product. So I brought along

copies of a draft of the new book I was working on called *The Starfish Files,* which I wanted to sell to companies as a handout for their managers to teach them about leadership. At the end of my talk, I held up a copy of the draft version of the book and asked audience members to give me their business cards if they were willing to read and review the book and send me feedback about how to make it better. I wasn't sure what kind of reaction I'd get, so I was amazed when almost everyone in the audience volunteered to review the new product for me. And they did: I received a lot of great suggestions and reactions via e-mail, and I used these ideas to improve the product before launching it. Note that my research was done entirely for free. I didn't pay them, nor did I hire an expensive firm to do formal research. I just asked for help, and people gladly gave it.

You can use the same technique yourself or have your sales, marketing, or service staff use the technique to find out what improvements your company can make to make customers happier. (I also recommend having senior managers or company owners conduct at least one in-depth customer interview per month to keep them in touch with reality.)

Try calling a few customers and asking them whether they're willing to participate in an informational interview to help you with your research into how to improve your product and/or service. I think you'll be pleasantly surprised at how many of them are willing and even eager to provide their input after they see that you're sincerely open to constructive criticism. Most customers feel like their opinions aren't wanted, and they're thrilled to find someone who cares.

To ensure that you or your people conduct successful customer interviews, try using the Customer Debriefing Form on the CD (filename CD0403) so you can adapt it to your specific needs and print multiple copies for use in interviews. My firm has used this form when training salespeople in *active research,*

which basically means any simple, hands-on ways to gather insights from your customers or others in your market. (My associate Charles Schewe calls it "walking the dog research" and advocates asking exploratory questions in casual, natural interactions with customers.)

The customer debriefing is a particularly good tool for doing action research, and it's one that I've used many times for my own business as well as for clients. Try it. I guarantee you'll discover at least one new and useful thing about your own business when you ask customers to open up and give you honest feedback.

Auditing Your Customer Service

How good is your service? One way to find out is to ask customers for an overall rating of it.

Surveys like the 7 x 7 survey in Figure 4-1 (and on your CD as CD0404) give you an idea of whether customers think that your company is good, fair, or poor to do business with.

Surveys like the template I provide on the CD allow you to "take the temperature" of customer service quickly and easily. If the answers aren't near the top of the scale, you know your patient is ill.

But then what? What if customers don't like you as much as you'd like them to? How do you know what to actually *do* about it? Well, you can always make a guess, try a change, and see if your popularity increases. But sometimes you can't make a good guess about what the root causes of low customer satisfaction or continued complaints are. Then you need to dig deeper, and that's where the *Customer Service Audit* comes in. It's a much more powerful tool than the 7 x 7 survey and can reveal information you didn't even know that you didn't know (got that?).

UPS always assumed that speedy delivery was the key to success. Competitors competed on speed, and customers always said they valued speed and were upset when packages came late. So UPS understandably focused on speed. Their drivers raced in and out of offices and up and down front porches trying to beat the clock. Then UPS talked to some customers who said they thought the drivers were in too much of a hurry to be friendly or helpful. Customers said they wanted drivers to stop long enough to answer questions and give advice. This response revealed an entirely different dimension of customer service that the company had ignored in its quest for speed. When the company bigwigs realized that the drivers' friendliness and helpfulness were important to customers, they changed the company's approach. The company gave new instructions to its drivers and gave them permission and training to provide more in-the-field customer relations and advice.

The "7 x 7" Customer Satisfaction Survey

1 = Strongly Disagree   7 = Strongly Agree

1 2 3 4 5 6 7   I am highly satisfied with all aspects of customer service.

1 2 3 4 5 6 7   I definitely will make more purchases from this company in the future.

1 2 3 4 5 6 7   I commonly recommend this company to other customers.

1 2 3 4 5 6 7   This company is highly responsive to customer needs.

1 2 3 4 5 6 7   This company's service is faster than typical of the industry.

1 2 3 4 5 6 7   This company's employees are helpful and cooperative.

1 2 3 4 5 6 7   This company is good at resolving problems for customers.

Overall Interpretation:

Overall score = _____ out of a possible 49 points. To convert to a percentage basis, divide score by 0.49. Interpret as you might a grade in a class. For instance, a score of 42 = 85.7% which is a B and not bad, but certainly leaves room for improvement. To have service that attracts new customers and brings back old customers for more, you probably need A level performance, which means a score of 45 or above.

Item-by-item Interpretation:

If your score is low on item:	You need to focus on improving:
1	Overall customer service; focus on the entire process and consider retraining all employees.
2	Purchase intent; focus on delivering a quality experience and product and following up to make sure users are happy with their purchase.
3	Referrals; focus on boosting positive word-of-mouth by raising overall quality and in particular by making sure you notice any problems or critical incidents and resolve each one positively.

Figure 4-1:
A general customer satisfaction survey that you can use.

4	Responsiveness; make sure you recognize and react to customer requests, complaints or problems quickly and visibly. Also train service employees to demonstrate more empathy (empathetic listening skills are needed).
5	Service speed; work on handling customer orders or needs more quickly and reliably.
6	Helpfulness; work on providing supportive service characterized by being accessible/available to customers and eager to meet their specific needs.
7	Problem resolution; make sure you have appropriate processes for identifying and resolving complaints or customer concerns, including ways of compensating customers for service interruptions.

Performing a customer service review

Probably a quarter or more of your customers aren't too happy with your product or service. And you won't know most of their concerns unless you look for them because less than 5 percent of unhappy customers complain. The other 95 percent of them are like the sunken part of an iceberg: They're a serious hazard to navigation, but nobody can see them — except maybe other customers. People are about five times more likely to tell others about bad experiences than about good ones. So those hidden grumblers are spreading the bad word without your knowledge. Time to find out what's troubling them.

How are you going to get to the bottom of hidden, complex customer attitudes toward your service? An audit is the best approach. A *customer service audit* uses a survey to explore the specifics of what customers want and how well they think you deliver what they want. Here's a five-step process for performing your audit:

1. **Identify specific attributes of customer service, like speed, friendliness, convenience, availability, or taking fast action on complaints.**

In other words, break down customer service into as many components as possible so you can get specific in managing them.

2. **Ask customers how important each specific attribute of service really is.**

   Some aspects of service are more important than others. And when you know what your customers value most, you know where to put your efforts so you can do the most good.

3. **Ask customers how well your service performs on each of those specific attributes. Do they think your company is doing well or not?**

4. **Think about it.**

   Specifically, look for gaps between customer priorities and your product/company's performance. If you're performing less than wonderfully on your customers' top-priority service attributes, you better work on those areas right now. If you're doing wonderfully on issues that they rank as low priority, you can slack off a bit in those areas, which can give you room to improve on their higher priorities. So think about what changes you can make to better match your service performance to your customers' service priorities.

5. **Make some changes.**

   Often, surveys and analyses like this one end with a nice report or to-do list. To make your audit pay off, you actually have to *make some changes* in how you deliver your customer service. So make an action plan, and then remind yourself to check on your execution next week, next month, and so on until you see real, lasting improvements in high-priority service specifics.

Using the audit template

Figuring out what to ask customers is the hardest part of doing a good customer service audit. This task seems easy, but don't be deceived. If you just ask customers about the obvious issues, you may miss something important! So take plenty of time to *brainstorm a long list of specific aspects of customer service.* Then ask a few customers whether you've covered everything and add any ideas that they suggest. A good, detailed list of what customer service consists of is the start of every great customer service audit. (And when you have yours ready, post it writ large where everyone who interacts with customers can see it routinely! Also, put it in your next marketing plan along with action steps on how to improve on all the items on the list.)

Here are some candidates, taken from a variety of businesses and industries, to get you started:

- Answering the phone quickly
- Apologizing for delays
- Being available when needed
- Being consistent and predictable
- Being creative at problem solving
- Being reliable
- Billing accurately
- Friendliness of personnel
- Getting a job done right the first time
- Helping to solve problems
- Honoring frequent-user offers fairly without tricky small print
- Informing customers quickly and fully about problems
- Keeping things neat and clean
- Making up for mistakes or delays with offers of real value
- Matching competitors' capabilities
- Matching competitors' prices
- Not arguing over who's responsible
- Not pestering with irritating sales pitches
- Not stuffing bills with junk-mail advertisements
- Not using rude letters to collect bills
- Not using rude phone calls to collect bills
- Performing only the necessary work
- Performing only the requested work
- Politeness of personnel
- Product/service ready when promised
- Product/service made convenient for customer
- Prompt warranty work
- Providing frequent-user benefits
- Providing loaner equipment when your customer's is being repaired
- Providing useful information
- Reminding customers when their products need maintenance

 ✔ Reminding customers when they need supplies

 ✔ Responding fairly to complaints

 ✔ Responding quickly to complaints

ON THE CD

You can copy this list (CD0405) or make up your own. Then ask a few customers to look at your list and tell you whether it describes the issues they care about. Encourage reviewers to point out any issues that may be missing; using their feedback is a good way to get the most complete list possible.

After you have a good, long list, you can prepare a survey and systematically ask as many customers as possible to respond to it. The survey should basically look like Table 4-1, whether you plan to fill it in yourself or have your customers do it:

Table 4-1	Customer Service Survey	
Customer Service Element	*How Important Is It?*	*How Do We Do on It?*
Politeness of personnel	__not important __slightly important __important __very important	__poor __fair __good __excellent
Getting job done right the first time	__not important __slightly important __important __very important	__poor __fair __good __excellent
Apologizing for delays	__not important __slightly important __important __very important	__poor __fair __good __excellent
Prompt warranty work	__not important __slightly important __important __very important	__poor __fair __good __excellent
Not arguing over who's responsible	__not important __slightly important __important __very important	__poor __fair __good __excellent
Things ready when promised	__not important __slightly important __important __very important	__poor __fair __good __excellent

Surveying successfully

The key to performing the survey successfully is to ask a bunch of customers. The best methodology lets you talk to your customers as easily and quickly as possible. If customers are willing to fill in a written survey and return it, then let them do it. (And your response rate will improve if you offer a gift, such as a coupon, pen set, or something relevant to your business, as a reward.) Sometimes, though, customers don't pay much attention to such requests, in which case, you'll need to ask them in person, by e-mail, or over the phone to answer some questions for you. Face-to-face interviews in which you explain that you're auditing your customer service and then ask customers to rate each statement while you fill in the form get reasonably high participation rates. Telephone requests in which you ask the same questions have somewhat lower rates. E-mail requests (if personal) get fairly high response rates. Mail requests get the lowest response rates, but because these surveys are the least trouble for you, receiving only 5 or 10 percent of mailed surveys back may not matter.

If you aren't sure which method works best or whether a particular method of administering the survey may be biased in some way, try two or three different methods. Collecting a bunch of responses is key. And be polite, always explaining who you (really) are, why you need the information (to improve your company's service), and always get permission to ask them some questions. Then at least you don't make any enemies, even if they decline to participate.

What's a "bunch of responses"? How many do you really need? Well, statistically, survey research firms often want to get several hundred or more responses. But then, they want to do fancy statistics in which they chop up the responses into little subsets by cross-tabulating one response against another, so they need big starting numbers. You probably don't. A dozen responses tell you something useful. Two or three dozen responses give you more certainty that the results accurately represent your customers. Don't be obsessive about getting responses; just get as many as you can in a few weeks of effort, at most.

Analyzing the results

When analyzing the results of a customer service audit, look for discrepancies between the first and second ratings: The first rating is the importance to the customer, and the second rating is how good your company is. Here are a few key points to remember:

✔ If your company is doing well on an important service attribute, you can leave well enough alone.

✔ If your company is doing poorly on an important service attribute, you need to improve your performance on it right away.

✔ If your company's doing well on an unimportant attribute, consider putting less effort and resources into it so you can emphasize a more important attribute instead.

Often you find that you're putting lots of energy into something that isn't too important to your customers and not putting enough energy into something else that really matters to them. For instance, in the case I describe in the preceding section, UPS had been focusing only on speed, not on helpfulness and friendliness. The sample results in Table 4-2 indicate the same results as well.

Table 4-2	Sample Results and Display Format	
Customer Service Element	*Average Importance*	*Average Performance*
1. Politeness	3 important	4 excellent
2. Right the first time	4 very important	2 fair
3. Apologizing for delays	3 important	4 excellent
4. Prompt warranty work	2 slightly important	4 excellent
5. Not arguing	4 very important	3 good
Average Scores	3.2	3.4

This table illustrates the common problem of overperforming on some elements of customer service and underperforming on others. Note that I give each rating a number from one to four using the following conversions.

1 = not important	1 = poor
2 = slightly	2 = fair
3 = important	3 = good
4 = very important	4 = excellent

That way, comparing the results on each item is easier. If your performance rating is equal to or above the importance rating, well, you don't have any trouble on that element. But if your performance rating number is below the importance rating, this result suggests that you need to make the item a higher priority.

Using numbers also permits you to average each customer response and compare your overall performance rating with an overall importance rating for all the elements you tested. This mathematical exercise is helpful, but don't let it blind you to item-by-item problems and opportunities to improve. In the example in Table 4-2, you can see that averages can be deceptive. Performance averages higher than importance. Does this high-performance rating mean everything's fine? Not at all! The higher average performance rating suggests that the firm is putting too much effort into some items. It's overperforming in areas where performance isn't very important to customers.

If you get a high average performance rating combined with overperformance on the most important service elements, then you're in a position to celebrate. But as long as you see underperformance on any important elements, you know you have an opportunity to improve your service.

Using Experimentation as a Research Technique

You don't always have to do a survey or ask customers for input in order to do good research. Sometimes all you have to do is carefully track what you do and what happens. This is the scientific method applied to marketing. For example, companies like Lands End or Staples that send catalogs to people on their mailing lists are always testing different designs and methods. Is putting the color-printed catalog in a brown paper mailing sleeve or letting the color cover show better? I don't know, but if you send some catalogs one way and some the other, and then compare the response rates, you'll find out in a hurry.

Identifying your variables

The first step in using a scientific approach is to identify your marketing variables. *Marketing variables* are any aspects of your product, service, or marketing communication that you can control and change and that may affect results. Variables for a mailing include the size of the envelope, whether it has a customized (personal) cover letter, and whether it has a special time-sensitive discount offer.

Varying those variables to see what works

After you determine your marketing variables, start varying them and tracking the results to see what works best. I do this in my own businesses. For example, on our Web sites, www.insightsfortraining.com and www.insightsformarketing.com, I discovered through experimentation that we get a lot more orders when we do two things. First, when we buy key-term listings through the Google and Yahoo search engines, they drive lots of traffic to our sites (if you want to do the same thing, check out their Web sites, www.google.com and www.yahoo.com, for information on advertisers). Second, when we have a special offer on our home page that entices people to make a purchase right away, our orders also increase. For example, we often offer a 15 percent discount on all purchases received by a specific date. These two variables — key-term bids and special offers with a time limit — combine to stimulate immediate credit card purchases over our Web sites. Without these variables, the rate of Web orders falls significantly. When we figured this out, we began using these variables to boost sales strategically whenever we needed more sales volume or wanted to attract attention to a new product.

I don't know exactly what your marketing variables are or what combination and approach will boost your sales most effectively, but I know that you can find out, if you take a scientific approach and are willing to experiment. Every business has its own successful marketing formulas, but each business has a different and unique set of formulas. You're responsible for doing the research and experimentation necessary to find your formulas. If you always take an inquisitive approach, you'll find and polish your own winning formulas.

On the CD

I put two key tools on the CD that come from the customer research chapter in *Marketing For Dummies,* 2nd Edition, because I think they're helpful. They are

- ✔ A diagram of the marketing research process, which maps how you should design and implement any survey or other research (CD0401).
- ✔ Seven Questions to Ask When Reviewing a Survey, which helps you avoid the errors that plague most surveys and make their results vague or misleading (CD0402).

The following CD elements pertain to the information in this book:

- ✔ Customer Debriefing Form (template) (CD0403)
- ✔ 7 x 7 Customer Satisfaction Survey (CD0404)
- ✔ Customer Service Audit (template) (CD0405)

Chapter 5

The Creativity Workshop

Say you have a great new band that you're promoting and you want to get sample copies of their new single out to teenagers inexpensively. If, say, 10,000 copies of the CD get out at low cost in a hurry, you're pretty sure you can generate interest in the band and build a following that will allow you to begin selling CDs through traditional record stores at a profit. But how should you do some sampling and attract teenage enthusiasts to the new sound?

This is a creative question that invites creative ideas. Maybe you should approach some record stores and ask them to place free samples on the counter for their customers. Or maybe you should give out the sample CDs in the summer at public beaches. Or perhaps you should send them by mail as a special benefit for people who visit the band's Web site and request a sample. Or maybe you shouldn't even give out CDs but should offer the music as a free download in digital format instead. What are your options? This question doesn't have one "right" answer; in fact, you may find many right answers. The end goal, though, is for one of your creative ideas to take hold and make an impact on your marketing.

In this chapter, I clue you in on just how important creativity is to marketing success, and I show you how to spur your creativity when you're stumped for more ideas. I also give you advice on how to manage a creative team or project, if you're given that responsibility.

Creativity's Impact on the Five Ps

In this chapter's introduction, I ask you to think about marketing music samples, but here's a real example of how someone solved that creative problem. Entrepreneur Jeffrey Arnold had the idea to put CDs on the lids of soda cups at fast-food restaurants. CDs are round and have a hole in the middle that correspond to the straw hole in a plastic lid for a large soda cup, so why not just stick the sample CD on the lid and give it away with a large Coca Cola? He liked the idea so much that he started a company called LidRock to help marketers take advantage of it. You can use the CDs to promote or sell movies, computer games, or music, and LidRock is piloting the idea right now with major fast-food chains. Will it catch on? I don't know . . . but you probably do, because you're reading this book some time in the future. Have you noticed this new way of distributing CDs when you've gone to the snack counter in a movie theater or when you've stopped at a fast-food restaurant?

The LidRock idea impacts two of the five key marketing variables: promotion and placement. (In Chapter 1, I discuss in detail the five key marketing variables, also known as "the Five Ps" — product, price, placement, promotion, and people — so flip back if you want more info on them.)

How can creativity impact the other Ps of marketing? Read on to find out.

I tell you lots of stories about creativity in this section because getting inspiration from others is often the easiest way to get your own creative juices flowing.

Product innovations

Products often come to life as a result of creativity. Someone innovates to improve a product or invent a new one, and the market changes forever. To see the power of creativity, all you have to do is think about the products that you use every day. Look around you right now and ask yourself how many of the products you see didn't exist ten years ago. Spotting dozens of new ideas with just a quick glance around is easy to do.

New products and clever variations on old products are the bread and butter of marketing. Some are made possible by new technical breakthroughs, but many product innovations have nothing to do with technology. Sometimes the innovations are fresh combinations or forms of traditional products and services. For instance, leasing used to be offered only for big companies that ran fleets of trucks or cars. Then someone had the bright idea to offer leases to car buyers, and he created a new kind of product — a car lease.

Yes, I agree, this example involves some innovation in how you price the product — in fact, this example used a new form of pricing to change the product. So this innovation uses a "hybrid" idea because it affects two of the Five Ps in combination. Creativity often defies categories, and that's okay. Why do you think they call it "out-of-the-box thinking?" People were thinking way out of the box when inventing products like the iPod, PostIt Notes, or the online auction.

Pricing innovations

Price-oriented creativity is at the heart of thousands of discounts, coupons, and other special offers.

The other day, I came across two little boys on the sidewalk who were raising money for their school's track team. How? They sold me a book of coupons along with a card and an ID number for a Web site, where I can go to cash in more discounts. A portion of the proceeds goes to the school, and the rest goes to the company that organizes the coupon booklet and runs the Web site. Now, getting me to hand over a $20 bill to elementary school students on the sidewalk may normally be a hard thing to do, but this official-looking package of coupons made parting with that money easy for me.

Sometimes you can make creative changes in when or how people pay rather than in how much they pay.

For example, the arm of my business that sends trainers to companies to lead workshops under contract has a problem that many such service businesses have: A client may call to book a several-day, expensive event, and we work hard to prepare for it. Then, at the last minute, the client cancels. Of course, if the client has an unexpected problem or priority and simply cannot pull employees out of work for three days to do the workshop, then they have every right to cancel. But what about us? We may have told other companies that we couldn't work for them that week because we were booked. Not to mention that we also spent time and money preparing for the event that now we won't get reimbursed for.

A few years ago, one of our associates suggested that we ask for half the fee in advance in order to hold a date and that we also add a clause to our contract stating that if the client cancels on short notice, we won't refund that portion of the fee. This strategy is a simple, creative way to avoid getting hit financially by clients who change their minds at the last minute; it's also allowed us to reduce the risks associated with scheduling expensive client events needing upfront investment and preparation. The alternative was to raise our rates to cover the risk of unpaid events because of last-minute cancellations. But higher rates may have made selling our services harder, so the advance-payment approach solved the problem in a better way for our clients and for us.

Here's another example from the Norton Museum of Art in West Palm Beach, Florida, that may inspire you. Museums can't live on ticket sales alone; they depend on people buying more expensive annual memberships. So when the Norton Museum has an especially big crowd of visitors on a busy weekend, the marketing manager sometimes hands out special coupons to visitors, offering a refund of the cost of the ticket they just bought if they apply it toward buying an annual membership. Usually some of them do, and the museum wins new members this way. Can you use a similar strategy to upgrade customers to more expensive or long-term purchases? It's certainly food for thought!

Placement innovations

One of my associates stayed at the W Hotel in Los Angeles last month and was impressed by the decor: tasteful furniture, lamps, and even trash cans; luxurious linens and pillows; the finest soaps and shampoos. You'd expect the finest at an upscale hotel, but the innovation she discovered was an elegantly designed catalog from which you can order any of the items in your room. Now that's a clever new way to sell bed and bath products!

I love paintings; I'm very visually oriented, as a lot of marketers are. So I sometimes stick my nose into art galleries, especially when I'm visiting a new city on business. But recently I discovered that I can take a virtual tour of the more valuable and impressive paintings that are for sale by galleries all across the country by visiting www.askart.com. If you have a computer with Internet access handy, why don't you go to this site now so you can see what a clever innovation it is? Visitors to this site can search for artists by name and view digital photos of any art they've created that's currently for sale. Galleries around the world are signing on to services like this one to post their offerings. I talked to several gallery owners who've tried it, and they report that within a year of going online their sales doubled and they began shipping art to distant customers who they'd never even met in person. Now, that concept is a great innovation in how art is sold. By placing the art on a Web site where anyone can view it without having to travel, galleries vastly increase the size of their potential markets.

In the future, I expect new art galleries won't even have expensive downtown exhibit spaces. Instead, they'll do almost all their selling over the Internet. Galleries may even be based out of a warehouse for all their customers know. What's the future of distribution in your business? Can you think of some ways to take costs out or reach more customers more conveniently? Creative placement is often behind the best business plans and the biggest profits.

Promotion innovations

What you name a product and what you say about it can make or break your business plan. Promotional creativity is the most important and attention-getting form of creativity in business. Turn on any TV and every time a show breaks for commercials, you can see dozens of examples of efforts to make promotions creative.

Miller Lite is an interesting example of promotional creativity in action. Once a dominant brand with a growing share of the beer market in the United States, Miller Lite fell on hard times for a while and watched its market share and sales slip. But the brand is currently staging an unusual comeback and is gaining share and growing its sales. How? Nothing about the product has changed — it's still distributed and priced pretty much the same. But the company is promoting it in new ways, and that strategy has made all the difference.

Miller Lite marketers realized that the growing focus on low-carbohydrate diets was important to the beer market. They tested Miller Lite and found that it had fewer carbs than other leading light beers. This finding led to a new emphasis in the product's advertising that helped Miller Lite attract new customers and grow its market share again.

Sometimes what you say doesn't matter as much as how you say it.

While Miller Lite was working to reposition itself as the tasty light beer with the fewest carbs, its sister brand, Miller Beer, was beginning to run ads emphasizing its individuality and independence. These concepts are, of course, personality attributes, so good, reactive advertising is needed to associate them with a product. Miller Beer is now making gains with a new TV ad in which a long row of men falls over like dominoes, one bumping into another in succession, until one of the men steps aside and orders a Miller. This ad says in a clever way that "Miller drinkers are different, independent, strong. They don't go mindlessly along with the crowd." A creative ad like this one, with its memorable imagery, can do a great deal to make a product successful. What can you do to present your own brand's personality in a creative, memorable way in your marketing communications?

Also look for creative ways to get your message in front of people. Take, for instance, an agency in New York City that's renting forehead space for logos (so now you see a company logo on people's foreheads as they walk around town). A bit crazy? Yes, but many good ideas seem that way, at least at first. Or how about the strategy of renting spaces for a new car in front of the finest restaurants in order to get it in front of prospective drivers?

People innovations

Here's a wild and crazy idea: How about having your CEO answer the phone for a day and, of course, why not give a new title to the person who answers your company calls? Perhaps VP of Customer Interaction?

In this age of computerized phone systems, having real, live, knowledgeable, friendly people answer customer calls is a radical idea. So few companies offer this service today that it could give you a real competitive advantage.

When, where, and how you have people interact with customers is a very important part of your marketing. You can do it innovatively and well or you can do it poorly. The difference between a bad server and a good one determines whether or not you go back to the restaurant a second time. At Pike's Place Fish Market in Seattle, the staff is encouraged to joke and clown around in front of customers, and this innovation has made the store a major tourist attraction and a multi-million-dollar success.

People can be your most important and valuable asset — but only if you can find ways to connect them meaningfully with your customers. Any ideas for your business? I hope so!

Being Creative but Also Practical

In business, I find that creativity needs to be a cyclical activity, not a continuous one. After you come up with and introduce a creative idea, you often want to repeat and perfect it, milking it for profits before doing the next creative thing. In marketing, perfecting an idea may mean testing several new creative magazine ads, discovering that one of them seems to *pull* (generate leads or sales) especially well, and then repeating the ad for the rest of the year or until consumers finally grow tired of it and stop responding well.

Being creative takes effort and money. A new idea for an ad or brochure requires someone to design it and print it, and that involves time, effort, and usually money as well. So focusing your creativity where it can do the most good is important.

Harnessing your creativity for profit

The pure artistic approach to creativity is just to be as creative as you can for the pure joy of it. In marketing, profit is usually the more dominant motive — although creativity should also be fun, because you can't come up with winning creative ideas unless you're in a good mood and are relaxed enough to free your imagination. A good way to keep creativity fun but also profitable is to decide what your creative goals are; then, be creative within the discipline of your business goals.

For instance, I sometimes lead brainstorming sessions for client companies. But I never do a completely free session; I always start with a clear strategic goal, such as

- ✔ Thinking of ways to freshen up an aging product
- ✔ Coming up with attention-getting ideas for a new promotional event
- ✔ Improving the company's Web site or printed brochures
- ✔ Designing a fun and effective new trade show booth
- ✔ Thinking of a better new logo and tag line to use on the company's letterhead and in advertising

Each of these topics can provide the focus and purpose to a wild and crazy brainstorming session. I've run sessions on each of these topics many times. Usually, I set a goal for the session, such as 100 new ideas for modernizing or renewing our product. A quantitative goal is better for creative idea sessions than a qualitative one; if you tell everyone that the goal is one really good idea, they'll self-censor their ideas and not be freely creative. You probably won't get any ideas. But if you say that the goal is 100 ideas, any ideas, it doesn't matter how dumb or crazy, you'll probably get 200 ideas. And ideas tend to build on each other, so as the group generates more and more, the quality begins to take care of itself, and you usually get at least a handful of really promising ideas out of the crop of hundreds.

Not getting carried away

My editors asked me to put this topic in. Editors often have to rein us creative writers in and keep us focused and disciplined. You may have to play editor with creative ideas in your marketing. An editor seeks the best and cuts the rest. Use this strategy with your creativity.

Sometimes a wonderfully entertaining, creative ad comes on TV and everyone talks about it. But here's the interesting thing: Half the time, people remember the ad vividly but aren't sure what product or company it's for. That creativity isn't useful because it doesn't connect the impression the ad makes with what the ad is selling.

To make sure that you aren't getting carried away, stop for a moment and ask yourself whether the creative ad, brochure, Web page, event, or whatever it is, is in danger of becoming its own product instead of selling yours. Try to avoid the trap of "creativity for its own sake." Entertaining or amazing an audience without making any sales is expensive. You aren't doing creativity just for the fun of it in marketing!

Tools and Techniques for Generating Creative Concepts

I use the term *marketing imagination* throughout this book, and this concept is probably the most important factor in marketing success or failure. Your ability to imagine new approaches is vital to your success as a marketer. The salesperson who invents a new opener or comes up with a new strategy for generating leads is the one who sells the most product. The distributor who finds creative new ways to serve customers over the Web gains on its competition. The small business that seeks new ways to promote its products or services makes a bigger impact at lower cost. And the advertiser who creates an imaginative message captures consumer attention and makes more sales.

In contrast, any marketer who fails to be creative or who tries to just use last year's formula or borrow directly from others is destined for failure. Marketing demands more creativity than any other business activity. So it only seems fair for me to help you be more creative in your approach to marketing. In this section, I give you some techniques to help you engage your creative imagination and come up with breakthrough sales and marketing ideas.

The creativity methods I discuss here are drawn from my work in corporate training. My firm puts on a number of creativity trainings and sometimes facilitates creative problem-solving retreats. In addition, it develops and publishes a variety of resources for trainers and managers in the area of creativity (see my book, *The Manager's Pocket Guide to Creativity,* published by HRD Press, for a larger collection of creative techniques). So I want to share the best of these many resources with you. I don't want you to feel stuck and unable to come up with fresh ideas. If you ever get to that point (most people do fairly often), dip into this section and reignite your marketing imagination!

Revel in the irreverent

Seek out and enjoy unconventional and crazy approaches. Any examples of how people can flaunt the rules of convention are inspirational. Even if they have nothing to do with marketing, irreverent attitudes can inspire your marketing imagination. For example, today's wild teenage fashions will end up in tomorrow's high-end clothing lines because most of these designers' new ideas are inspired by teenagers who are trying to break conventions, not make them.

When I get stuck on a marketing communication and can't seem to come up with a fresh idea, I like to watch a few scenes of the movie *Crazy People*. The movie is a comedy about an advertising copywriter who goes over the edge and gets sent to a mental hospital, where he and his fellow patients create such crazy and wonderful ads that his agency ends up begging them for more. The story is silly and it makes me laugh. After 15 minutes of that silliness, my mind is much freer and I'm able to think more creatively about my own ads or other marketing communications.

I recommend any comedy, whether it has something to do with business or not. Humor is based on unusual viewpoints, and it helps you loosen up and find your own creative perspectives.

I also recommend keeping an eye out for crackpots and others who do things strangely on the fringes of your industry. For every successful business, a dozen marginal ones operate outside the normal rules and rarely amount to anything. But sometimes these businesses have the weirdest ideas, and when you combine those weird ideas with a sound understanding of how the industry works, they may just lead to breakthrough insights. So don't forget to pay attention to the crazy people in your own industry. Sometimes they're better at inspiring your marketing imagination than more successful but conventional role models are.

Force yourself to develop alternatives

The quest for new and better alternatives is the essence of creativity. The marketing imagination is never content — it's always seeking new approaches. I remember one two-day product development session that I helped facilitate for Kellogg's, the breakfast-cereal company. Leaders of the company hoped to come up with one good new product as a result of the session. But which idea would be the winning idea? Hard to know. Best to make sure you have plenty of alternatives. So the group and I generated more than 900 new product concepts during our retreat.

Was coming up with so many good ideas hard? Yes and no. Generating the first five ideas was pretty easy, but in hindsight, they weren't worth a second look. Coming up with the next 20 ideas was much harder, but that list had hints of inspiration. But still nothing to write home about. We had to keep going.

After we got past the first 100, we were on a roll and could've kept inventing new concepts forever, if we'd had the time. In the long run, the few new product concepts that made it to the test market were in the high hundreds — so we'd already come up with hundreds of ideas before them. That means we may not have come up with *any* useable concepts unless we'd been as persistent as we were.

Perhaps this result also means that we could've come up with even better ideas if we'd developed twice as many . . . Oh well.

Don't overplan

Most experts tell you to write a careful plan. Marketing plans and business plans in general can help you anticipate the future and make sure that you're ready for it. But they can also destroy creativity. Plans hurt creativity in two main ways:

- ✔ **If you have to write everything down upfront, you won't have the opportunity to come up with creative approaches later.** The weight of the planning exercise deadens creativity. To decide all the year's marketing activities in just one week of planning is pretty hard. And it's certainly not fun. People who have to do that task aren't going to spend much time being creative. They're going to approach marketing in a mechanical way, looking up costs and writing them down one after the other until they've fulfilled their obligations.

- ✔ **If you have to follow a detailed plan, then the plan does the thinking for you and you miss the opportunity to learn, experiment, and invent as you go.** Rigid plans and microplanning that structure every decision and action are the enemies of creativity. They keep people from reacting and creating.

To make planning creative, leave room in your plan for improvisation. Sure, you face budget limits and you need to follow broad strategies that you expect to work. But also leave room for modifying the plan. I like to revisit my plans every month or two and, if I get a better idea, I simply rewrite my plan around it. Your plan is only paper. Throw it out if it's getting in your way and write a new one!

Also, make sure that your plans aren't too detailed. For example, specifying that you're budgeting so much for publicity, most of which should focus on generating press about your business activities, is one thing. That example is fine because it leaves you plenty of room to invent clever ways of getting publicity. But planning exactly how you're going to spend that publicity budget is quite another thing. For instance, if you specify one press release a month to the in-house press list of 250 names, you've just guaranteed that nothing imaginative will happen all year. Don't overplan!

Identify your personal barriers and enablers

A *creativity barrier* is anything that gets in the way of your creativity. And plenty of things can do just that. Being more aware of those barriers helps you learn how to avoid them or minimize their impacts. Here are some of the most common barriers:

✔ **Pressure to conform:** Thinking and behaving differently from others is taboo in many organizations and industries. This approach means that people are more conservative than they need to be.

✔ **Perfectionism:** If you worry too much about how well you perform, you'll be afraid to try anything really new. Sometimes I remind myself that when it comes to creative innovations, "If it's worth doing, it's worth doing poorly!"

✔ **Overconfidence:** It's easy to assume that you're doing the right thing without stopping to question yourself. Overconfidence keeps you from examining your assumptions or developing and considering alternatives.

When you know that a creativity barrier affects you, you can guard against it. Awareness is the key.

Creativity enablers are factors that help you be more creative. They work in the opposite direction of barriers, helping you overcome barriers and leading you to creative insights. Here are some of the more common enablers:

✔ **Open-mindedness:** An open, accepting approach to other ideas and methods is a great enabler. If you're open-minded, you often receive inspiration from others that you may otherwise miss.

✔ **Role models:** Creative innovators are great enablers. Try to find and spend time with such people. They can get your creative motor running in no time!

✔ **Persistence:** Perhaps the most powerful enabler of all, persistence keeps you trying even when your initial efforts at creativity fail. Often the only major difference between highly creative people and those people who aren't creative is that the creative people don't give up as quickly. Do you?

A lot of creativity trainings use this barriers/enablers model to help people identify factors that they need to focus on in order to boost their personal creativity. If you want to find out more about this topic, see my *Personal Creativity Assessment* booklet (published by HRD Press) for details and a self-assessment test. I put information about it on this book's Web site, `www.insightsformarketing.com`.

Incubate

Incubation is just what the term suggests. You sit on a problem or idea, keeping it warm, until it hatches a solution. But first, you have to lay that egg. In other words, start by focusing hard and furiously on your subject of concern. Research it thoroughly and bang your head against it over and over all week long. Wear yourself out. Then relax. Time to sit on the egg that you just laid. Take a little time off. Or work on something else. Just stop to have a quick look at the problem or to turn it over in your mind every now and then.

After you've let your problem or idea incubate for a while, you may begin to hear from it. It starts to call your attention back to it as new ideas and approaches come to mind. Then, and only then, is your idea ready to hatch. When you revisit it and give it your undivided attention again, you may find that you have more and better ideas than you had before.

Because incubation works so well, try scheduling your marketing development efforts to permit incubation. For example, rather than planning to spend three consecutive days writing a new brochure, why not schedule two days to study it and begin work on it, take three days off the project for incubation, and then one final day to complete your work? The result will be more imaginative and better because of the incubation period, yet you won't have spent any more of your work time on the project.

Break it down

When I get stumped on a project, I use a strategy called "breakdown brain-storming," and I've used it to good effect on many difficult tasks. The idea behind _breakdown brainstorming_ is to put some creative effort into thinking about the task itself rather than moving directly to formulating solutions. (You can find more information on this strategy in my book, _The Manager's Pocket Guide to Creativity,_ published by HRD Press.)

For instance, say you're working on a Web page and you want to do something creative and special. But what? You're stuck. So break down the task into as many subproblems or subtasks as you can imagine. Your list may include issues such as "attract people to our site," "make our site more entertaining," "create an opening page for the site that really wows people," and "find a game people can play on our site." Now you've broken the broad problem of designing a creative site into many smaller problems, some of which may fire your imagination more easily than the original problem did.

Compete

You're more likely to come up with a creative breakthrough when you have two or more individuals or groups working on the same creative task at the same time. So why not create a contest for yourself and a few other associates or friends? Pick a good reward — sometimes a joke reward is best. Give each person or group the same amount of time and the same starting information. Then compete to see who comes up with the best ideas!

Record more of your own ideas

You often have ideas that you discard or forget. If you get in the habit of recording more of your ideas, you may find that some of them are more valuable than you thought. Also, your marketing imagination becomes more active when it gets attention. By simply making notes or recordings of your ideas, you stimulate their production and soon generate many more.

I record ideas in several ways. I keep a large daily planning book, with room to write down not only my appointments but also my ideas. When I'm stuck, I flip back through the pages and pick out a good idea to follow through on. I also keep idea boxes where I can toss my notes or interesting articles that I clip out to stimulate my thinking. I have an idea box for each of my major projects. In addition, I keep a miniature tape recorder in my briefcase and often dictate ideas into it. Then I get the tapes transcribed so I can read them later.

Come up with your own system for recording ideas. Whatever works best for you is the right one, so try several. Or you can enlist others in your quest for ideas. You may want to provide everyone in your company with an idea journal and reward the best ideas in your monthly journal awards!

Look hard at your assumptions

Many smaller businesses assume that TV advertising is too expensive for them. That's a silly assumption. You can buy local television advertising very cheaply in most markets, and you can even find relatively inexpensive national cable ad slots. I'm not saying that all businesses ought to advertise on TV, but some businesses could and don't realize it because of their assumptions.

All marketers make assumptions and, in general, most of them are questionable. For example, assuming that your business isn't newsworthy is a common assumption, so your business never explores the potential of publicity. And many people assume that they can't manage word of mouth, so they do nothing to try to build referrals. Watch out for such assumptions! They keep you from considering many creative alternatives. You can create breaking news by sponsoring a benefit concert for a charity. You can encourage positive word of mouth referrals by offering a prize to the customer who brings you the most new customers. You can . . . wait, it's your turn to come up with an idea now!

Talk to ten successful people

I recently ran into a friend who's an artist. She complained that she needed to reach a broader market with her work but didn't know how to do it. She asked me whether any of my books held the solution. I hate to pass up a chance to make a sale, but I had to tell her no. The specific solution to marketing her work isn't found in *any* book. It has to come from her. It has to be something unique and creative. So where can she find the ideas she needs?

I suggested that she contact ten other artists and ask them how they market their work. Each one probably has a slightly different approach. By listening to each of their stories, she may begin seeing more possibilities than she does right now.

It's a wonderful discipline to go out and interview ten people and ask them how they do their sales and marketing. Put on your journalist's hat, take along a pad and pencil, and collect information about how other people do it. You're sure to come across something new and different that gives you a good idea for your own business.

Managing Creative Projects and Teams

When you have a group of people trying to be creative together, all sorts of complications arise. The first issue to watch out for is overly critical feedback. If one person tells another that an idea is stupid or won't work, the other person is going to hesitate to present more ideas. So try to instill an open-minded, positive attitude in your group of creative marketers. Praise creativity, even if it isn't practical. The more you recognize and reward creative behavior, the more creative ideas you'll have to choose from.

Next, recognize that different people are creative in different ways — and some people are more creative than others. The classic creative personality is very inquisitive, open-minded, and artistic, but not very organized or focused. Do you have someone in your office or on your marketing team who has great ideas and lots of imagination, is interested in all sorts of odd topics, but can't keep his or her desk clean? If so, this person is a great one to put in charge of looking for new product ideas or coming up with better headlines for new ads.

But don't ask this person to make sure that you meet all the deadlines for submitting ads to magazines on time. Obviously, for this part of the creative process, someone with a more organized personality and a clear focus is a better choice.

If you can, build creative teams out of people with contrasting personalities so that the team has all the complementary strengths needed to take a project from idea stage to execution. In marketing, you have to turn creative ideas into practical projects and complete them on time and within budget. This task requires a challenging balance of different kinds of personalities, skills, and roles. Some people can do all these things themselves, but most can't. Working with at least two or three other people whose creative profiles are different from your own is wise. Doing so makes passing the baton and filling all the roles needed to bring great ideas to practical fruition easier.

I include a great tool for managing creative groups or building creative marketing teams on the CD. It's called *Creative Roles Analysis,* and it's an assessment booklet that my firm uses in creativity trainings and retreats with clients (you can find it on CD0501). Normally, you'd have to buy the booklet from my firm, but you can print out as many copies as you need for each member of your staff or team so they can take the assessment and discuss who's best suited to play what roles on creative marketing projects. So if you want to really dig into the topic and discover more about your own and the rest of your team's creativity, print out this assessment and make sure each member completes it. (I also include instructions for interpreting and using the results on CD0501.)

On the CD

▮ ✔ Creative Roles Analysis (CD0501)

Chapter 6

Writing Well for Marketing and Sales

Sometimes marketing seems as if it's all about writing. I can't recall an ad in any medium that didn't have some writing in it, and many ads are dominated by writing. Similarly, coupons, contests, memberships, and other special promotions need a lot of clear writing to communicate their benefits and rules to customers. And sales rely on writing, too. Many people do sales approaches or follow-up proposals to businesses in writing instead of verbally, and sales materials always take written form. So, you can see why writing is an essential core skill for all marketers.

How do you go about the process of conceiving and writing great ads, direct-mail letters, brochures, or other marketing communications? Every good marketing communication starts with ideas that make it persuasive and effective. Marketing is all about communicating your offer in a compelling manner — a manner that gets attention and shapes opinions and behaviors. And that's a tall order! We ask a lot of our marketing communications, whether they're ads, mailers, Web pages, catalogs, brochures, or other forms of communication with our customers and prospects. So you need to do quite a bit of thinking in order to come up with ideas that really work. In this chapter, you discover some of the techniques that can really help you differentiate your communications from the pack.

Writing Persuasively

As a marketer, you need to create effective writing for ads, sales letters, Web sites, press releases, catalogs, and many other applications. Whether you do most of this writing yourself or use others to help draft it, you need to make sure that it's *good* writing. Your writing has to be clear, interesting, professional (no obvious errors, please!), and — most important — persuasive.

If you don't want to write yourself

Are you a good writer? I know that's a personal question, but you need to be honest about your writing talent. In ad agencies, specialists called *copywriters* do the writing — and they're excellent writers. But most people aren't. If you enjoy writing and are at least moderately good at drafting and editing clear, interesting copy, then by all means, read this chapter and write your own marketing materials, sales letters, and ads. I'm a writer (okay, I guess that's obvious), so I often draft catalog copy, ads, and letters for my own company as well as help my clients put marketing magic in their writing. But I know lots of great marketers and businesspeople who don't write well and probably never will. So, what can you do if writing isn't one of your strengths? Here are a few ideas:

- ✔ **Take advantage of books of business letters.** These books can provide a good starting point, allowing you to customize and refine a letter rather than having to start one from scratch. If you suffer from writer's block, a starting draft — even a poor one — may break the logjam and get you writing.

- ✔ **Make friends with writers.** Some people love writing and editing and enjoy the challenge of improving your copy. These eager volunteers can exercise their talents when they volunteer to help you write. Return the favor by doing something you're good at and they aren't; then everybody's happy.

- ✔ **Hire a writer.** Most writers are underpaid, so you can probably afford one. But don't assume that all writers can produce good marketing copy. A novelist writes 300-page stories, not short direct-response ads. Look at writers' portfolios and select the person whose portfolio includes the kind of writing that you need.

- ✔ **Hire an ad agency.** This strategy is the expensive approach, but sometimes turning the work over to the pros is a good idea. However, still insist on checking the portfolio of the copywriter assigned to your work and refuse to sign a contract until you have a writer who obviously can do just what you need.

✔ **Copy good writing . . . sort of.** Sometimes I clip a great ad or file a good brochure to use as inspiration the next time I need to do some marketing writing. However, I don't copy the writing directly; I only use it as a general model to inspire my own creative work. Copyright laws apply to any marketing materials or ads that you collect, which means you can't use the writing. Not even one paragraph of it. Remember in school how teachers taught you how to use source materials to write a paper but warned you not to plagiarize? Same rule applies here, except now you can go to court instead of the principal's office. So be careful when using other marketers' work for inspiration.

These strategies are for marketers who find writing painfully difficult. If you don't mind sharpening your pencil and crafting a careful paragraph or two, the rest of this chapter will help you make your marketing copy more effective. Oh, and even if you don't do the writing yourself, as a marketer, your job is to make sure that it's engaging and persuasive, so maybe you'd better read this chapter anyway! Someone has to manage the writing project and approve the final copy, and that someone should be you.

Engaging and persuading your audience

Basically, you can engage and persuade people in one of two ways:

✔ By appealing to them with a compelling, logical argument

✔ By appealing to them with an engaging story

Or you can use a combination of these strategies. But the point is, these two strategies are always options when you're communicating. And thinking about which option you might use is a wonderful source of inspiration whenever you need to create strong marketing communications.

In this section, I show you how to write incredibly effective *copy* (the words or story behind any ad or other marketing communication) that you can use for a print ad, a direct-mail piece, a brochure or catalog, a Web page, a broadcast fax, a radio or TV commercial, or whatever. The basic strategy applies to anything, even to a personal sales presentation. And the strategy's based on using these two very different ways of making a point when you communicate.

Straight facts or a little drama

Thinking about whether you want to make a factual argument in your ad or dramatize your point with some sort of story is always helpful.

In fact, every marketing communication has a factual and a fictional version that's just waiting for discovery. So which approach should you use? Or should you try something that's a combination of the two forms — part fact and part fiction? Simply posing this question opens up many possibilities to you as you develop your ad or other marketing communication.

Let me illustrate the difference between a factual and fictional version of a marketing communication. Imagine that you're designing a letter that you want to send to prospects of a training firm to introduce a new training program that teaches employees how to handle customer complaints effectively. I'll call this program Handling Angry Customers, or HAC for short. And I'll assume that it's a really great program and companies that use it to train their employees have happier, more loyal customers and make lots more money as a result. But how do you convince managers and training directors that HAC is a good service? What should the introductory letter say to catch their ears and get them interested in the training?

Just the facts, ma'am

Well, first, you may rough out a factual letter. A factual letter makes a logical argument, such as the following:

> *Dear Manager:*
>
> *Everyone knows that it costs ten times as much to win a new customer as it does to do business with an existing customer. Yet companies routinely lose their good customers because of errors or slip-ups that upset or anger those good customers and open the door for defection. What can you do to keep your customers from leaving you? What can you do to make sure that they buy more next year instead of less? What, in short, is the secret of high customer loyalty?*
>
> *People. It comes down to people in 99.9 percent of the cases, according to our extensive research. We studied the companies with the most loyal customers in a dozen different industries and, in every case, these winning companies have more sensitive, better-trained employees. Employees who know what to do when customers are upset or angry. Employees who know how to convert each problem into an opportunity to build loyalty instead of losing business.*
>
> *That's why we designed Handling Angry Customers (HAC), the radical new customer-service training that has a measurable impact on your customer retention rates — or you get your money back!*

Now, that argument is pretty powerful. It makes the case for the HAC service quite forcefully. And most people who want to describe a new service for business-to-business sales probably would choose a factual approach based on argument, just like this copy employs.

A flair for the dramatic

But remember what your ninth-grade teacher told you about all the different ways of making your point. You should also be able to present the HAC training program in a completely different manner using the tools of the dramatist and telling a story (or stories) instead of arguing the facts. For example, you may draft some copy for that direct-mail piece that goes like this:

> *Dear Manager:*
>
> *I want to share a little story that I think you will find interesting.*
>
> *Rick, the purchasing manager for SysTech, was a man of action. He hated to waste even a minute of his company's precious time. Yet today, he was doing something uncharacteristic. He was doing nothing. He had been doing nothing for four and a half minutes already, and it was obviously wearing on him.*
>
> *Rick was on hold. On hold with your company, to be specific. He was on hold because he had called to complain about a minor problem with the last order and been put on hold by one of your employees who didn't know how to handle the call.*
>
> *In contrast, your employee was quite busy. She was busy asking anyone she could find what to do. She had no idea how to solve Rick's problem. But she sensed the urgency in his voice, and she, too, was well aware of the ticking of the clock. Finally, after searching fruitlessly for the appropriate paperwork and getting a wide variety of unhelpful advice from her associates, your employee came back on the line. Five minutes and sixteen seconds had passed since she had put Rick on hold. You don't want to know what Rick said in reply when her first words to him were, "I'm sorry, Sir, but I can't find any record of that order. Are you sure you really sent it in?"*
>
> *Accidents happen, as the old saying goes. But whether you recover from them gracefully or lose a customer for life depends on how you handle those accidents. If that employee had only received basic Handling Angry Customers (HAC) training, she would have known not to put poor Rick on hold even for one minute. That violates the Adding-Insult-to-Injury principle, which says that you must handle all unhappy customers with a high degree of consideration and support. And never, ever, put them on hold or question their word when they are upset!*
>
> *But Rick doesn't care any more. He's already busy placing his order with one of your competitors. A competitor who has recently trained all its employees in the HAC program and is not likely to lose a customer over a minor problem. You may as well throw Rick's business card away. You're not likely to do business with SysTech again!*

This example uses a dramatic approach to make a point. It creates a plausible scenario that catches your reader's ear and draws her forward. It makes her wonder whether such dramas are playing out right now somewhere in her own business. And if so, well, she's certainly likely to question her staff's ability to handle angry customers and wonder if a little training may not be a wise investment. . . .

If you switch on your TV, you're bound to see a number of examples of both styles of advertising within a short period of time. Some TV spots make rational arguments, presenting facts and attempting to make you believe their product claims. Others present dramas, tell stories, and try to affect your attitudes toward their products by making their stories compelling.

Considering which option is better

Which works better, an argument-based communication or a dramatic one? There is no hard and fast rule. Sometimes one approach works better, and sometimes the other one does. So considering both options as you develop and test different versions of an ad is always wise.

To see how you may use this insight, return to the example of a company that wants to send out a letter to training managers and executives to introduce the new Handling Angry Customers training program. Rather than simply writing the standard argument-based, factual letter, I drafted copy for two kinds of letters — one with a fact-based approach and one with a fiction-based approach. One letter will work to the extent that its arguments are persuasive. The other will work to the extent that its dramatic scenario is compelling.

Dusting off your writing skills

Remember back in your old high school writing class when you explored the many ways of making a point through writing? Perhaps you had an assignment where you had to show how a character in a story feels when something bad happens to her. Well, you might just describe her feelings:

"She was hollow. Empty inside. She felt cheated and alone. In fact, she'd never been so down in her life."

Or you might create an imaginary scene that portrays her feelings:

"She slumped against the railing of the bridge, tears streaking her cheeks, tempted by the cold waters far below."

Both approaches communicate your point that the character is having a really bad day, but they do it in very different ways.

Which way is best? The approach you take depends on what you're trying to accomplish, the context, and the reader. It depends, in part, on your taste and style as well. There isn't necessarily one best way to make a point, but when you recognize and experiment with alternative approaches, you're more likely to find a good solution in any situation.

With both approaches in hand, I can test two very different types of letters. I can simply divide my mailing list in half, send out the two different letters, and wait to see which one more training managers respond to. Odds are, one letter or the other will pull significantly better. And if I hadn't written both versions, I never would've had a chance to find out which approach was best in this specific situation.

Always think "test" when you're working on a marketing communication. You can run one ad one week and another ad the next. You can mail or e-mail multiple letters by randomly dividing your list into sections. You can try different brochures on different customers or prospects. You can always find a way to experiment and compare multiple options. And when you do, you can discover far more than most of your competitors ever will, because most people aren't thoughtful enough to design even the simplest of experiments. This is one of the reasons why most people market in the dark.

Hybrid ads: Have your cake and eat it, too

Here's another way you can take advantage of the fact that ads can take either a factual or dramatic approach. Why not incorporate both approaches into one ad? Using this strategy, you may create a hybrid that works better than either form does on its own. At least it's worth a try. Why not test these three versions of any sales-oriented communication letters?

- ✔ A straight, rational, persuasive argument based on facts
- ✔ A dramatic ad that's based almost entirely on a story or scenario
- ✔ A combination of fact-based argument and a brief story to dramatize your point

After you create a factual and a dramatic version, developing the hybrid of the two is no big deal. Then you have three options of your sales communication to test, and testing them is easy because you can measure the response rates.

I prefer communications that combine argument and storytelling. I find the hybrid approach often makes the most effective ad or direct-mail letter. You can even use this approach on the Internet.

For example, you can include storytelling on a Web page or in an electronic newsletter. Whenever you have the opportunity to engage the reader long enough to communicate any details, a combination of argument and storytelling can work wonders. You can do it in a broadcast fax. You can use a picture that tells a story in a print ad, combined with written arguments. You can combine personal testimonials from happy customers with a factual description of the benefits of your product in a brochure. You have no limits when you're incorporating elements of both argument and narrative into a single marketing piece.

You can even incorporate both styles in personal selling by weaving some case histories or testimonials into a sales presentation. I'm always amazed at how seldom people actually use any form of storytelling in sales, yet it's an extremely powerful tool. In fact, I noticed over the years that the most successful salespeople tend to weave three or four stories into each sales presentation. They often use stories about other customers to illustrate a point. Similarly, some of the most effective sales collateral — brochures, catalog sheets, audiovisuals, and other materials that the presentation refers to — are full of stories. They may include actual case histories, customer testimonials, or generic stories written to illustrate how the product or service works. Never underestimate the power of storytelling when you weave it into sales presentations!

A work of art: Fact and fiction combined

When you create hybrid ad copy using both arguments and storytelling, you tap into both the rational and emotional sides of your customers with relative ease. Let me show you what I mean by creating a hybrid of the two approaches I showed you earlier for the Handling Angry Customers training program. I lead with the story version for the simple reason that people often react initially on an emotional basis and then engage their rational minds. So an opening appeal to emotion is a great initial attention getter. And a strong finish based on rational facts and arguments is a great way to cement those initial emotional responses by adding rational conviction to them. When I combine the two approaches into one (tightening them up a bit to avoid making the hybrid too lengthy), I get the following direct-mail or brochure copy:

> *Dear Manager:*
>
> *Rick, the purchasing manager for SysTech, is a man of action who hates to waste even a minute of his busy day. It is not like him to do nothing. But he has actually been doing nothing at all for four and a half minutes now, and it is definitely beginning to wear on him.*
>
> [Show picture of a man in shirt sleeves and a tie, phone to ear, looking at his watch in exasperation.]
>
> *Rick is on hold. On hold with your company, to be specific. He was put on hold when he called to complain about a problem with his last order — by an employee who didn't know how to handle the call.*
>
> [Show picture of frazzled employee, phone in one hand, making a palms-up gesture as if to say I have no idea how to handle this.]
>
> *If this were a real-life situation, you can imagine that your employee would be quite busy. Perhaps busy trying to track down the paperwork and figure out how to solve Rick's problem. Finally, after searching fruitlessly for the appropriate paperwork and getting a wide variety of unhelpful advice from*

her associates, your employee comes back on the line. Five minutes and sixteen seconds have passed since she put Rick on hold, and you don't want to know what Rick says in reply when her first words to him are, "I'm sorry, Sir, but I can't find any record of your order. Are you sure you really sent it in?"

Everything depends on the employee's response

Accidents happen, as the old saying goes. But whether you recover from them gracefully or lose a customer for life depends on how you handle those accidents. If the employee in the preceding story had only received Handling Angry Customers (HAC) training, she would have known that putting Rick on hold violates the Adding-Insult-to-Injury principle, which says that you must handle all unhappy customers with a high degree of consideration and support. And never, ever, put them on hold or question their word when they are upset!

A major source of hidden losses

Every manager knows that it costs ten times as much to win a new customer as it does to do business with an existing customer. Yet companies routinely lose good customers like Rick over slip-ups that anger those good customers and open the door for defection.

Did you know?

A large majority of unhappy customers give very clear signs that they are unhappy. Yet, according to our research, the vast majority of employees fail to pick up on those signs or respond appropriately to them.

What can you do to keep your customers from leaving you? What is the secret of high customer loyalty?

People.

It comes down to people in 99.9 percent of the cases, according to our research. We studied the companies with the most loyal customers in a dozen different industries and, in every case, these winning companies had more sensitive, better-trained employees. Employees who know what to do when customers are upset or angry. Employees who know how to convert each problem into an opportunity to build loyalty instead of losing business.

That's why we designed Handling Angry Customers (HAC), the radical new customer-service training that has a measurable impact on your customer retention rates — or you get your money back!

"My employees are performing 100 percent better since their HAC training, and I'm getting a lot of compliments from my customers. They really notice the difference."

— Charlotte McGwire, President, Global Food Supply, Inc.

You can take the first no-obligation step toward higher customer loyalty today by calling us or returning the enclosed postcard to get your Course Overview booklet and video today. And if you respond before the end of the month, you qualify for our introductory promotion, which locks in a 15 percent discount for any training events scheduled within the next six months. So please take a decisive step toward educating your employees by contacting us to preview or schedule the Handling Angry Customers training today.

Sincerely,

Millicent Marketer

V.P., Training Programs

About hybrid letter strategy

Before I go into the details of the hybrid story-and-argument strategy, I want to point out a few things that I did in this example to develop it a little further than the earlier ones:

- ✔ **Visuals:** I came up with some concepts for visuals, which I can use if the medium permits. A couple of simple black-and-white photos may work well in a two-page letter. If I adapt this copy to a brochure format, I'd probably opt for nicer full-color photos, budget permitting.

- ✔ **Headers:** I dropped in a few headers to break up the text, which makes it more readable. The headers entice the eye, drawing the reader into each section. They also tend to reinforce the points by hitting the reader over the head with them.

- ✔ **Text boxes:** I added two text boxes that readers can read independently of the main copy. The text boxes reinforce the copy and give readers with short attention spans something to jump to. Note that the first box offers another factual appeal. The second box is an emotional appeal based on a story. Specifically, it quotes a customer who's had a good experience with the product. Such testimonials are often very powerful and tend to be under-used in marketing communications.

- ✔ **Bold and italic text:** I added some bold and italics to the text to emphasize key points that I was afraid might get lost in the length of this piece. Be careful with any such embellishments, however. If you get too carried away, you may make the copy look silly and reduce its credibility.

- ✔ **Call to action paragraph:** I finished this letter with a final paragraph containing a *call to action* — details of what the reader can do next along with some incentive to do it now.

Developing a letter like this one to a high level takes quite a bit of care, but the effort is worth it when you get increased responses.

Combining an opening story with hard-hitting fact-based arguments and ending with a simple call to action should generate a nice response rate. Why? Because this marketing communication pushes two powerful buttons: It appeals to emotion and it appeals to logic. Which means it stands a good chance of creating immediate involvement with any reader who has reason to worry about how well his employees handle customer problems and complaints.

Think of getting attention as having full reader involvement — which means the reader is involved both emotionally and rationally. The preceding sample letter attempts to get attention and turn it into action by combining an emotional appeal (based on a story) with a rational appeal (based on factual argument).

What makes hybrid ads so effective?

I've demonstrated an obvious bias for hybrid ads, letters, sales presentations, and other communications that combine the best of fact-based argument with the best of narrative. Why is this strategy my favorite? Because it has two things going for it:

- ✔ **Creating a hybrid letter is usually the third step in a creative process.** Generally, people tend to create ads or ad concepts in the order I listed them in the previous section — that is, first, they create the rational argument based on facts; second, they create the dramatic persuasion based on storytelling; and third, they develop the hybrid that includes some of both tactics. Why do you have an advantage using the form that you created last? Because by doing so, you spend more time and invest more effort in your ad. You really had to work hard to develop two completely different approaches and then find a good way to combine them. So the hybrid form represents more creative energy and a higher level of involvement on the marketer's part. And, in general, when you put more of yourself into an ad, you get more out of it.

- ✔ **Hybrid ads take advantage of the fact that we humans have both a rational and an emotional side.** In fact, many scientists believe that arguments literally appeal to a different side of the brain than stories do. By combining appeals to both our rational and emotional sides, hybrid ads tend to cast the broadest net. And when both the rational and emotional appeals work well, these ads build the highest involvement on the parts of their readers, listeners, or viewers.

Getting Serious about Testing Your Copy

In the previous section, I show you how I combined a rational appeal with a story to make a direct-mail piece that has high impact. Good strategy, but will it work? Of course you never really know how it'll work until you try it. But you have no reason to market blindly. You can use a lot of easy ways to test what you've written and see how it performs. In this section, I show you a few of the best tests.

Checking your writing against screening criteria

One way you can test your copy is to check your writing against your screening criteria. To do so, develop some statements based on the criteria (these become your screening criteria) and then evaluate the writing against these statements. Ask others to evaluate your copy in the same manner, too. I show you how to check your own writing in the following sections.

Evaluating rational arguments and fact-based appeals

Ideally, your copy should be convincing and persuasive, and it shouldn't lead to counter-arguments. Your copy should also be believable.

Use the following statements as your criteria when evaluating writing with a rational appeal:

- ✔ I find this writing very convincing.
- ✔ I agree with the main points completely.
- ✔ I can't think of any reasons to avoid this product/service while reading/ listening to/viewing the copy.
- ✔ I don't feel like arguing with the writer/speaker.
- ✔ The writing makes sense to me.
- ✔ This ad is important.

Your goal is to create an ad that people don't feel like arguing with. Ads that generate the fewest counter-arguments are the most persuasive.

Evaluating emotional appeals and stories or case histories

An ad's emotional appeal, story, or case history should be engaging and interesting. It should engage feelings to a significant degree, and it should be realistic and believable.

Use these factors as your criteria when evaluating writing that uses emotional appeals:

- ✔ I find the writing compelling.

- ✔ The writing holds my attention.

- ✔ I feel that the copy describes a situation that could easily apply to me/my business.

- ✔ I like the ad.

- ✔ The ad is definitely true to life.

- ✔ I relate easily to the feelings of the people in this ad.

Evaluating hybrid ads

Hybrid ads involve both rational arguments and stories, so you need to evaluate them using both sets of criteria (in other words, all 12 questions). For ads that are purely fact-oriented or purely story-oriented, you can use just the six questions that apply to their specific form. Or, go ahead and evaluate each communication using all the questions, because you can't always be sure that you know what the ad's appeal really is. Figure 6-1 shows a form you can use to evaluate marketing communications based on the need for both rational and emotional appeals. You can also find this form on the CD (filename CD0601).

On the form, notice that I alternate the items measuring the effectiveness of your argument with the ones measuring the effectiveness of your story. The story-oriented items have odd numbers, starting with item number one. The argument-oriented items have even numbers, starting with item number two. So an ad that's effective as a story will score high on the odd-numbered items, for example. And a hybrid letter, such as the one I show you earlier for a customer-training program, will score fairly high on all items and receive a high overall score.

You can use this form to check your own work and refine your drafts as you work on customer letters or any other marketing communications. Or you can take your research to a higher level by soliciting customer input. Stay tuned for details.

Evaluation Form 1 (Argument/Story Effectiveness)

Please circle the number that best represents your feelings toward the marketing communication you have been asked to evaluate. Thank you for your help.

Scale: 1 = not at all to 5 = definitely

Item A

#1.	1 2 3 4 5	I found it compelling.
#2.	1 2 3 4 5	I found it very convincing.
#3.	1 2 3 4 5	It held my attention.
#4.	1 2 3 4 5	I agreed with the main points completely.
#5.	1 2 3 4 5	I felt that it described a situation that could easily apply to me/my business.
#6.	1 2 3 4 5	I could think of no reasons to avoid this product/service.
#7.	1 2 3 4 5	I liked the ad/marketing communication.
#8.	1 2 3 4 5	I did not feel like arguing with the writer/speaker.
#9.	1 2 3 4 5	It was definitely true to life.
#10.	1 2 3 4 5	It made good sense to me.
#11.	1 2 3 4 5	I could relate easily to the feelings in it.
#12.	1 2 3 4 5	It is important.

Figure 6-1:
Evaluation
Form 1
(Argument/
Story Effec-
tiveness).

Getting other people's opinions

Using the questions in Figure 6-1 to evaluate a marketing communication before you even try it out in the media or mail it isn't a bad idea. If you run your ad by a half-dozen or more people who are similar to your customers (or are your customers), you can find out what they think of it and, often, you find ways to improve the ad before you spend money and take the risk of using the ad.

I recommend talking to some of your friends in the industry and to some of your most friendly customers, as well as to some people you don't know quite so well, to sign them up for ad-evaluation duty. You can point out that the procedure is quick and painless, and they must simply look at drafts of marketing communications and then fill in a quick one-page-or-less question-naire by circling some numbers. So their duty is easy, and they get to have a peek into your marketing operations and may get some good ideas of their own. Or, you can sweeten the pot by offering participants a discount to make their participation more worthwhile.

Having a panel of even a few people who you can run your communications by before you finalize them is a really wonderful thing. In addition to asking your panel to respond to some specific questions, such as the ones I gave you earlier in this section, you should also spend a few minutes debriefing them in person or by phone to find out what they really think about your marketing piece. Try asking them to identify several things they like and dislike about the piece as an easy way to get them talking.

And while you're having people read and evaluate your marketing communi-cations, you can also ask them to make sure it's simple, error-free, and clear (some of the common problems that I always find myself correcting when I do communications audits).

If you really don't have the time to put together an informal audience panel to test your ad, at least test it yourself and get others within the organization to test it. Any evaluation is better than none!

Creating options and picking a winner

Another way to use research is to develop and evaluate three or more com-munication pieces. I know designing three ads, letters, brochures, or whatever is more work, but if you mock up three different designs and then compare them using evaluation questions (like the ones I gave you in the earlier sec-tion "Checking your writing against screening criteria"), you're more likely to end up picking a winner. Many ad agencies develop at least three different ads, and sometimes, as many as a dozen. Then everyone argues over which approach is best. If deciding which approach is the best is difficult, then you may have the luxury of multiple good options. But in my experience, one option often rises to the top, and it's rarely the first concept you developed. So creating more choices and testing your options before you make a deci-sion really does pay off!

Evaluating for High Involvement

Does your marketing communication get high involvement from your audience? In other words, do your readers notice it and become interested in it — that's *high involvement* — or do they just blow it off without paying much mind?

Because most people ignore most marketing communications, involvement is an important first step toward winning the customer. You need to win his attention and interest, and you need to get him involved in your effort to communicate.

In this section, don't worry about the content of your material or whether you convince people; just focus on how you build high involvement. High involvement is often essential, especially if you're designing an ad for a crowded place (like a magazine full of ads), where your biggest challenge is just winning some attention. A TV spot, a magazine or newspaper ad, a banner ad for the Web, (yet another) mailing, or an outdoor poster must grab attention and build involvement in a hurry or customers pass it right by.

So how do you create high involvement for an ad? Here's a hypothetical example:

> A picture of a crying baby will probably create emotional involvement, especially in parents of young children.

> A table that shows babies whose parents feed them organic baby food will have fewer health problems later in life than those whose parents feed them conventional baby food will get rational involvement.

> Combine the picture of a crying baby with the data from our imagined study showing that organic baby food is healthier, and you have the potential to capture full involvement because the ad appeals to both the rational and emotional sides of the parents you want to reach.

A number of large ad agencies actually measure rational and emotional involvement with questionnaires as a way of evaluating ads. Then they plot the results on a graph like the one shown in Figure 6-2. Ads that plot high and to the right win the most involvement on both dimensions. And these ads tend to be more effective, all else being equal, especially in situations where catching your target audience's attention is hard to do.

So here's another way to evaluate your own marketing communications or to have a panel or group of people representing your audience evaluate them: Simply ask people to rate each ad, letter, Web page, or whatever the communication is by filling in the Evaluation Form 2 (Emotional/Rational Involvement), shown in Figure 6-3. This form is available on your CD, in case you want to print some copies; the filename is CD0603.

If you're testing multiple ads or other marketing communications, simply ask your panel to evaluate each one using the same scale. On the CD, you find a form with room to evaluate up to ten options at a time, lettered from Item A to Item J.

Even if you have only one or two communications to evaluate, consider including others that you collected from the marketplace — especially ones that you think are effective because of their track records. Looking at the range of responses that customers give to a variety of options is always interesting, and doing so gives you some insight into how to interpret their responses. For instance, if people rate your new brochure design at 3.9 on average, and the average for competitors' brochures is only 3.1, then you probably have a winner, even though your absolute score isn't at the top of the 1 through 5 range.

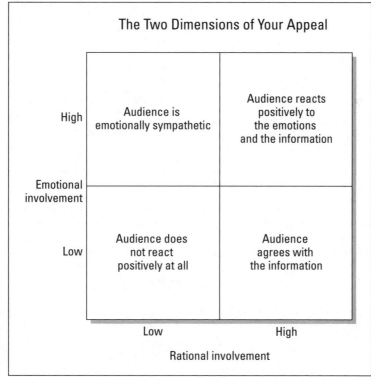

Figure 6-2:
The two dimensions of your appeal.

Evaluation Form 2 (Emotional/Rational Involvement)

Please circle the number that best represents your feelings toward the marketing communication you have been asked to evaluate. Thank you for your help.

Scale: 1 = not at all to 5 = definitely

Item A

#1.	1 2 3 4 5	I found myself caught up emotionally in it.
#2.	1 2 3 4 5	I was interested in the information it contained.
#3.	1 2 3 4 5	I got a definite sense of the feelings it is trying to communicate.
#4.	1 2 3 4 5	I could follow the logic of the argument easily.
#5.	1 2 3 4 5	It has a definite emotional appeal.
#6.	1 2 3 4 5	I thought it was well researched.
#7.	1 2 3 4 5	It captures my own feelings quite well.
#8.	1 2 3 4 5	It is a good source of useful ideas.

Figure 6-3:
Evaluation
Form 2
(Emotional/
Rational
Involve-
ment).

The evaluation form I provide in the preceding sections (Evaluation Form 1 Argument/Story Effectiveness) and on the CD (filename CD0601) for measuring customer involvement has four items that measure emotional involvement and four that measure rational involvement. To keep the form simple, I made all the odd-numbered items measure emotional involvement and all the even-numbered items measure rational involvement.

If you want to maximize involvement, you may want to score reasonably high on both the odd- and even-numbered items. But if you designed your communication to have either a highly emotional or a highly rational appeal, don't expect to score high overall. Instead, look for top marks on the items that measure the dimension of involvement that you're shooting for.

Interpreting Your Ad Research to Select or Refine a Design

In this section, I examine the data from three different ad designs, each one a draft of a possible direct-response ad designed to run in the Sunday magazines of various newspapers. I'm just going to describe these ads, not show them, because I want to focus on how you interpret research about people's reactions to them.

✔ The first design uses an eye-catching photo and a brief story as its focus.

✔ The second design presents several little-known facts and builds an argument for the product based on them.

✔ The third design is a hybrid of the first two, combining a smaller photo and brief quote from a customer with a short discussion of relevant facts.

Here's how a panel of 15 prospective customers evaluated each ad on the customer involvement scales (see the previous section for more details on this scale) and also on the emotional/rational appeals scales (see the earlier section "Checking your writing against screening criteria" on story-based versus argument-based appeals). I simplified the results by coding them as L = low, M = medium, and H = high.

Ads	Average Scores			
	Appeal		Involvement	
	Story	Argument	Emotional	Rational
1. Photo/story	H	L	H	L
2. Facts/argument	L	M	L	M
3. Hybrid of 1 & 2	M	M	M	M

You can see that the panel's reactions to the ads are nicely summarized in a table like this. At a glance, you get a feel for the strengths and weaknesses of each of the options. The first one had high appeal as a story and also achieved high emotional involvement. It bombed on the other scales, though, reflecting its lack of hard information. The second ad got medium scores for the appeal of its argument and for its ability to involve people rationally, but it bombed on the other scales because it lacked emotional impact. And the third ad, the hybrid ad, received medium scores across the board.

So which ad is better? A conservative marketer probably would pick the third ad because it seems to have something for everyone. I usually favor hybrids with a combination of stories and arguments and the ability to create both rational and emotional involvement. My choice based on this data, however, is definitely the first ad. I like to see exceptionally high scores on anything, even if they require a sacrifice on other dimensions. Grabbing attention with an ad is hard, so one that packs an emotional punch is obviously a good choice.

If you're still worried about ad number one's low scores on the argument and rational involvement scales, well, feel free to fiddle with it and do some more testing. Perhaps you can make it just a bit bigger and work a line or two of copy in at the bottom with some compelling facts. Even an asterisk with a footnote citing some facts or statistics may raise those low scores to the medium range without diluting the ad's emotional impact and bringing down its other scores. So you can fiddle with it and try to formulate a better hybrid ad, but I wouldn't fiddle too much. An emotionally powerful ad is a rare commodity, and you may mess it up if you add too much to it.

Designing for Stopping Power

Another important consideration for any marketing communication is how well it screams for attention. Not all marketing communications need to shout out to their audience, but many benefit from the ability to grab attention. *Stopping power* is the ability of a marketing communication to attract immediate notice. To command attention.

What does your logo look like? Do people stop and give it a long look because they find it interesting? Do they want to open an envelope because the logo on the outside is striking and catches their eye? Well, maybe not — most logos lack stopping power. But I wanted a logo for my business that would grab attention. I fancy myself as competent in the field of marketing communications, but still, my company used rather dull logos for a decade before I finally got one that had some stopping power. And I must confess, it wasn't my idea at all. One of my employees, Stephanie Sousbies, pointed out that a symbol we used on the cover of a workshop binder was stronger than our current logo and suggested that we try that one instead. Then we hired a very experienced (read expensive) graphic designer to take the basic design and improve it so we could use it in both black-and-white publications and color. Now the design serves as an eye-catching and memorable logo on our letterhead, all our products, mailings, ads, and Web sites. Figure 6-4 shows this logo in its black-and-white form, and whenever you visit this book's Web page at www.insights formarketing.com, you'll see it in color.

Figure 6-4:
INSIGHTS
logo,
grayscale
version.

INSIGHTS
for Training & Development

What gives this logo stopping power? In part, its use of the human eye as a symbol. Humans are genetically coded to look at eyes. And to achieve stopping power, what you want is to get people to look at your message. A human face does the same thing, and sometimes you see a face used in an ad or brochure as a way to get people to stop and look. In our logo, however, the graphic designer combined an eye with a triangle — which is a more dynamic form than a square or circle and tends to get a longer look. And he drew the eye part way outside the triangle rather than framed inside it. This element adds interest and movement, and it symbolizes the proverbial "out of the box" approach in a novel way.

Does sexy sell?

Another sure way to give any marketing communication stopping power is to put something sexy into it. A lot of naive marketers try that ploy. If you show some attractive people in suggestive positions or even just put the word "sex" in the headline, people will take a quick look to see what's going on. But generally sex has nothing much to do with what you are communicating, so that sort of stopping power doesn't work well. People just move on again after they realize you've tried to trick them into paying attention.

So now that you've read an analysis of the visual elements, notice that the name also ties in very well: INSIGHTS, as a business name, suggests that the company is always thinking hard and looking for good ideas and solutions. The designer used bold, clean capitals for the word, which helps draw attention to the logo. And of course, the name and the logo both incorporate references to sight in their own different ways, helping to catch the mind a moment after the imagery catches the eye.

The "stop and stare" factor

I'm quite pleased with the impact that this name and logo have had since my company adopted them. A lot of people tell us that they like our logo and name, and even those people who may not be wild about them at least notice and remember them. And that's the advantage of stopping power.

Stopping power's great virtue is that it gets you in. And when you're in, when you've captured the attention of a prospect, then the rest of your design can go to work.

Putting a sexy photo on the outside of a direct-mail envelope probably won't increase the response rate, and it may get you into a lot of trouble. Stopping power isn't really that simple.

To really generate stopping power, you need to give any marketing communication seven different qualities. (By the way, I got these ideas originally from Hanley Norins of Young & Rubicam.) Here are the qualities an ad needs to have in order to generate serious stopping power:

- ✔ It has to be dramatic.
- ✔ It has to demand participation.
- ✔ It has to stimulate some emotion.
- ✔ It has to make people curious.
- ✔ It should surprise people.
- ✔ It needs to communicate in an unexpected way.
- ✔ It should violate convention.

Do your marketing communications have stopping power? Maybe, but probably not. Most communications don't. In fact, if you think about this concept, it's impossible for most communications to have high stopping power. Stopping power requires qualities that make the communication stand out from the crowd. So, an ad with stopping power is always going to be a rare trait.

When I think about stopping power, I often consider an eighth criterion that Y&R didn't include in their original formulation of the concept. I believe that *beauty also has stopping power* — a lot of stopping power. When a product design is beautiful (occasionally this is the case with a new car, for example), the thing to do is just show the product in the ads. Its beauty will make people stop and look. If you don't have an inherently beautiful product or if you have a service that people can't easily see or you can't easily photograph, then consider finding a beautiful image to *represent* your product (see Chapter 9 for details).

Measuring stopping power

As in the previous sections, where I use evaluation forms to rate communications on their appeal and involvement, you can use a simple evaluation form to measure a communication's stopping power. What you can measure, you can manage, so when you start evaluating your communications with the stopping power form, you may find yourself working more stopping power into your marketing. You can give more stopping power to any ad, letter, telemarketing script, sales presentation, Web page, fax, business card, advertisement, or other communication. And stopping power always helps get attention and gives your communication the opportunity to do its job.

Applying Great Writing to Your Web Site

Open up any of your own Web pages and take a hard, objective look at them. Are they visually appealing, drawing your eye in so that you want to read what's on-screen? If not, add a unifying design element, like a central photo or a bold headline. Or, reduce the clutter and make it clean and easy for readers to approach.

Next, read the first text that catches your eye. Is the text clear? Interesting? Brief? Does it make you want to read more? Probably not. Most of the writing on the Web is just terrible. Really awful. Unclear, too complicated, and full of errors of usage and grammar. I've never met a Web site I didn't want to edit. Here's a quick checklist of things to work on if you want to try to improve the clarity and appeal of your Web site's text:

- **Can you reduce the number of words?** On the Web, shorter is usually better. You can tighten your text by eliminating unnecessary words and by choosing words that express your meaning more succinctly.

- **Can you make everything crystal clear?** It's amazing how hard it is to understand all the writing on the average Web site. That's because company insiders (like you) who write the text have a hard time imagining how ignorant someone like me can be when visiting the site for the first time. I just went to www.3m.com to see what this major company was up to, and I encountered the cryptic message "Aldara cream now indicated for AK" on its home page. I hate to be ignorant, but what's Aldara cream? Does 3M make it? Does "now indicated" mean it has some sort of regulatory approval for use? And what's AK? Part of what makes this message confusing is that it's next to messages about carpet cleaners and toilet bowl scrubbers — not the most logical place to boast about a new medication, if that's what the cream is. Next time you look at your own site, imagine how it may read to someone like me who has fresh eyes and little or no knowledge of your business.

✔ **What's the point?** Every Web page, like any form of writing, needs to have a clear point. The topic sentence. The main claim to fame. What is it? I rarely can tell because Web pages tend to be divided into lots of little sections and zones, and each one competes for attention with all the others. Make sure you have an overarching message (see Chapter 2 to work on your marketing focus if you're not sure what your most important message should be). Your home page ought to devote at least one-third of its area to conveying a message about what makes your company or service special and brilliant. And you need to mention this message in variations as reminders on most of the other pages on your site, too. *Focus* is the key ingredient in great Web writing!

✔ **Can you reduce errors?** Oh, sure, your site doesn't have any typos, inaccuracies, nonfunctional links, or other errors . . . but do me a favor, and just check it carefully one more time anyway. Thanks!

Avoid these common pitfalls and your Web writing will be as tight, appealing, and effective as the rest of your marketing communications. And remember to make sure you have factual arguments that persuade logically and/or good feelings and interesting stories that appeal emotionally in everything you write for marketing. Stories can work well on Web pages, just as they can work well in sales materials, direct-mail letters, or personal sales presentations. Call them cases, keep them short, and you can work dozens of them into your Web site. There's nothing like a good story to create high involvement and make your point persuasively.

A Final Check: Auditing Your Marketing Communications

One of the services my firm offers to clients is a complete audit of all their written sales and marketing communications. When we do these audits, we always find that we can improve these communications by

✔ **Making the writing briefer:** If you can shorten the number and complexity of words, you make the communication easier and quicker for customers and prospects to read. Those changes mean more people will read and understand your message. And that's a good thing. A very good thing.

✔ **Correcting errors:** You may think accuracy isn't an issue, but I'm often surprised at the number of errors that I find in marketing communications. Trust me, somewhere in your printed materials or on your Web site or in an ad, your products or services are misrepresented. Wrong names, inaccurate technical details, incorrect addresses or product codes, and old prices may be creating confusion and losing the company sales.

✔ **Identifying omissions:** In every company I audited, I found many places where the information was insufficient for customers or prospects to take the next step toward purchase. Sometimes in our evaluations, we add something as simple as a contact address or phone number; other times we need to provide instructions for how to select the right product or option. But the most common of all is that we have to explain what the company is and does.

For example, I have a nice golf umbrella from a company that I'm helping with its marketing communications. The umbrella has stripes in the company colors and has the company name on it. But unfortunately, most people don't know the name, so when they see the umbrella, they have no idea what the company is or what it does. This umbrella is a simple little giveaway promotion, but it won't do any good until the company adds a tag line explaining what it is, plus some contact information so prospective customers can find it by phone or on the Web.

✔ **Achieving consistency:** Each individual marketing message is a part of your overall message, and you need to view each one that way. In my audits, I often find that pointing out major and minor inconsistencies in how the client communicates is necessary; then I ask the client to come up with suggestions for standardization. When a client communicates a consistent message, each individual communication helps create and maintain a strong, professional image in the marketplace, instead of creating a weak, inconsistent, or confusing one.

✔ **Improving persuasiveness:** I'm amazed at how boring most marketing communications are. I like seeing writing jump up off the page or the computer screen and seize the reader by her eyeballs. When I audit clients' communications, I often flag dull or unpersuasive communications and work on giving them more power to grab attention and shape attitudes and actions. Marketing communications should be active, not passive!

I'm sharing these common corrections to marketing communications with you so that you can try to fix the problems yourself. Perform your own audit of every piece of written (or scripted) marketing communications your organization does, looking for ways to make it the best it can be.

On the CD

Check out the following files on the CD-ROM:

- ✓ Evaluation Form 1 (CD0601)
- ✓ Two Dimensions of Your Appeal (CD0602)
- ✓ Evaluation Form 2 (CD0603)

Chapter 7

Using Testimonials and Customer Stories

*W*ouldn't it be nice if a dozen of the best-known and most admired people in your industry wrote you personal testimonials saying how special your product or service was? Wouldn't it be great if the top people from the best companies in your market gave you permission to print their endorsements in your company literature and ads? And wouldn't it be great to have excellent customer quotes, lauding your business or product and saying how superior it was to all the competition?

Each of these examples shows the power of personal references, testimonials, or quotes. If a credible, objective party says "buy," prospects are going to listen. In fact, ads, sales sheets, brochures, letters, and Web pages are all more effective when they include a quote or case history.

Effective Use of Testimonials — a Real-life Example

Some marketers have used customer quotes and testimonials for years, especially in direct-response print ads, brochures, and letters. But most marketers ignore this powerful technique. The company Modern Memoirs is an exception to the rule that marketers tend to overlook references and testimonials, and its director, Kitty Axelson-Berry, reports that quotes and examples from past clients are instrumental in attracting new customers to her writing, editing, and publishing service.

Modern Memoirs specializes in "commissioned personal memoirs," meaning books about you or someone important to you that are generally made for limited, personal distribution. Actually, the business creates all sorts of personal books, from family cookbooks to books celebrating the first years of a child's life to the classic personal memoir or family history.

The company's products are obviously quite personal, and they require a fair amount of personal involvement and expense as well. How does a prospective customer become comfortable with the idea of signing a contract? How does he know that the staff of Modern Memoirs will handle his project with sensitivity and skill? Knowing that other people have already taken the plunge and emerged happy with the book of their dreams is the best evidence. So Modern Memoirs uses a variety of customer quotes and stories to let past customers tell prospective customers about its business.

For example, in one of its brochures (a three-fold colored piece printed on standard 8½-x-14-inch paper), you find photos of some previously produced books and a detailed description of one that reads:

> MEMOIRS by Doris P. Lebow, a full-length memoir hand bound in leather and paper, artfully combines 18 hours of as-told-to personal reflections with 29 photos, 40 letters of personal correspondence, 62 favorite recipes, three genealogy charts, two maps, and a family medical history.

That's a packed volume, and it's a good example of the firm's work. The example gives prospective customers a very clear idea of what's possible, along with the reassurance that others have trod this path successfully before them. To include a photo and description of this work in its brochure, Modern Memoirs had to ask the client for permission. But, in general, customers readily grant their permission when they're happy with the project and proud of their own work. In fact, Modern Memoirs' contracts typically include a clause giving the company permission to show the book to others as a sample of its work. (Figure 7-1 illustrates two of the inside panels from this brochure, and you can find more of the brochure on your CD. Look for file CD0701.)

m o d e r n   m e m o i r s

To produce a printed work worthy of its subject, we have developed a four-step research and production process.

First, we conduct a series of in-person interviews with the individual, in consultation with family members and friends as appropriate. Full confidentiality is assured.

Next, all materials are transcribed, edited for clarity and continuity, and fleshed out with supplementary materials, including photographs.

Then, all text and related graphic elements are integrated and printed to laser copy for review.

Finally, using camera-ready flats and Syquest disk, the books are custom printed and bound in leather or fiber, according to preference.

MEMOIRS by Doris P. Lebow, a full-length memoir handbound in leather and paper, artfully combines 18 hours of as-told-to personal reflections with 29 photos, 40 letters of personal correspondence, 62 favorite recipes, three genealogy charts, two maps and a family medical history.

Modern Memoirs documents an individual's unique life experiences. These could include:

- Adventures
- Romances
- Customs
- Stories from childhood
- Careers
- Achievements
- Set-backs
- Turning points
- Medical history
- Genealogy charts
- Letters or manuscripts
- Ethical wills and crucial instructions

In addition to the commissioned as-told-to memoir, Modern Memoirs has developed a unique format that transforms awkward family photo and record albums into readily accessible print volumes. Using a mix of photos and text, the *Children's Book Series* specializes in preserving a child's earliest experiences, experiments and areas of expertise.

Hendrix's Book recounts a little girl's first three-and-a-half years, in 32 pages of text, 28 photos, two drawings and a footprint.

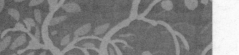

Modern Memoirs also provides editing and/or publishing services for personal manuscripts of all lengths and topics.

Figure 7-1: The Modern Memoirs' brochure.

Borrowing a Page from Books

The book business uses testimonials frequently. Some authors plan their cover quotes before they even write their books. Publicists rush advance copies or bound galleys of books to key reviewers early in the book-production process in the hope of snagging a quote from a favorable review in a well-known newspaper or magazine. And authors network madly to line up the addresses of experts and celebrities and then shower them with letters and samples of their writing in the hope of getting cover quotes from the rich and famous. When you see several impressive quotes on the outside of a book, you know that the author or his or her publicist devoted dozens of hours to securing those well-chosen words.

When Harvey Mackay was writing his first book, *Swim with the Sharks Without Being Eaten Alive,* he launched a major campaign to line up celebrity endorsements. If you ask enough people, some of them are bound to say "yes" just because the exposure is good for their image, too. Well, Mackay asked lots of people for quotes, many of them well-known celebrities. And more than 40 gave their testimonials for promoting what went on to become a runaway bestseller. The reading public had the distinct impression that Mackay was already a celebrity himself, even though in truth, he had networked to most of those respected, successful endorsers and didn't know them personally.

You can find a contemporary example of effective use of testimonials on the Web site, www.rdpr.com, which caters to authors. If you click your way into the site and find the "Resources" button (click that, too), you can see how this firm uses five to ten quotes from happy customers to describe each of its products and services. The quotes actually provide enough substance that they take the place of the normal descriptive copy and do the selling themselves. This example is a very effective way to use quotes to sell products and services on the Web.

Why Quotes Work

Why go to all the trouble to secure a few brief quotes? Because a good quote sells.

Basically, the idea is to let someone the prospect *believes* do the selling instead of you. You're the marketer. Nobody is going to take you seriously when you say that your product or service is superior.

To make the quote powerful, you need to get some quote or story from a source that the prospect will believe, and you need to make that quote or story available to a prospective buyer at or near the point of purchase. (The *point of purchase* is the time and place where the prospect makes a decision that affects your sales.) When people are at the point of purchase, the timing is right: They're interested in what you have to sell, and they're ready to consider your offer seriously. At this moment, they want to believe in your product or service. If they find your claims credible, they'll probably buy your product or service. But prospective customers are naturally suspicious, and this is the time when testimonials, other evidence of product quality, and believability are the most powerful. For instance, testimonials can reach out to someone who's just picked up a book and is considering purchasing it but isn't quite sure whether the book will really meet his expectations.

A few years ago when I wrote the book *Motivating & Rewarding Employees* (Adams Media), I put extra care into the project to make sure that it offered fresh new insights and methods for managers. I was actually very pleased with how the book came out and felt it was my best book to date. But if I had said so in my introduction, who'd believe me? The author is hardly an objective source, nor is the publisher. If the publisher puts "You've got to read this book!" on the cover, prospective readers naturally wonder why the publisher thinks it's a must-read — and readers are liable to conclude that the reason has more to do with the publisher's desire to sell a bunch of copies than the quality of the product.

So who could sing the praises of *Motivating & Rewarding Employees* in a credible manner? How about people whose names or titles indicate their objective expertise on the subject matter? So I sent copies of my manuscript to a dozen people who I thought might be willing to see their names on the cover, and most of them sent useful quotes back.

These quotes were very helpful in marketing the book because they helped prospective readers and reviewers get a sense of what made the product unique. They were well worth the 15 to 20 hours I spent calling, e-mailing, faxing, and sending overnight letters to line them up. In fact, I don't have a definite way to measure, but I'm pretty sure these quotes boosted the book's rate of sale in bookstores by at least 25 percent.

To secure these quotes, I put together an impressive package describing the product to give contributors the feeling that they were lending their names to something that would make them look good, too. And, in the long run, I ended up using my personal network to secure each and every quote. Some of these people know me pretty well, and others know someone who knows me well. In general, getting a quote is easiest when you have some type of connection between you and the contributor. Your own happy customers are easy to ask for quotes.

Using Quotes in Catalogs

Earlier in this chapter I said that testimonials work well at the point of purchase when someone is considering buying a product off the shelf. But there are many other possible points of purchase. Sometimes people make their purchase decisions while in front of a salesperson; sometimes they decide when they're in front of their computer looking at a Web page; and sometimes they decide when they're reading a direct-mail piece, such as a sales letter or catalog. All these instances are points of purchase, so using testimonials or customer stories in them can be effective as well.

Catalog shoppers often need supporting evidence when they're examining the claims about a product in a catalog. To them, a product may sound good, but is the catalog overstating the product's virtues? How can the shopper be sure? Again, a testimonial from an expert or a quote or example from a satisfied customer at this point of purchase can lift sales by helping the involved shopper believe the marketing claims.

When you're selling expensive products or services to businesses, providing enough evidence to make your claims believable is especially important.

Human Resource Development Press (HRD Press) publishes catalogs that sell a range of products and services to companies for use in training employees. Some of the many products in their catalog are relatively inexpensive and easy for a prospect to buy. Other products are complex or expensive enough that sometimes the catalog includes some evidence from experts or users to help make its case. For example, Figure 7-2 shows a page from an HRD Press catalog that features a fairly expensive training product and a book that ties in with the product. The designer gave considerable space on this page to testimonials, displaying them next to each of the products that the page features. The testimonials help establish the credibility of the products.

LEADERSHIP

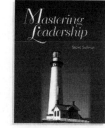

National Finalist at the Vision Awards!

 VIDEO

Mastering Leadership
By Steve Sullivan

If you are looking for a powerful video message to add impact to your leadership and management skills workshops, preview *Mastering Leadership* today! You will find Steve Sullivan's inspiring program unparalleled in its ability to educate, entertain, and energize.

Filmed on the majestic coast of Northern California, this new 33-minute video describes the essence of leadership: energizing people by instilling a sense of purpose for the organization or team. Steve Sullivan discusses the galvanizing factors that are needed for successful leadership.

Mastering Leadership will add impact and inspiration to your ongoing leadership training programs. The video is perfect as a wrap-up segment, or an after lunch energizer. Or you can use the participants booklets, slide masters, and leader's guide and make *Mastering Leadership* the major component of your workshop.

Mastering Leadership costs less than half of comparable videos and makes a cost-effective addition to your video resource library.

The Complete Package includes:
Exhilarating 33-minute video, and five participant booklets with assessments.
(additional booklets **$6.95** *Order code: R92-MLPB)*

Facilitator's Guide, Disk with slide masters.
(additional disks **$65.00** *Order code: R92-MLSM)*

One copy of Leading at Mach 2, *written by Steve Sullivan.*
(additional copies **$17.95** *Order code: R92-LM2)*

Complete Package. **$295.00** *Order code: R92-MLCP*

This is what the experts are saying about *Mastering Leadership*—

"Steve Sullivan has mastered it all."
Dana Mead, Chairman and CEO, Tenneco

"Extraordinary! *Mastering Leadership* was the highlight of our leadership conference."
Tom Beckett, Director, Yale University

"Your *Mastering Leadership* video program has made training almost as easy as breathing."
Anna Lossius, Vice President, Fleet Bank

"In our executive seminar series, *Mastering Leadership* was the highest rated program ever!"
David Jones, Chairman of the Board, Southern Gas Association

"Wow! Our people can't stop talking about your program. Welcome to the team."
Peter FioRito, Vice President, IBM Global Services

—Now see for yourself!

"After reading *Selling at Mach 1*, I flew halfway across Canada to hear Steve Sullivan speak. Now that I have finished *Leading at Mach 2*, I would fly halfway around the world."
**Al Alexandruk
CEO, The Prolific Group**

Leading at Mach 2
By Steve Sullivan
Leading at Mach 2 is a 23-year "work-in-progress." Not until Steve Sullivan had excelled as an Army Ranger, Senior Corporate Executive, Entrepreneur, and nationally recognized Motivator did he feel qualified to address the issue. Now, after a lifetime of getting results at accelerated speeds, this award-winning author's recipe for success is no longer a secret. If you thought leadership meant "being the boss," *Leading at Mach 2* gives you ample reason to think again.

To Order Call 800-707-7769 or Fax 888-374-3488

1

Figure 7-2:
Leadership Training Products in an HRD Press catalog.

Seeking Customer Testimonials

So if testimonials and customer stories are so effective in lifting sales at the prospect's point of purchase, why don't marketers use them more often? In truth, this technique is a relatively rare marketing strategy. Most businesses market their products without testimonials. I think part of the reason most marketers don't use testimonials is because they're not aware of the power of this technique. Marketing or advertising courses at business schools don't teach this technique, and marketing textbooks don't cover this topic, either. Plus, this strategy isn't a common practice among marketers and managers. And because using testimonials is an uncommon strategy, most people are unclear about how to use them. They aren't even sure who to ask for a quote or how to ask them. In this section, I show you how to obtain good, useful customer testimonials.

Whom to ask

The first thing stopping many people from lining up testimonials is that they aren't sure whom to ask for quotes. So that's the first thing to clear up. Basically, *you can ask anyone who has a legitimate, authoritative opinion* about your product, service, or business. If someone obviously should have an opinion, then you can certainly ask him for his opinion. Here are some of the more common prospects to consider when seeking a testimonial, case history, or other useable contribution:

- ✔ Your customers
- ✔ Friends in management positions in businesses or in other positions of recognized authority, such as accountants, doctors, or politicians
- ✔ Experts in your industry or technology, such as well-known authors, professors, or journalists
- ✔ Anyone who runs a consulting, real-estate, or insurance firm; they're always looking for exposure and the public often sees them as experts
- ✔ Anyone you can get to sample or review your offerings (such as in a test market, in-store sampling, or introductory promotional offer)
- ✔ People who are sufficiently well known and routinely get such requests and have an established system for handling them
- ✔ Editors of newsletters, magazines, or e-newsletters about your industry

You have or can make plenty of opportunities to talk to people in most of these categories. So asking them for their opinion on a specific question concerning your business can be perfectly natural. Take advantage of these opportunities to pop the question and see what raw testimonials you can harvest just by shaking your tree a little.

Other people who you'd like to ask may not be within your circle of regular contacts. Don't despair. If they're well known, they're no doubt used to such requests. They may have a publicist, secretary, or assistant who handles requests for testimonials or other public appearances routinely. Just call or ask around until you find out what the proper approach is, and then send a professional written request. With celebrity endorsers, you may want to suggest some simple phrases or quotes that they can consider using if they don't have the desire to write their own from scratch. Also, be sure to describe the sort of use you think you'll put their quote to, with specific references to how neatly and professionally you'll present it and how many people you expect to see and read (or hear) it. That way, the big fish can decide more easily whether this is a good exposure opportunity for her.

When you approach a well-known individual for a quote, your odds of success are a lot lower than when you approach your own customers or other people you already know. Also, the turnaround is going to be considerably slower. But don't worry. If you keep trying, you'll probably line up one or two at a minimum. And even if you don't, customer quotes are often more believable and more compelling than celebrity endorsements anyway.

Don't be too pushy when asking people for quotes. Some people just don't feel comfortable lending their names. Often lower-level employees in a company don't have the authority to lend their names and titles to others without clearance from their bosses, which isn't that easy to secure. Other people are simply not into the idea of participating in your project and don't have any interest in seeing their names in your marketing materials. That's fine. Don't bug these noncontributors. For every one of them is another person who loves your product or service and likes taking part in anything that gives him or her exposure. Just keep looking until you find people who are happy to contribute. They're out there for the finding. And so few people ask for their contributions that they'll probably be honored when you ask.

Stay far away from people who raise the question of payment. Anyone who says, "Sure, I'd be willing to give you a quote. How much are you offering?" isn't thinking about the opportunity in a helpful way. They don't see it as a simple favor that may come round to help them some day in the future. They're trying to milk the situation for a few quick bucks. People who think that way are likely to come up with other ways to bother you for money in the future. And besides, you won't really get an objective testimonial if you pay for it. So when you bump into someone who wants to profit from your request for a quote, just thank them kindly and back out as gracefully and quickly as you can.

What to ask for?

The next stumbling block that stops many people from getting testimonials is that they don't know what to ask for. Basically, *you can ask people for any information or opinions that wouldn't embarrass them in public*

But (and this is a big but), your request needs to be very specific. Specificity makes your request easier to answer and less easy to object to. Specific requests include

- ✔ The person's opinion of your product or service
- ✔ A description of how he or she used your product or service and what happened as a result
- ✔ The person's view of where the industry, product category, technology, or economy, or whatever is going
- ✔ Information about which of your products or services he or she uses
- ✔ How often he or she uses your product or service or how much of it he or she uses
- ✔ Why he or she uses your product or service
- ✔ What he or she thinks the best things about your product or service are
- ✔ Who he or she would recommend your product or service to
- ✔ What he or she would recommend your product or service for

And the less well you know someone, the more specific your request should be. You can always ask a close friend for a reference, and they'll generally say, "Sure, just tell me what you want me to say." But people you know more casually are not likely to be as easy to work with. To them, a general request for a favor like that may seem inappropriate or difficult. So be more specific as you work outward from your immediate circle of friends and associates.

Ensuring a helpful response

Why is being specific in your questions so important? Think about the difference between asking someone for one of these specifics versus just asking them for a recommendation or testimonial. Imagine you know me vaguely as one of the owners of a business from which your business buys some computer repair services. You don't normally think about me or my services unless you have a problem with your computers. But today, you've just received an e-mail from me asking for a personal quote from you recommending our service to other businesses.

What will you do with this request? Probably nothing at all. Perhaps a flat refusal, but you don't actually want to be rude. So probably nothing at all. You could dash off a hearty recommendation and send it back by e-mail, but that scenario's not very likely because the request is so broad and poorly defined. What should the recommendation say? How long should it be? How should you write it? If you just ask someone for a vague recommendation, you're asking her to do something that is difficult and poorly defined — and something that doesn't offer her any obvious, major benefit to justify the difficulty of the task.

Now try a more specific request using one of the suggestions from the preceding list. Imagine now that I e-mailed not a generic request for a recommendation but something like:

> *Dear Ms. Franklin,*
>
> *As one of your regular suppliers for several years, I am writing to ask if you could tell me what sort of companies you think our computer repair services are especially well suited for. Would you recommend them for large companies? Small? High-tech? General? Do you think the companies need to have a lot of technical expertise to take full advantage of our services or not? Your opinion would be especially helpful right now as we are preparing our marketing plan and designing our marketing materials. Just a quick sentence or two is all we really need, because I'm sure you are busy. Thanks so much for your input!*
>
> *Sincerely,*
>
> *Chip Smith, Owner, ABC Computer Services*

This e-mail script asks for one simple, clear thing: Who the customer would recommend your services to. That's a very easy question to answer for any reasonably happy customer. You're likely to get a positive response, such as the following:

> *Dear Chip:*
>
> *Got your note. Happy to help but in a hurry. Basically, I'd say ABC's services would be useful for any company within this geographic area, as long as they have computers that need maintenance. I think your service is great! By the way, can you remind Joanne that she is supposed to get us a bid on a new graphics workstation? Thanks.*
>
> *Anne Franklin*

Congratulations! You just landed a testimonial in the raw. It may not look like much right now, but with a little work it will become a powerful marketing tool.

Processing the testimonial

To "process" this raw testimonial, first you need to isolate and refine the language. Here's the part that contains the answer to your question:

> *"Basically, I'd say ABC's services would be useful for any company within this geographic area, as long as they have computers that need maintenance. I think your service is great!"*

This recommendation is a start, but it isn't quite as short or punchy as it needs to be. And tightening up the text a bit by cutting superfluous words (like *basically*) and by substituting briefer words or phrases for lengthy or poorly chosen ones is perfectly reasonable. Just don't make the recommendation say anything that it didn't originally. For instance, you can't add "I love this company" if that thought wasn't there to start with. But you can massage the text into the following form without violating the spirit of the original quote:

> *"ABC's services are great! They're useful to any company in the area with computers that need maintenance."*

I moved up the bit with stopping power and changed "would be" to "are" because present tense is always stronger for testimonials. And now that I isolated and cleaned up that offhand sentence from the middle of your customer's busy e-mail, the quote is beginning to show some real promise as a marketing communication.

Seeking permission to use the testimonial

But your testimonial still isn't finished because *you do not yet have permission* to attach its author's name to it. So you need to e-mail the source again, this time asking for permission to quote their earlier e-mail. You may do so using a script such as:

> *Dear Anne,*
>
> *Thanks so much for your e-mail. I'm attaching that bid Joanne promised you. It took her longer than she expected, but the good news is she found some alternatives that offer the same performance at a lower cost. One of our bigger suppliers is discounting several high-end models to get rid of back inventory, and we can pass the savings along to you.*
>
> *Your answer to my question was very helpful. Thanks for participating. It helps us refine our strategies, and I'm also considering including a few quotes from customers in our next brochure or other marketing communications. With a little editing to shorten it, the answer you gave reads, "ABC's services are great! They're useful to any company in the area with computers that need maintenance." If you have any objection with our referencing*

this quote or would like to review specific uses of it, please let me know. Otherwise, we will include it in our upcoming brochure, alongside some other quotes. Thanks again for your help.

Best,

Chip

I scripted this reply carefully to keep it low key. I don't want to put images in the customer's mind of her name and quote being plastered all over late-night television or on a huge billboard beside the freeway. I want to keep the reply professional and cool in tone so that she just glances at it and thinks, "Wonder why they want that? Not much of a quote really. But it is what I said after all, and what harm can there be in it?"

Note that you have two choices in how you solicit quotes. The first option is to ask a specific question in order to generate a quote (as Chip did in the preceding example), and then — if you like the quote — seek permission to use it in your marketing. A second approach is to ask upfront for permission to use a quote, and then ask specific questions to generate one. If you're sure that the person will cooperate, try the latter. If you aren't so sure what response you'll get, try the former. Then you don't have to deal with the embarrassing situation of having to decline using a quote because it isn't as positive as you'd hoped!

Assuming that you solicited a quote first — one that you like — you have more than one way to ask for permission to use it. You can "assume" permission and just write to confirm, as I illustrated in the preceding example, or you can assume that you don't have permission and ask for it. The following example (another basic script you can use for a follow-up letter) represents the latter approach. This script takes a slightly different tack in other ways, too, emphasizing the positive responses from customers, which tends to make people feel good about being part of the event.

Dear X:

Thank you for your response to my questions. I appreciate your help and am frankly amazed by the many positive responses my request generated from our customers. Although we certainly intend to continue improving our services over time, it is gratifying to know that so many customers currently have positive things to say about our business.

I'd like to include your quote in our future marketing materials and would appreciate it greatly if you'd confirm that this is acceptable in a return letter, fax, or e-mail. And, in addition, if you'd like us to include some background information about your business or products, send that along as well.

Once again, thanks for your assistance. Your participation in this outreach project is greatly appreciated, as is your continued business. Do let me know if we can do anything more for you.

Sincerely,

X

If you don't mind being just a little bit pushy, you can end your communication to a prospective recommender by telling him to contact you if he objects to you using the quote, the way I did in my sample e-mail reply to Anne Franklin. Then, if you don't hear back, you can reasonably presume that you have the person's permission to use it. But if you think that customers may object to that approach, end the e-mail with a request that they respond one more time to confirm their permission to let you use their quotes. Then you have to wait for their replies, and some percentage of them won't ever get back, forcing you to either give up or to go begging with a reminder e-mail or phone call. But some customers *will* return a confirmation. After all, the quote is in their own words, and they already sent them to you, so saying that you have permission to quote them isn't a big step.

Either way, if you ask enough customers to start with (say, at least ten), in the long run you should end up with sufficient authority to include quotes from some of your customers in future marketing communications. If you line up even three or four quotes with this technique, you're in a position to harness the power of testimonials in your marketing.

What if some people get cold feet but you liked their initial quotes? Even if some people balk at permitting you to use their names, you can still find good uses for those quotes. After all, they're legitimate quotes, and you have (I hope you have!) hard copies of the source e-mails, letters, or written notes on the phone conversations in your files. So you can use the quotes, attributing them to a general description of the person and/or company. "President, financial institution" or "Bank Executive" may do fine if the local bank's president ducks your requests and never confirms that you can attribute her quote directly to her. A quote is a quote, and it can add value to marketing communications even if you have to attribute it to an anonymous "Regular Customer."

Actually using those testimonials

The final step is putting those quotes to good use in your marketing efforts. Put them together on a single sheet of paper so you can get a good feel for how they read and can decide what order you'd like to see them in.

You really have no limits to how you can use these quotes. I like them sprinkled in ads, brochures, and catalogs. They add a lot of credibility to direct-mail offers, and you may even consider putting some on the outside of your envelope to increase the likelihood of potential customers opening it.

Testimonials can also appear on Web pages to good effect. If you get enough material, you can even have a button on your site labeled "Customer Testimonials" and allow viewers to click through to an entire page or more of such quotes. Web sites don't usually include any customer testimonials; maybe it's time for you to break that mold.

Letting Testimonials Stand on Their Own

Another idea is to create a flier, poster, or point-of-purchase pamphlet or sign made up almost entirely of testimonials. The testimonials can actually become the core of such marketing communications instead of just decorating and lending strength to communications that have other core content.

I have an example of a marketing piece for my own business, created by Rocks-DeHart Public Relations, in which testimonials make up an entire page. In fact, it's the second-most important page — the back page of a catalog. (***Hint:*** The most important page of a catalog is the front page, of course, followed by the back page, and then the inside covers and the center fold, where the catalog falls open naturally. Design these pages to draw people into the rest of the catalog — and use testimonials on these key pages because of their power to engage the reader.)

Adding a tab or button on your Web site's home page that says "What Our Customers Are Saying," and behind it, a pop-up box or a printable Portable Document Format (pdf) sheet with lots of testimonials can be extremely powerful. And if you have some longer case-history type customer stories, also add a tab or button to your Web site called "Customer Case Histories." Write these stories either in third-person point of view, as if in a newspaper, or in first person, as if the customers are telling it. And, of course, get written permission for your quotes and keep the permission on file.

Avoiding legal traps

Many countries regulate advertising, so you always have to be careful to make honest, well-supported claims in any marketing communications. This point is certainly true for testimonials. A number of major ad campaigns ran into legal trouble by putting misleading or false statements into the mouths of celebrity endorsers. In a landmark case, the singer Pat Boone once endorsed an acne medicine called Acne-Statin in TV ads in the United States. He said, "With four daughters, we've tried the leading acne medication at our house, and nothing ever seemed to work until our girls met a Beverly Hills doctor and got some real help through a product called Acne-Statin." The U.S. Federal Trade Commission (FTC) investigated

this testimonial and concluded that it was misleading. Not all of Boone's daughters had used the product in question, and none of them had serious acne problems. The FTC forced the ads off the air, the company got in trouble, and Boone ran into some legal complications of his own. Lying in advertisements isn't nice, and it isn't legal, either!

You can avoid such problems if you don't do it the way Acne-Statin did. For instance:

✔ **Don't pay for your testimonials.** Get only genuine quotes from happy customers or others who are expressing their honest opinions for free.

(continued)

(continued)

- ✔ **Make sure that they say things that are patently obvious, that reflect the truth, and are statements that you can easily substantiate.** Customer opinions about the quality of your service are easy to prove if you have the letter on file. But don't ask your customer to give you a testimonial saying, "100 percent of leading doctors say that using their product will make you immortal." In other words, be reasonable in what you claim or ask others to claim.

- ✔ **Let them express their own opinions instead of having them state facts.** For instance, if Boone had said, "As a father of four girls, it's my strong opinion that Acne-Statin is the best product and I encourage my children to use it," then all that the advertising company would have had to substantiate was that he had encouraged his children to use it. To substantiate that fact, all the company needed was a simple note in his handwriting

to his daughters saying, "Why don't you try this product? I think you'll like it." And, as for his opinion that the product was the best in its category, well, that statement is just his opinion. As long as he didn't say the same thing about the competing products, no one was likely to challenge his opinion.

Another legal issue concerns the provider's rights to his or her quote. If a person says or writes something, he may have legal rights to it under copyright law, and he may make some claim to such rights if he thinks the quote is of value to you and your company. So, you need to make sure that you get permission to use the quotes in your marketing. *In writing.* And keep a record of your request as well as the customer's reply so it's clear that you're using his quote as you said you would and as he said you could. A nicely maintained file of your correspondence is good protection. And so is good legal advice — from a lawyer, not some hack author like me.

Using Customer Videos and Photos

Candid customer comments or reactions on video or audiotape have many of the same virtues and uses as written testimonials. You can use them to create effective radio or television ads, and you can use them in a promotional video you distribute to prospects if you do business-to-business marketing. Some private schools and colleges now hand out videos to prospective students, and these videos are a great medium for some candid reactions as well as for testimonials from students and alums.

I also encourage you to consider using customer footage on your Web site. The technology exists to put short (keep it short, please!) clips of video or audio recordings on sites and to make them available at the click of a button. People love watching TV, and they'll gladly sit and watch short videos on your Web site. Videos pull people into a site, increase the amount of time that they spend there, and also increase the credibility of your marketing claims.

Photos of customers combined with their quotes or comments are also powerful marketing tools. You can include them on a Web page, in a catalog, in print ads, and even on a product's packaging.

Photographing endorsers

I like the idea of using a customer's photo, perhaps with a short quote in her own words. You see this technique in some print advertising for consumer products, although when major advertisers do it, the presentation is so slick that you're never sure whether the person is a real customer or a paid model, which reduces its effectiveness. The best photos are honest, genuine ones. They show a real person, hopefully a reasonably attractive and friendly one, but not some smooth-skinned model who looks like all the other models in the fashion magazines.

If one or more customers agree to be photographed for your ad, catalog, Web page, or other marketing communication, remember that you have to do all the work involved. You must hire a professional photographer who routinely does portrait work outside the studio. You want the photographer to take portraits of your customer, so make sure that you find a photographer with plenty of comparable work in his portfolio. Then arrange a time for the photographer to visit the subject at home (if the ad is for a retail product or service) or at work (if the ad is for a business-to-business product or service). Assume that the photographer will need about an hour to get a decent shot and that the session will cost you anywhere from $100 to $500, depending on the photographer that you hire.

I think that digital cameras make everyone a photographer because you can see the image right at the moment and take more if you didn't capture just what you need. I suggest a corporate digital camera that everyone is allowed to borrow so you're sure to get an ongoing archival and promotional file to assist in marketing. Photocopy a pile of permission forms that employees take along with the camera to make it easy to obtain releases from the subjects of the photos.

Make sure that you get the subject to give you written permission to use her image in your marketing. Having a lawyer draw up a simple release form for your subject to sign may also be wise.

Making candid customer videos

TV commercials using customer testimonials are among the most effective ads. Not flashy, but effective. They don't win design awards in the advertising industry, but they do win high believability ratings from viewers — especially when they use candid testimonials.

What is a *candid testimonial?* It's what a customer says and does before you tell him that you're recording him. For instance, a car dealership may have a hidden video camera on the floor of its showroom aimed at a centrally placed new model that looks really great. An employee can monitor the camera's view from a nearby office or a hiding place on the showroom floor and when a shopper approaches the new model, the employee turns the camera on and hopes for a good reaction. Perhaps the shopper does a double take upon opening the driver's door and says, "Wow! I gotta have one of these!" and then jumps right in. And the video camera captures it all. Think how much more effective a commercial would be if it had a few candid reactions praising a new model instead of a fast-talking salesman in a cheap suit!

You can also create more heavily managed situations designed to increase the chances of usable responses. For instance, you can set up a booth in a mall where you display samples of a retail product and invite people to interact with it. You can even have someone who knows where the camera is engage these people in conversations, asking them what they think, to make sure they deliver some lines in the right place — facing the hidden camera and/or microphone. Similarly, you can demonstrate a business-to-business product or service at a trade show in a booth that's set up for recording. Getting some footage of candid customer reactions to a product or service isn't too hard if you do some advance planning.

Don't forget to ask permission!

The key is obviously to ask whomever you quote or photograph for permission for whatever use you have in mind. Be specific and clear about what you want to do. Ask in writing and get a written response, preferably with the person's signature (e-mail is a little less solid from a legal perspective). And when you're going to use a photo or video — in other words, the person's likeness — then you need to be extra careful about getting appropriate permission. In the paperwork, make it clear that you'll be using his likeness. Also, consider getting legal advice, especially if your organization makes enough money to be an attractive "deep pocket" target for legal actions.

After you record a candid customer reaction, look at it immediately and see whether it's any good. If it's inadequate, just plan to discard it and don't trouble the customer for permission. If it may be usable, however, immediately speak to the subject.

Explain that you're doing a candid camera operation and that you caught the person's reaction on video. If possible, keep the video rolling as you explain so that you can record his reaction to supplement his written permission. Thank him and treat him kindly. Try to encourage his natural tendency to be amused and pleasantly surprised. If he's mad, apologize and promise that you'll discard the footage. Then get rid of him and go on to the next subject. But if he doesn't seem to mind, secure his permission right away to use the video. Ask him if you can use the tape in future marketing communications. Get his "yes" on tape, and then have him sign a permission form and make sure that everything is clear.

He may want to see a copy of the finished ad or whatever the product will be. This request is certainly reasonable, and you should promise to send it to him as soon as it's finished.

If you're going to describe the person providing the testimonial as being affiliated with an organization, make sure that the person has the authority to give you permission to mention the organization's name, too. A senior executive obviously has this authority, but if you interview a mailroom clerk at a big company and plan to run a quote from him in which you describe him as an employee of that company, you'd better check with the company's publicity department first. The company may have a policy against endorsing products or services, and you don't want to find out about it after you've printed a thousand brochures.

A word about video quality

Make sure that you use high-quality video cameras to record customers' candid reactions. The average Super-8 home video camera doesn't produce as fine an image as you'd probably like to use, even for local television advertising or a company promotional video. A High-8 camera with plenty of light may be good enough, and it doesn't cost much more than an average Super-8 camera. And if you have access to professional quality digital cameras, they're obviously even better. Sometimes a local television station or college is willing to rent out cameras and, in larger cities, many audio-video supply houses rent equipment as well. Or, if you have a big enough business that you can afford to use a professional production studio, just turn the filming over to them and tell them to get high-quality, usable footage of customers or you won't pay them for their work.

Keep in mind the importance of good lighting, whether you make the video yourself or hire a crew to do it. Basically, all cameras, including digital video cameras, take better pictures when *more light* is available. If you can shoot under bright indoor lights or outdoors on a nice day, you're likely to get a video that looks good. If you film in a dim interior room or at night, the video footage won't look good. Bright light not only gives a good, sharp image, it also permits greater *depth of field* (in other words, the depth is in focus). In dim light, the camera has to adjust itself (or someone has to adjust it) by opening up its *aperture,* or the hole that lets light come in. And the wider the aperture, the more shallow the area that's in focus. So the foreground and background of a scene are blurry when the light is dim, but increase the lighting, and everything jumps into sharper focus.

If you want to use sound (such as the customer's voice), plug a good quality microphone into the camera and hold the mike near the sound source. Don't count on built-in camera mikes; they aren't good enough for most marketing uses. Sound should be clear and crisp enough to match the clear, crisp visuals from that good camera you're using in bright light.

And Now for an Easy Alternative

You may want to harness the power of customer testimonials without actually securing any. That's impossible. But you can do some next-best things that work pretty well. The best alternative to getting customer testimonials is to create a plausible fictional situation in which you create a customer character or characters. Then you tell a story, perhaps using dialogue or quotes, that conveys an accurate picture of what makes your product or service great.

Basically, what you do is substitute fiction for nonfiction. Many consumer ads use fictional scenes and characters to make their points. Simply turn on a TV or radio and take in a few dozen ads, and you'll come across at least a few of this type.

You can also create dialogue between fictional characters. Radio ads in which two people talk about a product are fairly common and can work well. These ads often attempt to be humorous, and sometimes even are, but don't have to be. As long as the characters personify the feelings of the listener, the listeners may identify with them just as strongly as they would identify with real customers.

Selling Services with Customer Stories

Services are intangible. You can't take them for a test drive or kick their wheels. You have to imagine them. When people shop for services, they often have difficulty deciding whether what they imagine is really appropriate and whether it will have sufficient quality to meet their needs.

For example, how do you know that a bank can handle your business checking account well? You don't. You just assume that a bank with a well-known name and a well-built branch is able to provide basic banking services. You're using two symbolic indicators of the quality of the bank's service to aid your imagination: its brand name and its facility. Other indicators of the quality of its service, such as how professional the tellers appear and how nice the checkbooks and checks they offer are, also may influence you.

Whenever people shop for a service, they rely significantly on such indicators of service quality. For this reason, service marketers are supposed to "manage the evidence," which means making sure your lobby, brochure, staff, and other visible elements are professional and appealing. And that's good advice. But I like to add another strategy, which is to let the people who actually *know* how good your service is give evidence to customers who want to find out.

Customer stories and testimonials are especially powerful when you're marketing services. Some consulting firms use them to good effect by including brief case histories of past client work in their brochures or presentation folders. The Jack Morton Company, a specialist in marketing events and promotions, uses this strategy very effectively. Some years ago, the company went to some of its best customers and obtained permission to write descriptions of specific projects that it did for those clients. The Jack Morton Company printed each project description on a single 8½x11-inch sheet of glossy paper and included a color photo to illustrate it. The clients agreed to let the company use their names and stories in these marketing devices. When future clients want to get a better idea of how this company's services work, they can simply read actual, real-life stories from past clients. Powerful evidence indeed.

On the CD

Check out the following items on your CD:

- ✔ Modern Memoirs brochure (CD0701)
- ✔ Script for soliciting a testimonial (CD0702)
- ✔ Testimonial response script (CD0703)
- ✔ Letter script for testimonials (CD0704)
- ✔ Catalog page from Human Resource Development Press (CD0705)

Part III
Advertising Management and Design

The 5th Wave   By Rich Tennant

"Have you noticed how sophisticated streaming media advertising has become in elevators lately?"

In this part . . .

Do you ever advertise? If not, I can honestly say that you better think about starting because there are few businesses that couldn't benefit from well-designed, carefully placed advertising. If you do already use this powerful medium, then you no doubt know how expensive it can get and how hard designing an ad that really achieves its business objectives can be. Careful planning — which I show you how to do in Chapter 8 — is the answer to these problems. Ads can accomplish a lot of profitable objectives, but only if you clearly define them upfront and then design your campaign appropriately.

Ads absolutely *must* be well designed. They need to look good, read well, sound great, catch the eye, make a lasting impression, and be the stuff of dinner conversation. In short, ads have to be powerful. In Chapter 9, I share my best ideas and techniques for building powerful ads that really make an impact on your customers and on your sales. Promise me that you'll read it carefully and that you won't ever run an ad that lacks power and punch.

Chapter 8

Planning and Budgeting Ad Campaigns

*D*esigning an ad is hard enough; so now for the bad news. Before you start designing your ads, you really need to create an advertising campaign. An *advertising campaign* is the big-picture plan (with budget) that you develop to help you decide who you want to reach with your ads and what you want those ads to communicate. The campaign you develop for your campaign should give you some clear targets for how you'll get a good return on that spending. Without a clear campaign, your ads may be beautiful, brilliant, or clever, but they won't necessarily make you any money.

In this chapter, I help you plan how much you want to spend on advertising and how you want to spend it. You can easily spend more money than you've imagined in your wildest dreams because ads can be very expensive. I show you how to set some practical parameters on your advertising campaign to make sure that you're laughing, not crying, all the way to the bank.

Start with what you know

It's a funny thing, but think about it: In business, true wisdom comes down to knowing what questions to ask. Your advertising campaign will be more successful if you ask yourself questions, such as, "What ads should we run?"; "How much should we spend?"; "How much will it cost?"; and "Will it pay off?"

You may find these questions difficult to answer. If so, don't panic. (Well, not quite yet.) Instead, back up. Take things more slowly and build on what you know. The only good plans are ones based on solid experience. If direct mail works pretty well for you and you have some letters that seem to pull, plan on sending out more letters like them. And you can base your sales projections on past experience, which improves your odds of making an accurate guess about future performance.

But if you've never done any TV ads, don't plan to put 45 percent of your budget into TV commercials next year. You don't know enough yet to make a good plan. Instead, plan to find out about TV. Budget a small amount — only as much as you can afford to chalk up to experience — and spend it finding out how to make TV ads that work. If you come up with a formula that really does seem to work, well, then you can consider rewriting the plan to incorporate a more ambitious TV campaign.

So when you plan your advertising, make sure that you're building on experience and not just guessing wildly. Also, make sure that you know what each dollar is supposed to accomplish so that your plan has realistic returns in bottom-line sales and profits.

Defining Your Overall Advertising Goals

Why advertise? Unless you have a clear purpose, there's no point. Many businesses advertise for poorly defined reasons. I've heard lots of managers say things like, "We do some advertising just to keep ourselves visible, but I don't think it affects our sales." Or, "We try to match our competitors' advertising because customers expect it." Or, "We've always done advertising; I don't know if it really works, but we're afraid of what might happen if we stopped."

What would happen is that they'd save the money they're now throwing away on advertising. I can guarantee that an advertising budget isn't doing anything helpful if you don't even know what it's supposed to be doing. Advertising for its own sake never achieves anything worthwhile; it just fills up the media with mediocre ads that nobody really notices. Only advertising that you specifically design and place to achieve an important business objective is worthwhile. Other advertising (most advertising) doesn't accomplish anything worthwhile because it doesn't set out to accomplish anything worthwhile.

Here are some examples of objectives or goals that advertising can help you accomplish. Pick one of the following goals or one of your own making, and make sure all your ads serve this purpose:

✔ Remind people of your product, service, or brand so they continue to buy and use it regularly.

✔ Show why your product, service, or brand is better than competitors so that you can capture a bigger share of sales.

✔ Explain or inform by sharing information about your offering so that prospective customers realize that you have something they can use.

✔ Give people an urgent reason to buy right now (such as a limited-time offer) in order to stimulate a short-term boost in the number or the size of purchases.

✔ Project a positive, appealing personality or image in order to build loyalty and increase sales gradually but durably over time.

✔ Support distributors by driving customers to them in order to increase purchase through your distribution network and to stimulate the distributors to work harder on selling your offering, too.

✔ Expand or shift your market by showing why you're appropriate for a group that hasn't paid much attention to you in the past so as to generate sales in a new market.

Having a Specific Objective for Each Ad

My whole approach to advertising is based on selecting a meaningful objective for your ad to achieve. You're supposed to design and test the ad against this objective (see the section "Testing Your Ad Design Against Your Objective" later in this chapter), and if the ad proves worthy, use it hard until you achieve the objective or the ad stops working toward that objective. This tactic is a simple, focused, businesslike approach that doesn't waste money on fluff advertising. But objective-driven advertising is only as good as the objective. So I figure I'd better give you some more help choosing a good objective. In this section, I show you how to link some common advertising objectives to specific, measurable outcomes. This idea is helpful because it gives you an easy way to see whether or not an ad is successful.

Looking at some useful objectives and hopeful outcomes

Table 8-1 provides a selection of useful marketing objectives, each linked to an indicator you can watch to see whether the ad works. To make your advertising objective-driven, simply select one (or at most two) of these objectives and keep it clearly in mind throughout the advertising process.

Table 8-1	Useful Ad Objectives and Their Desired Results
Objective	*How to Know Whether You're Achieving It*
Boost sales	Sales rise when and where the ad runs.
Generate calls	The telephone rings off the hook.
Generate by-mail responses	Responses come in by mail in large numbers the week after the ad first runs.
Introduce new product	Requests for and press coverage of the new product increase significantly right after the ad appears.
Switch customers from competing product	Sales go up as a result of switching.
Encourage word of mouth	Current and past customers begin to talk, stimulating sales to people who say they "heard about you from someone they know."
Increase your share of market	Your sales grow faster than the leading competitors' sales.
Recruit new distributors	You hear from multiple distributors who are interested in working with you.
Help build sales by building image or reputation	Sales grow gradually but definitely do grow, along with rapid improvements in image and enhanced reputation.
Attract more upscale buyers	You sell higher-priced products or find that you can raise your prices or no longer have to negotiate as many discounts.
Attract a different group of customers	Your sales to the new group increase.
Cross-sell new product to current customers	You sell more of the new product to your current customer base.
Get more shoppers to visit your store(s)	Store traffic and sales figures increase.

Notice that every objective in this table links to a specific outcome that you can track to see whether you achieved the objective. If you see movement in the measure, then the ad is working toward its objective. If you don't, then the ad isn't working, and you need to improve it or scrap it in favor of a new design.

Notice also, however, that most of those indicators that measure the success of an ad are a little hard to measure precisely. In fact, sometimes they're very hard to measure accurately. Sure, you can track your sales with accuracy, but can you track the rise in sales resulting from one particular ad? Not unless you can hold everything else you do constant. Experiment by changing only the ad, if feasible. But sometimes you can't help changing many different marketing initiatives at once. So which sales came from the new ad versus your catalog, the latest updates to your Web page, the trade show you were just at, or the better system you created for tracking your own leads and remembering to call them back? Sometimes you can tease out the answers but not always.

The ultimate objective, of course, is to generate sales from your ads. For example, if you run an ad designed to get more people into your store, the ultimate objective is to increase sales in that store. So you need to measure the ad by its impact on sales as well as on any more specific and short-term measures, like number of people visiting a store. Notice that I added a desired outcome in each of these descriptions of an advertising objective. Each statement includes some what-to-do information and also some indicator of how you know whether it's working or not. I want you to be this specific when you define your own advertising objectives. That way, you can create or purchase advertising that has a very clear purpose in mind, and then you're able to watch its performance and see whether it's doing what you said it ought to. One of the most fundamental rules of good management is that accountability is important — and advertising is certainly not above this accountability rule.

Keeping your objective on track with the ad planning process

The most effective ad campaigns result from well-defined objectives, careful objective-driven design and, often, redesign until the marketers know that they have a winner. Figure 8-1 shows the process in a nutshell.

Now I want to tell you what you should do with this six-step process. This process isn't a description of the typical advertising process that you can just look at and say, "Oh, okay, I guess that's how they do it. Now I'll get some people to do it for me." Most people don't use this process to create advertising. Instead, I give you a prescription for avoiding the typical process in order to achieve much better results than average. So you need to use this six-step plan to truly drive your own advertising process. Whether you're working on your own, hiring experts at each step, or a combination of the two, you need to take the process in hand at each step and make sure that it's doing what it's supposed to do.

The Ad Planning Process

1. Define useful objective(s).

2. Design to objective(s).

3. Test against objective(s).

4. Redesign based on test(s).

5. Maximize run of perfected ad.

6. Terminate ad as soon as it stops achieving objective(s) or as soon as the objective(s) are no longer important.

Figure 8-1:
Designing ads that really work.

That means you need to remind yourself and tell others (probably over and over) that you want them first to make sure that they have a good, meaningful, profitable objective for your ad to accomplish. Then, when they convince you (or you convince yourself) that the objective is on target, you need to make sure that the pursuit of that objective drives the design stage. Don't let people waste your time showing you ads that look nice but aren't relevant to your objective.

By the way, insist on following this same process for any advertising or Web page design you do. Just because stuff on the Web is virtual doesn't mean that you can get away with using lower standards for it. The money you spend on the Web — and hopefully *make* on the Web — is certainly not virtual.

Testing Your Ad Design Against Your Objective

So how can you make sure that your advertising is the "right" kind, the kind that is profitable because it achieves important objectives? Well, an awfully good place to start is to set out one or two important objectives and then design ads to achieve those objectives. Last, you simply track your progress toward those objectives to see whether your ads work. If not, pull the darn things in a hurry, redesign, and try again.

When the design is finally appropriate and looks like it ought to achieve your objective, you still have to drive the process aggressively or you won't get a good result. Your next step is to test the ad against its objective. *Test* means find cheap, easy ways to see whether or not the ad seems to work. Now, advertisers hate to do that, and people who sell advertising hate to see you do that. Nobody wants to test; they all want to just run with it and pray it'll work. But your money and your fate is at risk, not theirs, so you must insist on testing. Here are a few testing tips:

- ✔ To test a mailer, do a mock-up and test mail it to a small list of people. If you get a low response rate, redesign. If you get a good response, do a larger-scale mailing.

- ✔ If you're testing a print ad, don't let anyone talk you into buying 20 insertions in five different newspapers. Just buy one or two insertions in one paper, and see what happens. If the ad doesn't seem to do anything and nobody notices it, redesign. If the ad works wonderfully, run it on a larger scale.

- ✔ If you're testing an idea for a television commercial, don't let anyone talk you into an expensive production and a massively expensive, multi-city prime-time run. First, try a low-cost, quick-and-dirty version of the commercial that you can make at the studio of a local cable station (especially when you're marketing a smaller business and can't afford to do high-production-value ads until you know that the concept works). Test the inexpensive commercial cheaply by running it a few times in local markets. For a hundredth or even a thousandth of the cost of a typical campaign, you can find out whether that TV ad concept is capable of achieving your objective. If not, go back to the drawing board. But if it does do well, now you know enough to try risking some serious money on a larger-scale, more professional TV campaign.

- ✔ Whatever kind of ad you're testing, run it by some people who are representative of your target market. Ask them what they think. See whether they even remember what the ad said. See whether they feel excited about doing what the ad asked them to do. See whether they understood the darn thing. And whether they noticed the special offer you included. Heck, see whether they even noticed what product or company the ad was for. Asking people to review your ads is a great way to get some informal, early feedback before you risk using the ads on a quick, small-scale run in the media. Big companies use formal advertising tests with elaborate statistical analyses, but any company can do informal ad testing — although few do.

When you finally find an ad that seems to work, once again you need to take charge and stick to the process. An effective ad is a rare and wonderful thing. Enjoy it. Show it off. Get the most you can out of it. Try it lots of ways and places. And don't believe what those experts tell you, because as soon as an ad begins to really work, they'll start talking you into replacing it. "Don't want the market to get saturated," they'll say. Or, "Ads rarely run for more than a few months without redesign. Have you thought about the next one yet?"

The truth about ad-to-sales ratios

I want to debunk a myth that leads many otherwise sane managers into wasting their money on pointless advertising — and sometimes into underfunding really effective ads. That myth goes under the rubric of the advertising-to-sales ratio. *Advertising Age,* the weekly news bible of the North American advertising industry, publishes a periodic compilation of the ad/sales ratios (sales revenues divided by ad spending) of companies in a wide variety of industries. Advertising agencies use these ad/sales ratios, so they have a sense of how much they can expect companies to spend on advertising. But too often agencies take these ratios too seriously and use them as guidelines when designing advertising budgets.

The idea that businesses should spend *x* percent of their revenue on advertising is widely accepted in the field of marketing, but it's totally absurd. This idea encourages spending for the sake of spending. "Gotta spend that 6 percent somehow. Let's blow it on some TV." This idea is a silly myth. There's no magic ratio of ad spending to sales. There's only advertising that pays off and advertising that doesn't. If you do poorly defined, purposeless advertising, it won't pay off, whether you spend 10 percent of your sales or a fraction of a percent. If, on the other hand, you come up with advertising that really works for your business, then why would you limit it to a certain percent of sales? Far better to do as much of it as you can, building your business at an optimum rate as a result.

You'll know when you need to replace that ad. Replace it when it no longer achieves its objective. For instance, sales will slip or something else obvious will happen. You won't get as many orders, leads, calls, or visitors to your Web site. But until then, give the poor thing a chance! It may take you a long time to come up with another winner, so ride this one for all it's worth.

Budgeting Based on Objectives

I get many calls from unhappy marketers who are stuck with the unpleasant chore of writing the advertising budget for the next quarter or year and don't know how to do it. Good news! When you design ads using this objective-driven method, you're halfway toward completing the most sophisticated and effective method for writing an advertising budget.

Larger companies with major advertising programs used to budget based on a percentage-of-sales target (where they were determined to spend *x* percent of sales on ads, just because that was the convention in their company or industry). In the last decade or two, most larger companies switched to an objective-and-task method. With this method, companies simply decide what advertisements they need to achieve their objectives. Next, they add up the costs of these ads and get their budgets. If the budget is more than the company can afford, the bigwigs argue about the number and adjust it to reflect affordability. In this case, they have to accept that they probably won't achieve their full objectives.

Playing with variables

The basic idea is to budget based on what you have to do in order to achieve a specific objective. For example, say that your objective for next year's advertising is to double your sales. You have some ideas about how to do that because you tested some ads and found that they can bring in more sales. So now you simply need to work out a program that gets those ads in front of enough prospects to bring you all the sales that you want.

To double your sales, you probably have to reach at least twice as many prospects (more than twice as many if the quality of the prospects goes down). So how much advertising do you need and where should you place it to achieve those goals at a reasonable price using the ad designs that you think will work? Work through a plan, estimate the cost, and see whether it's profitable at the level of sales you anticipate (and perhaps at a more conservative forecast of sales, too, just to be safe). If the plan meets your budget, it's a go. If not, redesign.

How do you redesign an advertising campaign to better achieve your goals and make it more affordable? You can fiddle with one or more of the following:

- ✔ **Increase ad effectiveness.** Try different ad designs, media, or timing. Some work better than others, so you need to experiment to find out what the winning formula is for your business.

- ✔ **Decrease the cost of ads.** Try different ad designs, timing, or media, again with the goal of finding out what works best. Except now the priority is to test cheaper options and see whether they're effective enough to improve your bottom-line advertising results.

- ✔ **Increase your profits.** Try raising prices or lowering costs so that your profit margin is greater — which probably means improving product quality in customers' eyes.

The preceding variables are the main ones that affect the profitability of your advertising campaign. Play with them until your plan and budget work.

Using an Advertising Objective Worksheet

To create a budget for your advertising expenditures, I recommend you do it in two steps. First, fill in one or more Advertising Objective Worksheets (available on the CD as filename CD0801). These worksheets build up your planned campaign based on an objective-and-task approach, so they're consistent with the advertising process I describe earlier in this chapter. They also produce a more realistic and effective plan than you're likely to get using other methods.

Design your ad campaign one ad at a time, estimating the costs and results from it, and then add more ads until you get bottom-line totals that meet your business needs (what revenues and profits are you counting on from this campaign?). Adjust the mix of ads in your worksheet until you're satisfied that you have a good selection of ads that achieves your goals efficiently (with a good return on your advertising investment).

I included spreadsheets on the CD for both the Advertising Objective Worksheet and the Advertising Budget (filenames CD0801 and CD0802) so you can create these products quickly just by entering the numbers you want into these Excel spreadsheet files. The advantage of using these spreadsheets is that the formats and formulas are all worked out for you already. All you have to do is describe your specific ads by entering appropriate numbers in each boxed cell.

Filling out the worksheet

The Advertising Objective Worksheet is a helpful tool for analyzing specific ads and for summing up their overall impact on your marketing program. For the sake of analysis, an "ad" means a specific advertisement run in a specific medium a specific number of times. So, in a budget for my own training-materials company, for instance, I may define ad number-one as: "4-x-4-inch ad on Conflict Assessment, three months in *Training* magazine." And I may define ad number-two as: "Direct-mail script #22, to house list with new catalog." To keep track of these specifics, I wrote a clear description of each ad in the "Description" column of the spreadsheet.

When you use the Advertising Objective Worksheet on your computer, you'll see (to the right of the "Cost of Ad" column) that the spreadsheet calculates the return on investment for each ad. If the result is 1, the ad breaks even, which means that its expected revenue-generating power is equal to its cost. If the result is above 1, you're making a profit on the ad. If you aren't sure which ads (combinations of a specific ad design and insertion in a medium of your choice) to use the most, then look at this column and repeat the ads with the highest returns on investment.

If you aren't sure what to enter under the "Reach" (number of prospects) column in the worksheet, ask whoever sells space or time in the advertising media of interest to you. Almost all media you buy ad space from will have statistics on whom they reach, and they almost always give away detailed profiles of audience or readership for free to anyone who's interested in advertising with them.

Note that the worksheet defines reach as the number of *prospects,* not just the number of warm bodies. Sometimes these numbers are the same, sometimes they aren't. For instance, if you're promoting a product that mostly women buy, then you want to enter the number of women (your prospects in this case) who read a magazine into the Reach column, not the total number of people in the magazine's readership.

If you aren't sure what to enter under "Cost of Ad," again, consult the people who sell advertising space. They're happy to quote you prices for various options. And don't be afraid to negotiate; the salesperson may not reduce his prices, but then again, he might!

Making good estimates

If you're including direct mail or other forms of advertising that don't involve a third party selling access to the medium on your Advertising Objective Worksheet, then you need to come up with your own cost estimates. Get quotes from the post office, printer, or any other contractors you plan to use. You can use the worksheet to calculate returns on a lot of marketing communications, not just ads, because the principle is the same — that you want to justify each marketing communication in terms of its impact on customers and its financial returns.

You can estimate all the rest of the numbers you need to enter in the worksheet based on you or your company's experience. If you've never done any advertising before, you'll find guessing all the numbers you need nearly impossible. You won't have a clue what percentage of people who see your ad, get your letter, or view your Web site will actually respond by inquiring for more information or by sending in an order. Nor will you know what percentage of the people who responded to an ad actually ended up closing an order. It may be 100 percent, but with some forms of advertising and some sorts of sales, response rate will be considerably less. Again, some advertising experience in the medium is vital, so if you don't have any benchmarks to rely on, first do some very small-scale test runs of ads to find out how they'll perform.

Similarly, until you've done some similar kinds of advertising to similar sorts of people, you probably won't have a feel for how many repeat purchases you can count on from the average person responding to a specific ad. You simply have to accumulate that knowledge through a series of experiments before you really understand all the variables enough to make good guesses about repeat purchase rates. That's why you need to develop and test all ads using the six-step Ad Planning Process (see the beginning of this chapter). Using this process allows you to accumulate enough insight to design fairly complex and varied advertising plans. But don't expect to bypass the learning stage and produce accurate, effective plans and budgets overnight.

If you haven't done much advertising in the past, develop and test just one ad at a time. Grow from it and master it before trying to plan and budget many more. And even if you do quite a bit of advertising already, don't expect to suddenly leap into three or four new types of advertising overnight. Give yourself time to apply the Ad Planning Process and learn as you go, adding perhaps just one new "trick" each time you redo your budget.

Using an Advertising Budget Worksheet

After you've carefully planned and developed a number of different types of ads, you'll have a good idea how to use these ad forms in your marketing. And when you've analyzed how you can use each of these types of ads using the Advertising Objective Worksheet, you'll have a good feel for how they may add up to an advertising campaign that helps you achieve your sales goals.

Now you can finally summarize all this good thinking in the classic advertising budget: a simple listing of the totals you plan to spend in each medium by month for the coming year. On your CD, you can find the Advertising Budget Worksheet (filename CD0802). It's also summarized in Table 8-3. This form is a convenient tool for summarizing your advertising plans because it already has the formulas built in to sum up each column and row and to calculate the overall annual budget for all your advertising.

Table 8-3	Outline for an Advertising Budget	
Category and Item	*Past Year Spending?*	*Next Period Spending?*
Advertising Management and Design		
Fixed monthly consultation or service fees for ad management		
Design and production of ads		
Brand/identity research and/or design (design services)		
Web site improvement to present brand identity better		
Total Advertising Management and Design Costs		
Ad Campaigns		
Expenditures on advertising in trade magazines		

Category and Item	Past Year Spending?	Next Period Spending?
Expenditures on advertising in newspapers		
Expenditures on advertising on the radio		
Expenditures on advertising on television		
Expenditures on billboards/outdoor ads		
Signs on buildings, vehicles, and so on		
Point-of-purchase signs and displays		
Total Cost of Ad Campaigns		
Direct-response Advertising		
Compilation and maintenance of in-house lists of customers		
Purchase of mailing, telephone, or e-mail lists		
Purchase of software and hardware for list management		
Design services for direct-response advertising		
Production costs for printed mailings		
Mailing costs		
Fax costs		
Telemarketing costs		
Telephone answering services, outsourced, and inbound calls		
Payroll costs of in-house staff, incoming calls		
Staff time/cost for responding to removal-from-list requests		
Total Direct-response Advertising Cost		
Total Advertising Expenditures		

A good advertising budget is the end result of a lot of careful experimenting, learning, and analyzing. When you've done this preparation, figuring out what you want to spend on advertising is easy. Remember what I said about advertising-to-sales ratios and how you shouldn't use them to decide what to spend on advertising (if you don't remember, that's okay; check the sidebar "The truth about ad-to-sales ratios" earlier in this chapter)? Well, now that you finished all the preparatory work, I think you can finally take a peek at your ad-to-sales ratio, so I include an automatic calculation of it at the bottom of the Advertising Budget spreadsheet (below the portion that gets printed). If your ad-to-sales ratio is in the 2 to 12 percent range, you can probably ignore it (because most campaigns fall somewhere within this range). However

✔ If it's smaller, you have to ask yourself whether you're being too conservative.

✔ If it's higher, stop and check your assumptions. Are you really getting a big return on the ad spending you've planned? Are the prices you've been quoted reasonable? Is the program profitable? Okay. Then never mind that high ratio. Maybe you're just making a bigger investment and getting a bigger return than the average marketer. If you've found a good way to make money, why hold back? However, when ratios get much higher than 12 to 15 percent, you're obviously spending quite a bit of your revenue on advertising. So just make sure that you know why and are happy with that level of investment.

On the CD

Check out the following items on the CD-ROM:

✔ Advertising Objective Worksheet (CD0801)
✔ Advertising Budget Template (CD0802)

Chapter 9

Shortcuts to Great Ads

. . . .

In This Chapter

▶ Do-it-yourself ad templates

▶ Creative ad concepts

▶ Attractive images to make your ads draw

. . . .

Creating a fabulous advertising campaign is easy. All you have to do is hire designers from a big New York ad agency and give them an unlimited budget to come up with incredible concepts. Then you can just sit back and review their proposals until they come up with a real home run. (And you can spend several million dollars to run TV spots during the Super Bowl and another few million to flood consumer magazines with full-page print ads, right?) But what if you don't have the resources or budget to throw the best designers on your project and let them loose? I certainly don't have a million dollars to spend on a 30-second TV ad. How about you? What if you want to find less expensive ways to create some effective ads for a more small-scale or modest campaign?

There are plenty of shortcuts to great advertising. And many ad campaigns stand out by attracting interest and having exceptional impact without costing an arm and a leg. Creative smaller ad agencies sometimes can create a high-impact campaign on a low-impact budget, and do-it-yourself marketers sometimes hit home runs (or at least a flow of singles, which can get you around the bases) — without hiring an agency or designer.

In this chapter, I help you design print ads and mock them up or even design them fully, using nothing fancier than a basic computer running Word. You can even use this chapter, along with a blank sheet of paper and a pencil, to lay out ad concepts. Then, get someone else to translate them into their final form.

Do-It-Yourself Shortcuts

One of my favorite ways to think about a new ad I need to design is to leaf through a copy of *The New York Times Sunday Magazine*, studying the ads and pulling out examples of ad layouts that I think may fit my needs. (I like looking in the *Sunday Magazine* because its advertising space is expensive, so I usually find a lot of carefully designed ads that inspire me.) Of course, you can't just cut someone else's brand name out of an ad and paste yours in. But you can get lots of starting ideas for different ways to approach using a rectangular space to communicate your message and achieve your advertising objective. (Don't know what your objective is? Flip back to Chapter 8 and get one; then come back here to figure out what ad design can best achieve your objective.)

The tried and true visual appeal ad

If you look at a large number of print ads in any well-read consumer or professional magazine, you'll begin to see some basic ad templates repeated over and over, each time with a fresh new combination of imagery and language. Most commonly, many consumer magazines run one- or two-page full-color ads featuring a striking or beautiful photograph with a simple headline that usually contains a play on words to help catch and hold attention. The ad always includes the brand name and the tag line explaining the brand's basic brilliance and appeal. (If you don't know what makes your product or service brilliant, go back to Chapter 1 and find out so you can write a simple, compelling, one-sentence description of why your brand is great.) And at the bottom, the ad may have a sentence or two of explanatory copy.

This basic visual ad template works for fashion clothing, automobiles, cosmetics, travel destinations, and life insurance. It may work for you. Start by seeking a photograph that is glue to the eye — something that you can somehow relate to the essence of your appeal. Go to stock photography Web sites (see the upcoming list) and rifle through them to see whether something strikes your fancy. Then work up a headline that relates the image you choose to your brand. If you decide to use a stock photograph in your ad, just contact the stock photography house directly to find out what it will charge for your intended usage (the cost typically ranges from as low as $100 to as high as $1,000, depending on what you have in mind).

You can view and license the rights to photographs at Web sites such as

- www.ablestock.com
- www.corbis.com
- www.comstock.com
- www.indexstock.com
- www.1stopstock.com

Become a desktop publisher

Increasingly, entrepreneurial marketers are designing their own print ads and submitting them in Word or the Acrobat Portable Document Format (pdf) output option that Word now includes. Consult the people at the publication you want to advertise in (or the printer you want to hire to produce your brochure or catalog) to find out the easiest and most inexpensive way to submit your ad designs.

Many publications (including magazines and newspapers) can help you perfect your ad design if you give them the basic layout, images, and language you want included. (They may charge extra for this work, but even so, the cost is still cheaper than working with an agency.) So don't be afraid to ask for help and find out what your options are. If they want your advertising business, let them work for it!

The design and layout, along with the visual images and good *copy* (the writing in your ad), are the keys to a successful ad. Putting the ad together and getting it printed is important, too, but not nearly as important as the basic design. So, as a marketer, you can influence the impact of your ad by being closely involved in developing winning ad concepts and designs. Once you have a good idea, you can find lots of people who are willing to help you execute it.

There are lots of good photographs on the Web and in magazines and books. Use these sources to look for the kind of image you want, but then go to a seller of photographs and buy something similar. Don't try to use "found" photography that someone else may feel he owns, unless you pay him a one-time fee or royalties for each use based on a legal contract between you and the owner/distributor of the photo. Purchased photographs from the stock photography suppliers in the previous list aren't really too expensive to use, but defending a copyright lawsuits is.

And don't forget the obvious: A good, clear photograph or drawing of your product is often the best art for an ad. If you have a product that's even slightly photogenic, maybe you can just use a good, clear photo of it and not bother with purchasing any other art.

Some basic ad templates

Here are more basic designs that you can use as a starting point for your own ads. Each design is a fairly common type of ad, which can work quite well when you combine it with the appropriate words and images. So if you have some ideas about what you want your ad to achieve, try laying it out in one or more of these templates to get a decent rough cut of a design quickly and easily. (All the following templates are on the CD as Word files that you can copy and edit.)

Image ad template

CD0901 has a basic Word template, shown in Figure 9-1, for laying out an ad designed to communicate your brand's image to strengthen awareness and interest in your brand. If your objective is brand building, this format may work for you. Find a great image to help you show others what you think makes your brand appealing or special (see the list of Web sites in the previous section for sources of photos); then tie the image to the brand with clean, simple language in your headline and copy.

Headline Sets a Tone or Uses an Analogy

Beautiful photo or illustration here

Minimal copy designed to simply echo the visual feel and look in appealing words goes here (use expanded spacing for easy reading)

LOGO
(Make it clearly visible)

Short, elegant phrase highlightinng the brand's image
www.yourwebsite.com

Because... include a catchy phrase based on the analogy to help explain your illustration

Figure 9-1: Ads that use the image template catch the eye and emphasize the brand's essential appeal.

Many successful image ads use a central metaphor or simile tag lines to connect the product to an unlikely object, place, or event, which may then become the central photograph or drawing in the ad. For example, a marketer of birthday or party supplies may want to say that her Instant Party Kit is "Like a Carnival in a Box." With this simile in mind (this tag line is a simile because it uses "like," otherwise it's called a metaphor), you can visualize ad concepts such as an illustration showing a wild Brazilian carnival scene, visible through the cracked-open lid of a plain brown cardboard box.

One way to come up with a good comparison for a metaphor or simile image ad is to start by naming one or more qualities of your product that you want to communicate in the ad. Next, brainstorm other things that exemplify these qualities. An elephant represents a long memory, for example, so an auto mechanic service that maintains full service records on your car in its database may want to use an image of an elephant sitting behind a service counter. The headline may be, "We Remember," followed by body copy saying something like, "When did you last change your oil or charge your AC? What grade of oil got the best mileage in your car? Where did you put those snow tires? Do you still have any warranty benefits? What can you do when you lose your car keys while visiting Aunt Matilda, two states over? Whatever your problem, however foolish you think your question may be, don't hesitate . . . *Call us.* We remember!"

Okay, you get the idea. Now come up with a comparison for your own ad campaign.

Informative ad template

CD0902 is a template for an ad that emphasizes information about the product. What are its important features or benefits? How does it work? If you have a good story about your product, this ad design allows you to tell it clearly and well (see Figure 9-2).

Headline Goes Here
(Make it informative, about some appealing fact)

Small Headline
Overview of product or service here here here here here. More specific information here vfv dfsflkh sgsdg;j safdf jhk; dsgfdsl kfdsfmn.

Specifications:
- detail 1
- detail 2
- detail 3
- detail 4

(Let this text lead to the smaller headline and additional details in the right-hand column.)

Product photo or usage illustration (color or black and white)

Descriptive caption

What Customers Are Saying

"testimonial"

"testimonial"

"testimonial"

Smaller Headline
about important technical details that differentiate this offering from others and make it better. Text text wara afdas.

Detail photo or diagram

BRAND NAME

Contact information here here here

Figure 9-2: The informative ad template emphasizes information that helps the reader see why your offering is special.

You can lay out an informative ad in lots of ways. If you feel that the design in Figure 9-2 is a bit too technical, try the option in CD0903, which floats a series of product or usage photos around a column of simple explanatory copy.

To design an effective informative ad, first make sure that you're clear on what's special and important about your product from your customer's point of view. Get in touch with your special brilliance (see Chapter 1), and then select three or more facts that communicate this brilliance convincingly. For instance, if your service is faster than your competitors, use facts like the following:

- ✔ Average response time for new service requests: 3.5 hours
- ✔ Winner of multiple industry awards for the quality and speed of our service
- ✔ Money-back guarantee if we take more than 24 hours to respond fully to your request

These facts make the case in a compelling manner, and they all support the core claim to fame the ad is trying to communicate. Don't let your facts wander off topic or you dilute the ad's impact rather than strengthen it.

Call-to-action ad template

Another option is to design your ad so that it asks the viewer to leap into action and request information or make a purchase right now. CD0904 and Figure 9-3 show a basic call-to-action ad template that you can use to stimulate leads or sales by adapting it to your product. Before you do, think hard about what incentives you can give the viewer to act immediately. Your objective is direct action, so you need to include some extra benefit or reason for them to act, beyond the basic benefits of your product or service.

You can ask the viewer to take action in a lot of ways, but these types of ads generally have these elements in common:

- ✔ A strong basic appeal with both emotional and intellectual reasons to choose the product or service
- ✔ Added incentives to buy right now, such as a special time-sensitive discount or free add-on product or service included in the offer
- ✔ Direct request or command to act; for example, to call a toll-free number or go to a Web site and enter a special code to take advantage of an offer
- ✔ Clear, frequent, and varied options for contacting you and placing an order or requesting more information

If you can offer options or choices, include them in your ad, too, because choices tend to increase the response rate. CD0905 is a template for a call-to-action ad that's, in essence, a minicatalog, showing multiple products from which the viewer can select.

Main Headline (Short & Eye-Catching)
Secondary headline (explanatory, draws reader in)

Call to action in a short, clear opening paragraph saying exactly what you sell and why they should buy it right now.

Supporting information giving benefits, testimonials, or other evidence to help close a sale or stimulate a visit to your Web site.

Additional benefits or special offer associated with this ad to encourage them to take action immediately. **Number to call.**

Illustrative photo or drawing, black and white or gray scale art

Small, short caption

Company Name Here

www.yourwebsite.com
Toll-free phone number

Figure 9-3:
Ads using the call-to-action template ask the viewer to take action and make a purchase right away.

Creating Ad Concepts for Fun and Profit

The ad templates in the previous section are layouts that show you how to create an ad in two dimensions using text and images. But every good ad has an important third dimension: the *conceptual dimension*. Your ad needs to engage readers on the conceptual level by grabbing their attention, stimulating their senses, or engaging their creativity. It needs to make them think, feel, laugh, or maybe even cry.

The conceptual dimension of advertising is what gives an ad power. A clean layout and design helps the concept jump off the page and into the viewer's mind, but only when you have a conceptual design for the ad in the first place. So now I'm going to take you beneath the surface of your ad to help you explore the conceptual dimension of your design.

Some ads start with a basic objective and graphic design, whereas others may start with the concept and then let the form follow naturally. Designing ads is a creative job, so don't feel you have to do it in any particular order.

How do you find a great ad concept that will give your ad design that extra zing needed to really make it work?

Creativity is a good source of conceptual design. Think of something special that's easy and cheap to do, and you'll have a high-impact ad for less. But that's a tall creative order, otherwise everyone would already be doing it. So I better give you some help. I have two cool ideas that aren't overused. They're novel approaches that rely on free content to give your ad more stopping power and to hold attention. By using found content, you short-circuit the problem of having to develop great creative content of your own — which can be hard for even seasoned advertisers and is certainly difficult for the amateur designer.

- ✔ In my first idea, I create ads that evoke a strong sense of mood by using words associated with that mood.
- ✔ In my second idea, I create ads that communicate a mind-catching thought in the form of a wise quote.

In this section, I show you how to use these two shortcut design concepts. They're very flexible and adaptable. In fact, these concepts fit every business. And because copy, not art, drives these concepts, you can easily adapt them to many media, and they' re relatively cheap to execute in any medium as well.

The mood ad

The premise of the *mood ad* design (which you can use for any medium, from print ads to Web pages to brochures, radio, or even TV) is that you can position your offering in an appealing way by setting an emotional tone. The way the mood ad templates I provide for you do this is through the power of language and color. For instance, you can drop the color if you're doing black-and-white print. And you can add music or convert the words from print to voice if you're working on TV, radio, or the Web. In this section, however, I illustrate the mood ad concept for print.

The basic approach to creating mood ads is to use an umbrella word like "reliable," along with various synonyms, such as "dependable," "careful," and "trustworthy." This concept uses words to evoke a strong feeling and to associate it with your product or service. (I'm describing a print ad concept, but you could possibly turn it into scripts for radio by simply reading the list of words.) Figure 9-4 is a simple ad concept designed to convey the reliability and dependability of a service or product. This concept may be especially appropriate for a business service or a workhorse product used over and over at work or at home. Remember this ad is just a concept — you can play around with it by adding color, changing the layout, adding a paragraph or two of explanatory copy, or doing whatever strikes your fancy.

Perhaps you can combine this concept with the informative ad template in Figure 9-2, using "RELIABLE" as the headline and some of the synonyms for it as the secondary headline (like "Dependable, Persistent, Consistent, Safe"). Then the rest of the ad may include text describing product or service features and qualities that make it so reliable, along with customer quotes that emphasize reliability. You can take this concept many places and, wherever you go with it, you'll get a strong design that conveys the concept of reliability in every element of the ad's design.

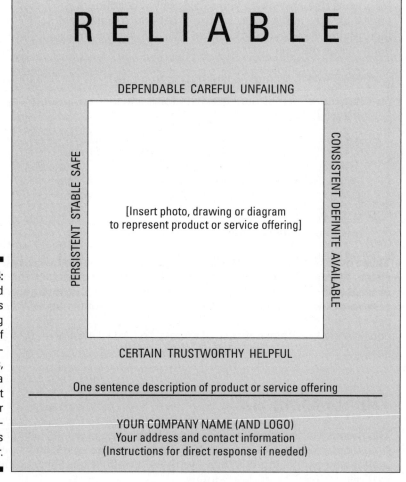

Figure 9-4:
This ad creates a strong sense of trustworthiness, which is a perfect concept for a business-to-business marketer.

RELIABLE

DEPENDABLE CAREFUL UNFAILING

PERSISTENT STABLE SAFE

CONSISTENT DEFINITE AVAILABLE

[Insert photo, drawing or diagram to represent product or service offering]

CERTAIN TRUSTWORTHY HELPFUL

One sentence description of product or service offering

YOUR COMPANY NAME (AND LOGO)
Your address and contact information
(Instructions for direct response if needed)

I once used the mood ad concept to advertise a service plan for a company that sold capital equipment to businesses. Those at the company felt that their service plan offered better support than their competitors did and wanted to convey this advantage. The key word they felt captured their attitude toward customer support was "concern." They were concerned about each customer and stayed in close touch with each one to make sure everything went well. Figure 9-5 shows a basic layout concept for a service-plan brochure that uses words to convey the feeling that the company stands behind each customer and takes a personal interest in his success.

Perhaps you want to create a mood ad of your own. Many possible feelings or meanings exist beyond the ones I illustrate here. Another nice thing about this mood ad design is that it's very easy to write new ones as needed. All you really need is a book of synonyms, such as a thesaurus or my favorite, *The Synonym Finder* by J.I. Rodale (Warner Books). Search the main entries for a word that appeals to you as a possible headline. Then examine the synonyms for it to find a dozen or more that add strength and depth to your ad. Incorporate these synonyms in the design however you want. Here are some good design options:

- Wrap words around an illustration to frame it (as the templates do).

- List the words in a long string to form unusual and powerful body copy or script.

- Ask a question, and then let viewers answer it by checking boxes next to words ("Is your ISP reliable? If so, then surely you'd describe it as _careful, _trustworthy, _stable, _available, _safe, _unfailing, _helpful, and _supportive. What? Didn't check all those boxes? Maybe you'd better give us an e-mail. That is, presuming your current service will let you.")

- Make a collage of words or a string of words (like in the design for a brochure cover in Figure 9-5).

These design concepts all harness the power of emotionally evocative language. Words are extraordinarily powerful: They can create a definite mood or feeling about your business or its product or service. And mood ads harness this power in simple ways that don't require sophisticated design skills or even much talent. In other words, they give you a relatively big impact considering how easy they are to create. That's the kind of marketing I like best!

The wisdom ad

The premise of the *wisdom ad* design (which you can use for any print media from display ads to direct-mail letters, brochures, catalogs, and sales collateral) is that people like ads that give them the gift of wisdom. People value wisdom because it's in short supply.

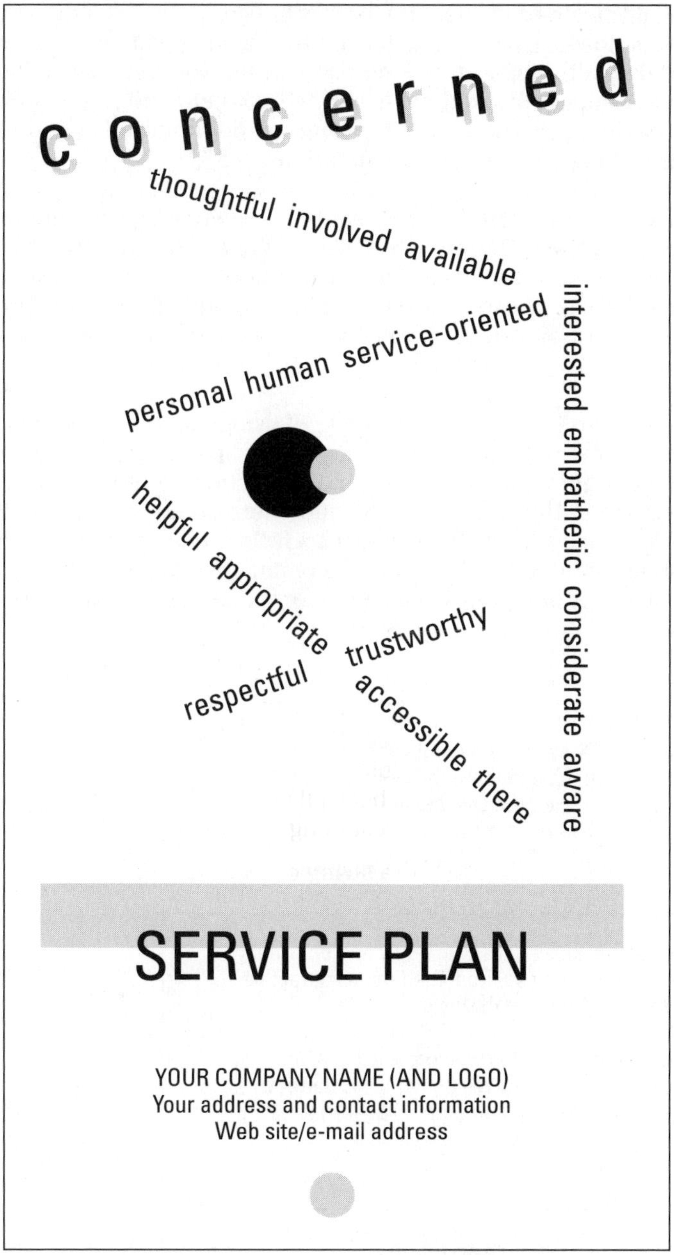

concerned

thoughtful involved available

personal human service-oriented

interested empathetic considerate aware

helpful appropriate

respectful trustworthy

accessible there

SERVICE PLAN

YOUR COMPANY NAME (AND LOGO)
Your address and contact information
Web site/e-mail address

Figure 9-5:
This
brochure
template
expresses
positive
feelings
associated
with good
service.

So where can you find servings of wisdom to include in your ads? My strategy
is to go to the classics. People always like a great quote from a master writer
or thinker, so a wise thought from literature can give your ad stopping power
and increase its value to readers.

Figure 9-6 illustrates a wisdom ad, proportioned for use as a display ad in a magazine or newspaper. This ad has no traditional headline to catch the eye; instead it uses a thought-provoking quote as its stopping power. If you use short quotes and attribute them accurately to their authors, you usually don't need to obtain reprint permissions. You can find thousands of quotes to choose from in any dictionary of quotations.

Note that the ad in Figure 9-6 is still at the concept stage. It's not designed fully. You may want to bump up the size of the quote at the top to make it really stand out. You can also add an illustration of Sherlock Holmes. Or maybe use a stock photo of a wise-looking owl and let the copy run over or reverse on top of part of the photo. The concept just gets you started; the execution is up to you.

The ad in Figure 9-7 is another example of using a quote instead of a headline. Many people like such quotes and may even clip the ad just to help them remember the quote. I've written a middle section of body copy in which a short message to the reader ties the quote into some positive attribute of the marketer's offering. This strategy takes a little creativity but it's a lot easier than writing a compelling headline or coming up with an original hook. All you have to do is find your hook in the form of an appealing quote and then tie that quote in to your products or services.

Figure 9-6:
Print ad relating the timeless quest for truth with the quest for better products.

> **"It has long been an axiom of mine that the little things are infinitely the most important."**
>
> **- Sherlock Holmes**

We hope you'll take a moment to enjoy and consider todays's word to the wise, from the famous detective created by Sir Arthur Conan Doyle.

And perhaps you'll find this wisdom applies to our [product/service] as well. We endeavor to perfect the many details that our customers tell us make all the difference between an ordinary and a great experience.

WORDS TO THE WISE
from [Company Name]
[Contact Information]

"The real question is not
whether machines think
but whether people do."

- B.F. Skinner

We hope you'll take a moment to enjoy and consider
todays's word to the wise, from the famous behavioral
scientist who raised his daughter in a laboratory box.
But we don't believe Skinner's doubts are valid, at
least not when people put their minds to something
that concerns them greatly. Certainly our customers
are quite thoughtful when it comes to deciding which
[producer/service] to select. And they tell us they
appreciate our thoughtful approach to design as well.

WORDS TO THE WISE
from [Company Name]
[Contact Information]

Figure 9-7:
This ad both
amuses and
compli-
ments the
prospective
customer.

I also designed these ads as if they were part of a series called "Words to the
Wise." The idea behind this series is to offer readers new quotes on a regular
basis so they develop a habit of looking for the next "Word to the Wise" ad. It's
a concept, anyway — and it may work for you, if some other reader doesn't
use it first!

Using quotes in brochures, catalogs, and newsletters

Elsewhere in this book, I go on and on about the value of customer quotes. I
like quotes! In general, an audience of any ad is more interested in anything
that was *not* written by the ad designer or marketer. They don't care what *you*
think. They know you're after their wallets. So whenever you find a way to
make a quote from someone else relevant, go for it. (Use quotes from famous
people because their quotes are generally in the public domain. If the source
is dead, you can be doubly sure she won't object to you quoting her. For a
customer quote or a quote from a magazine or newspaper, get specific, written permission from the person quoted or the publisher.)

Yet another easy ad concept

You may also consider other devices to create sustained interest in your advertising. For instance, why not hire a starving novelist to craft an interesting short story, and then run brief installments of it in a series of ads? Engagement devices like this are effective and are limited only by your imagination and willingness to break out of the normal advertising formulas.

A great way to integrate relevant and compelling quotes is to go to a dictionary of quotations and find something compelling. Using a wise quote is the basic premise of the wisdom ad concept I describe in the preceding section, and it's also the concept behind the brochure cover design in Figure 9-8. In this design for a simple two-fold, three-panel brochure printed on 8½-x-11-inch paper, the cover features two quotes that are relevant to the service the brochure advertises. The figure is just a cover concept (or you can repurpose it to be a print ad concept), and you can lay it out to be visually appealing using color, interesting/large type, an illustration, and so on. A version of the figure appears on the CD in file CD0906; I played with color and type to give it more visual appeal. You can find lots of ways to turn a concept like this into a finished product through creative design.

The quotes are interesting in their own right, especially to people who are wrestling with how to become more successful in their career and life — and those people are the target audience for this particular brochure. I designed the ad to promote the services of a personal coach (someone who helps people get organized and get ahead). So using wise thoughts about the nature and meaning of success are very relevant to the service and make the brochure valuable and intriguing to the target audience. Carrying the concept to the inside pages of this brochure makes sense, and so does sprinkling several more good quotes around it.

Notice that by simply changing the two large-type words that form the title, you can adapt this design to many different businesses. A computer consultant can simply use words describing his business, such as "computer systems" or "successful training solutions" to adapt the cover to fit the business. Then in the interior copy, you can pick up the theme of success by showing how each of the services the consultant offers helps companies achieve success. You can always come up with creative ways to adapt a good ad concept to your particular business and market!

"The common idea that success spoils
people by making them vain, egotistic
and self-complacent is erroneous; on
the contrary it makes them, for the
most part, humble, tolerant and kind.
Failure makes people bitter and cruel."

- W. Somerset Maugham

P E R S O N A L
C O A C H I N G

HELPING CLIENTS ACHIEVE THEIR GOALS

YOUR COMPANY NAME (AND LOGO)
Your address and contact information
Web site/e-mail address

"Success is relative:
It is what we can make of
the mess we've made of things."

- T.S. Eliot

Figure 9-8:
A concept
for a
brochure
that makes
good use of
quotations.

Visual Shortcuts to Great Ads

In the preceding sections, I share concepts and templates that make use primarily of advertising copy (or the written word) for their effectiveness. Often, the easiest way to create a high-impact ad cheaply and quickly is to simply write clever copy. But you can also find many wonderful ways to make an impact using art. Visual appeal can transform an ordinary marketing message into an extraordinary one.

So now I want to look at some strategies for creating powerful ads, catalogs, brochures, Web pages, or other marketing communications in a hurry or on a tight budget by using beautiful visuals.

If you want to make a big impact with a gorgeous photograph but need to work fast or on a tight budget, you probably don't want to hire a professional photographer. Your best bet in a hurry is stock photography, and you can find many vendors on the Web, so don't be afraid to go shopping for a great image (see the beginning of this chapter for some links or visit www.insightsformarketing.com for updated links).

Think about the visual appeal of your ad this way. Every year, people buy expensive calendars featuring fine photography and hang them up where they look at one image for a full month. These same people are routinely exposed to many hundreds of ads each day but do their best to ignore and forget them. What's the difference between the calendar they pay for and treasure and the ads they ignore? One has beautiful photographs; one doesn't. So if you want people to treasure your marketing communications instead of ignore them, try giving people what they want — something beautiful.

Using a beautiful landscape photo

My office has a pretty big library of books on marketing and advertising, and I just went through the indexes of a bunch of them looking for the word "beauty." It's not there. Go figure. What I figure is that most people aren't designing their marketing materials (or even their products) to be beautiful. They're trying to make ads effective, clever, or shocking, but not beautiful. So you can use that strategy with the confidence that you won't have a lot of competition in using this shortcut to great advertising.

You can offer customers beauty in plenty of other ways, as well. You don't have to confine yourself to photographs! A beautiful storefront, office space, or even an especially elegant business card can create an aesthetic impact that pleases and impresses prospects and customers. Yet how many of the spaces where businesses receive or serve customers are actually made to be truly beautiful? A flowering plant or small garden, a gorgeous painting, photo or art poster, a fresh coat of paint and a little trim — all are small investments in adding beauty to the customer's world.

Here's an ad concept: Why not select a really attractive photo of a beautiful natural landscape? The headline can say "Have a Great Day!" In the bottom right-hand corner, you can put "Brought to you by . . . " and add your logo or company name, plus a short one- or two-sentence update on what you're doing or any new upgrades or additions to your product line. Start this copy with "Now offering . . . " or a similar phrase.

 Keep the ad copy minimal, and let the beautiful photo be your gift to customers and prospects. Don't clutter your photo with too many advertising messages, either. An ad like this achieves the objectives of burnishing your brand image and generating goodwill among customers and prospects, and both of these objectives can help you close sales and retain customers later on.

Portraying an attractive person

People look at other people. We're socially oriented; we can't help it. In particular, photos of people playing, laughing, and having fun tend to attract viewers. Also, photos of children and babies are naturally attractive. And handsome or attractive people tend to draw and hold attention. But this doesn't mean that you need to fill every ad with sexually provocative images. Besides, that tactic isn't very effective unless your product is relevant to sex appeal (like cosmetics).

One way to use the natural appeal of people is to have a head-and-shoulders photo of an interesting or attractive person, using him or her as your spokesperson for your print ad. The spokesperson can say something in first person, like "I'm glad I switched to (name of your company or brand)." Placing that message in a bold headline, over an interesting, animated face, draws most viewers down to the copy to see why the person is happy he or she switched to your product.

Another classic concept is to have models using the product rather than just showing the product by itself. People bring ads to life. Whenever possible, include photos of interesting people to draw the eye and engage the viewer.

Inserting a humorous cartoon

Humorous cartoons clipped out of newspapers or magazines cover many office bulletin boards and home refrigerators. People like a good cartoon. So another simple way to attract viewers to your print ad is to include a good cartoon. This idea is easier than it sounds. Web sites like cartoonbank.com, www.glasbergen.com, www.pritchettcartoons.com, www.cartoonwork.com, and www.tedgoff.com cue up thousands of humorous cartoons and give you the option of licensing them for professional use in an ad, newsletter, mailing, e-mail, or Web page. Have a look. You just need to think of some way to relate your product or service to a humorous cartoon, and you have yourself a great ad concept!

On the CD

Check out the following items on the CD-ROM:

- An image ad template (CD0901)
- Informative ad templates (CD0902 and CD0903)
- Call-to-action ad templates (CD0904 and CD0905)
- Tall ad or brochure cover (CD0906)

Part IV
Power Alternatives to Advertising

The 5th Wave   By Rich Tennant

"I don't know, Art. I think you're just ahead of your time."

In this part . . .

Ads are powerful, but they aren't the only way to skin the marketing cat. Other elements of your marketing communications are vital, too. In fact, these elements can sometimes take the place of (expensive) advertising. In this part, I start by discussing the power of your brand — the recognizable name or visual symbol that customers come to know, trust, and love. I show you how to present this brand identity consistently in everything you do, starting with the basics of business cards, letterhead, e-mails, and faxes. I also explore the important new topic of presenting your brand on the Web.

Brochures, product sheets, catalogs, and other printed marketing materials are also powerful tools in your marketing arsenal, and I recommend that you examine every one of your printed materials carefully using Chapter 11 as a guide. I've never met a company whose sales I couldn't boost simply by revising its brochures and other printed materials. Speaking of printed materials and the Web, I include a chapter on newsletters that I hope will get you thinking about how to harness this economical and effective medium in your marketing program.

And last, but by no means least, I highly suggest that you spend an evening studying the chapter on publicity and working up a media kit and list so you can begin getting your business the press coverage it so richly deserves. Publicity is the wild card of marketing — the marketing "ace in the hole" — the secret that savvy business owners know about and I want you to know about, too. If you manage to get some good editorial coverage in the media, it can be worth literally hundreds of thousands, maybe even millions of dollars of advertising, and it's virtually free.

Chapter 10

The Basics: Branding through Business Cards and Letterhead

*W*hen you go into an important business meeting or sales call, you know that you need to look good — professional clothes; clean, attractive hair; a nice smile; good manners; and no body odor. Most people with any business experience learn to follow these rules of personal presentation fairly quickly. (More or less — I do wish that people would be a little more careful to dress conservatively and professionally whenever they have a connection or sale to make!)

But when you're presenting yourself at arm's length through marketing materials, people are far, far less professional. Try to keep in mind that your business card, letter, brochure, catalog, or other materials *represent you* to potential customers. Most businesspeople tend to impose a lower standard on these materials than they would on themselves if they were there in person. But in truth, an even higher standard is necessary and appropriate. Why? Because you aren't there to make your case. And no matter how well designed your marketing materials are, they're a poor substitute for human beings. So your marketing materials need to be really top-class to do the job.

In this chapter, I show you how to take a close look at how your brand looks, starting with an examination of the brand identity and then making sure your business cards, stationery, labels, envelopes or boxes, faxes, and e-mails all convey your identity clearly and well.

Who Are You?: Establishing Brand Identity

Who are you? Your name and face are instantly recognizable to anyone who knows you. People who don't know you can easily begin to recognize you from your unique combination of name, face, and voice. You have a clear identity as a human being — so clear that telling you apart from anyone else on the planet is easy.

Well, maybe I'm exaggerating. If your name is John Smith, then you may not be too distinctive by name alone. But add your face to the name, and now you're truly unique. People are expected to be unique and easy to identify. It is confusing and even upsetting when someone doesn't look like a unique individual. We don't want clones running around — they seem creepy. I should know: I'm a twin. When I stop to get a cup of coffee at the general store in the small town that my brother lives in, I usually create social chaos. People come up to me and say hello, and I have no idea what to say back. Or they look at me quizzically, turn away, and then look back, not quite sure whether they know me or not. You want to make sure your product or service is so clearly identifiable and so well known that you never have such problems in your marketplace.

To evaluate the strength of your corporate identity, consider the following questions:

✔ Does your letterhead look unique and is it easy to identify at a distance, like from across the room?

✔ What adjectives would someone use to describe your company if she could work from only a copy of your letterhead?

✔ Does your logo look more attractive and professional than your competitors' logos?

✔ Does everything you send through the mail, fax, and e-mail show your logo and identifying information in a clean, consistent, and attractive manner?

✔ Do you include your *corporate identity* (logo, name, and so on) on all packaging and products in an appealing and consistent way?

✔ Do you and all other representatives of your company carry attractive business cards in a proper case to give out whenever you have an appropriate opportunity?

✔ Do your e-mails include your corporate logo, name, and contact information consistent with your letterhead and business cards?

These questions help you identify immediate issues or opportunities in how you present your identity to the world. Marketing is in the eyes of the beholder, so you must make sure that everyone interacting with your firm or any of its products, services, publications, Web pages, ads, or other marketing materials sees your unique identity clearly and fully.

The best-looking logos, the most appealing names, and the strongest presentations of identity are usually associated with winning companies and brands. Like it or not, appearances matter. I always urge my clients to make sure that they look like the company they want to be, not the company they were three years ago when they last ordered stationery.

In the remaining sections of this chapter, I ask you to take a close look at some of the most important elements in your public presentation of your marketing identity.

Creating Your Name and Logo

Whether you're selling your business or a specific product, your name and logo is key. Coca-Cola has a striking identity: The brand is easy to recognize anywhere, any time. The Coca-Cola Company writes its name in a distinct way that makes its name into a logo design, and it always has color.

Nike uses another strategy. The company doesn't always write its name the same, but it always has the distinctive swoosh logo nearby. The swoosh brands every product the company designs and also appears on the company's letterhead, business cards, and so on, giving the company one of the best known brands in the universe.

Close your eyes for a moment and try to visualize the logo or name of your local telephone company, bank, cable TV company, and local taxi company. How many of these logos and names pop right to mind, appearing clearly and easily in your mind? Not all of them, I bet. Depending on where you live, maybe one or two logos or names are so well designed and consistently portrayed that you can actually visualize them instantly without a hint or other aid.

Now take an objective look at your own marketing identity. Do people instantly recognize or easily visualize your name or logo, as they do with Coke or Nike? If not, you need to work on your identity.

To pump up your identity, give your company, product, or service a clear, clean, visual signature. Always write your company's, product's, or service's name the same way, and make it look good. No, make it look great. If you don't know how to design a great signature or logo, I recommend hiring a graphic designer who can show you a portfolio of really impressive logo and identity work.

Assessing your identity

Take some time to make sure your marketing identity looks really good. A good marketing identity is one that

✔ Makes a strong, positive impression on all who see it.

✔ Portrays you, your firm, service or brand as you aspire for it to be. This way, if your

business actually grows and achieves higher levels of success in the future, it will grow into your logo and look, not out of it.

✔ Is highly memorable and easy to recognize, even from a great distance.

✔ Is consistently displayed wherever you have an opportunity to do so.

Many printing shops offer free or almost-free design services as a way to get you to give them your order. But you won't get a good design this way, unless you come to them with a really clear vision of what you want and manage the design work carefully.

"Selling" Your Business Cards

Your business card is often the first contact someone has with you or your business. Sometimes your business card is the only marketing communication that a prospect has, so you want to make sure that it follows the rules of good marketing communications by building both emotional and rational involvement. That means it needs to communicate the information that a prospect needs to figure out what products or services you have and how he can contact you easily.

Making a good overall impression

Don't forget that your business card has to appeal to prospects on a basic emotional or intuitive level, too. Imagine someone looking through a pile of cards that includes many competitors of yours. Why would a prospect pick out yours? What about your card makes it call out to people?

Basically, your card needs to make a powerful, positive, personal impression. However, most cards don't. Most are quite dull. Even the ones that are clean and professional generally emphasize information and ignore the need to make an impression.

Different cards for different occasions

You can even consider *custom cards* for specific occasions. When I go to trade shows or conferences, I sometimes have a designer or someone handy in my office make up inkjet-printed business cards specific to the event. (Your Word program has a template that works with Avery Clean-Edge printable sheets of business cards, so you or someone adept at designing can print up a few dozen sheets for any special occasion. Buy the sheet pack for your type of printer, either laser or inkjet.)

When I returned from a conference of human resource directors, where I ran a workshop on identifying and developing high-potential employees, I knew what would happen to the business cards that people collected at this kind of event: They'd land in a big pile that you'd go through afterward; half the time, you'd look at a card and say, "Now who was this person? Why do I have this card?" So I handed out cards that not only identified me and my business but that also included the name of my workshop and the conference's name and date. That way, people could easily recall me, no matter how big their piles of cards or how poor their memories. I'm sure I was the only presenter at that conference who actually had cards custom made for the event, so that helped my card stand out from the others, and it was probably why I got a number of good calls from participants in the months after the event.

To make a good overall impression, strive for a sophisticated, professional image — with something different, such as a better-quality paper, a more beautiful logo, an unusual vertical layout, a useful fact or inspirational quote printed on the back, or an attractive use of color to highlight your company name or logo. Above all, focus on a well-presented company name and logo.

Hold on! Just because you want to make a powerful, personal impression with your card, don't do anything crazy. You don't want to make a *negative* impression! An overly colorful, flashy card with a photograph plus gold-, red-, and green-colored print is not the way to attract attention. Keep the design clean and professional, and make sure it fits your market and exceeds your customers' expectations.

Deciding on design details

When designing your business cards, remember that you want your card to make a good impression and to include enough information so contacting you is easy. But at the same time, you don't want to overload your prospects with so much information that the card is confusing. (A good general design template for business cards is available in file CD1001, by the way.)

The standard size for business cards in the United States is 2 x 3½ inches. Businesses usually have their cards printed, as opposed to copied, largely because printing is more durable when handled a lot. How you set up the original design depends entirely on how you're getting the cards made.

Choosing flat or raised ink

You can get business cards printed in either flat ink or raised ink. Flat-ink printing is just the standard printing. In raised-ink printing, the printer uses an ink, dusts it with a plastic powder, and heats it in an oven that melts and expands the powder, giving the type a raised look and feel.

Almost all printers offer both types of printing for business cards, and the choice you make is largely one of taste. Personally, I don't like the look and feel of raised cards, but many people prefer them.

Here's my favorite, if you want serious elegance: Ask your printer to help you find a specialist who will make a die (metal stamp) of your logo, and have it embossed on your card, along with flat ink printing of the business name, tag line, and your name and contact information. It takes longer to make and is more expensive, but it really stands out.

Setting your margins

Printers like to have space from the edge of the design to the edge of the paper. The amount of space needed varies from printer to printer — anywhere from ⅛ inch to ¼ inch. To be safe, leave ¼ inch in all directions (see Figure 10-1) because paper can sometimes shift from side to side when going through the press, and this space assures that the cutter won't clip off any text that's too close to the edge of the card.

Figure 10-1:
Don't let your card design get too close to the edge of the card.

John Smith
President

EMail: info@bfox.com

Brown Fox
and company

12 Acme St.
Smithville, OH 12345

123/456-7890
Fax 123/ 456-0001

1/4"

1/4"

Pondering paper stock

Print your business cards on a heavy paper, such as #65 cover stock. Also, using matching paper stock for your business cards, stationery, and envelopes is a good idea because people associate each with the others and see all of them as part of a clearly defined professional presentation and image (see Figure 10-2; you can also see a full-color version on the CD if you open CD1002). Some papers differ in weight but match in color and finish, so you can easily match your cards with the lighter paper of your letterhead.

Some printers offer package discounts on letterhead, envelopes, and cards when you order them together, so getting them all printed at the same time is often cost-effective.

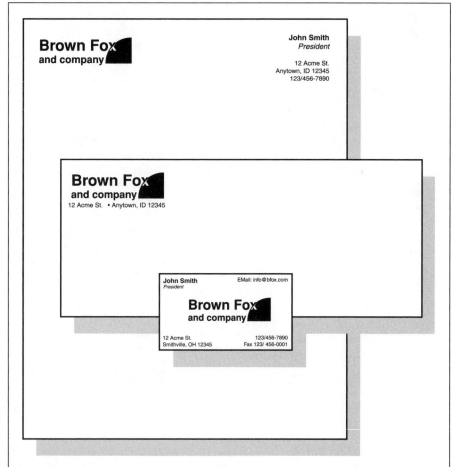

Figure 10-2: Consider how your letterhead, envelopes, and business cards look when seen together.

Designing Your Letterhead and Envelopes

Like with business cards, letterhead and envelopes may be the first encounter someone has with your business, and first impressions are obviously important. But even if customers have done business with you for some time, the look and feel of your stationery has a subtle but powerful impact on their attitude toward you. Good letterhead can help retain a customer or stimulate a referral. So, like with business cards, letterhead is a surprisingly important marketing investment. Make sure you have a clean, impressive design that impresses customers favorably.

And don't overlook the importance of an envelope design that calls out to be opened. Important prospects get too much mail. Why should they pay any special attention to your envelope? Because it appears professional, impressive, and looks more interesting and useful to them than the average junk mail they receive. Or does it? Better take a cold, hard look at your envelopes and see whether they're up to the challenge!

Conveying your image through paper and print

If you're a stockbroker or a business consultant, you may want to have an established, conservative look for your design, ink, and paper selections. Communicating a sense of stability and longevity can be important in these fields. What sorts of type, ink color, and paper say this the best? Perhaps Times Roman lettering, centered in a traditional style at the head of the paper, printed in conservative black ink on an old-fashioned creamy paper with some cotton fiber in it, also containing a watermark. Such a paper is more expensive than lighter, more modern papers but is consistent with a conservative, solid, sophisticated image. (Make sure you order blank sheets, too, to use for second pages because a regular piece of white paper doesn't match.)

What should an art therapist choose for stationery? Well, an art therapist needs to select an image that's both playful and supportive — soft, reassuring, but a bit artistic and fun, too. How about a full-color rainbow as the logo, which brings in the artist's palette but also evokes thoughts of calmness, good fortune, and healing (because rainbows come after storms)? As for paper, perhaps an attractive, soft, woven paper, again in a conservative off-white or creamy color, but perhaps this time with some little flecks of color in it?

You need to project a clear, strong personality each and every time you present your business. Capture and convey your brand personality in your letterhead, envelopes, and business cards. Even if you don't work with an expensive designer, take the time to explore many options and make a thoughtful selection of paper, ink, type, and logo (if you use one). Extra care and a little extra investment here go a lot further than most people realize to help make sales and marketing successful.

Here's an idea you can act on easily, with or without a designer's help. Go to a larger print shop and select a distinctive paper for your business. Something that you feel has a unique, appropriate, and appealing look and feel to it. Then order letterhead, business cards, envelopes, and even labels all on this distinctive paper. This subtle design element can boost the image and appeal of a business.

Getting your message across through faxes and e-mails

Many businesses use decent letterhead but send faxes using a generic cover sheet with designs (please avoid the templates in Word!). Other businesses improvise and use a blank sheet of paper to create inconsistent and unprofessional looking faxes.

You can simply use your letterhead for faxes, centering the header "FAX MEMO" at the top of the page, with the date centered in smaller type below it. Then use the standard memo format of left-justified To:, From:, and Re: lines, including both the name of the person the fax is to and her fax number. At the bottom, beneath your signature, provide your own fax number if the contact address on your letterhead doesn't include it. You can also say in a "Note" at the bottom, "3 more pages to come" or whatever, to make sure she receives all the pages you send.

If you send a lot of faxes, you may need a special fax form. This form can be on regular white paper (because the paper doesn't go through to the recipient anyway), but it must have a faithful reproduction (in black-and-white line art) of your logo and identity; in other words, you want it to look pretty much the way it does on your letterhead. Add any lines for including fax-oriented information, such as who to call if the fax doesn't come through correctly and how many pages the recipient should expect. If the document's important, you can also provide alternative ways of seeing or receiving it, such as providing an e-mail address that the recipient can contact if she wants you to send it electronically (a good option when the recipient may want to edit or work with your material).

Sometimes (like when sending a multipage contract) you need a cover sheet to explain what's coming by fax. I recommend that fax cover sheets look like letterhead, except that they say "FAX COVER SHEET" at the top, centered (or wherever it doesn't interfere with your letterhead design), and have a short table (boxed in) with all necessary fields of information where you can write in. Don't let the tail wag the design dog. The key point is to make sure the fax presents your identity well, just as your letterhead and business card do. (And don't overuse the fax cover sheet. If you have just a short note to send, make it a one-page fax memo, as my earlier design notes. Don't send a cover sheet that says "one page to come" when all you need to send is a memo.)

Placing Brand Identity on Your Web Site

I want to compliment UPS for being a good example of how to present the corporate identity on a Web site. If you go to www.ups.com, you see a montage of images (at least at the time of this writing), with a beautiful version of the UPS shield-shaped logo prominently displayed on a dark field. The logo seems to pick up a little light from above and positively shines out at the audience. Click on any of the many tabs and navigate through pages for different countries and services or go to the corporate page, and this nice version of the UPS logo is always prominently there to greet you. That's how Web sites should handle logos and identities, but most sites don't do it nearly that well. Does yours?

In a much more modest example, all the corporate Web sites for my business consistently use the company logo, at least on the home pages. As a reader, you may already be familiar with www.insightsformarketing.com. Notice that the eye and triangle logo appears prominently in the banner on the top. If you go to the sister site for our corporate training and consulting services, www.insightsfortraining.com, you see a home page design that's somewhat different in color and details but still displays the logo consistently and in the same place. Similarly, at our online store for corporate trainers, www.trainingactivities.com, the site prominently and consistently displays the logo.

Web pages allow for excellent graphics with high resolution, strong colors, and good backlighting on the viewer's computer screen. So use graphics to present your logo attractively. Every Web page can help build the strength of your marketing identity. Make sure yours does!

On the CD

Check out the CD for the following materials:

- ✔ Sample Business Cards (CD1001)
- ✔ Sample Letterhead, Envelope, and Brochure (CD1002)

Chapter 11

Essential Brochures, Catalogs, and Spec Sheets

. . . .

In This Chapter

▶ Deciding which marketing materials you need

▶ Designing brochures that make an impression

▶ Knowing when to use digital brochures

▶ Creating catalogs, booklets, and books

▶ Making spec sheets

. . . .

As a consultant, I usually get new clients through referrals or people who've found out about me through my books and booklets, Web site, catalogs, or have read about me in the news (see Chapter 14 if customers don't read about you in the news as often as you'd like them to). After I talk to a prospective client and he sees that my firm can be of help, he invariably asks me to "send him something." This request may mean that he expects a proposal letter with a suggested program and pricing, but it always means that he expects an impressive folder stuffed with sheets describing specific services or programs, a brochure with our background and approach, plus examples of past clients, and an assortment of press clippings. The nicely designed and printed brochure and spec (or specification) sheets, all in full color on coated paper (which looks shinier and crisper than plain uncoated paper), makes the mailing look professional and reassures the recipient that we are "real." Increasingly, my company's including a CD with video, too (I talk about CD and DVD supplements to or replacements for the conventional brochure at the end of this chapter).

In this chapter, I help you work on brochures, spec sheets, catalogs, and booklets, all of which are essentials of a good marketing program. I also touch on modern CD and DVD versions of the introductory brochure, which are, in my opinion, the most exciting new direction in brochures.

Considering Your Needs

So how do you know which kind of marketing materials you need to create a brochure, spec sheet, catalog, booklet, or flier? Well, a brochure, spec sheet, and flier are really just variations of the same theme. In these materials, you include essential information about your offerings, plus additional information and images to attract and hold interest. If you only need one page of information and plan to place it beneath a letter or in a pocket folder, then you can just design a one-page spec sheet (for technical information) or flier (which will have more interesting information and/or images than a spec sheet). But if you have more information and need multiple pages or if you expect to fold the material for mailing or displaying in a rack, then create a brochure layout and design. Another consideration to keep in mind is that brochures — when done well — can look more sophisticated and professional than sheets.

When you want to include a lot of information, such as descriptions of every product in a line, a brochure may get a bit overstuffed, so you probably need to make a catalog or booklet instead. What's the difference? In producing them, not much. Both a booklet and a catalog contain multiple pages that are bound together by center folding and stapling or by spiral binding or glued *perfect binding* methods (how paperback books are made; see the sections "Captivating Catalogs" and "Booklets and Books" later in this chapter).

When multipage publications focus on portraying and selling an assortment of products, they're usually called catalogs. So if you have an assortment of products, you probably need a catalog. But don't overlook the less common option of a booklet or a book. (A booklet is a center-folded and stapled short book, which you can make more cheaply than a bound book.) For example, if you run a boatyard, you could compile a book on how to maintain your boat, geared to boat owners. Booklets and books can work wonders in generating interest in what you do and position you or your firm as experts in your field.

Beautiful Brochures

"We need a brochure." That's the most common request that a marketing consultant or designer hears from clients. Seems like everybody needs a new brochure, and I think I know why: The old ones aren't working. Maybe they don't have much impact or maybe they don't look very good. Maybe they don't contain the company's latest information or products. Or maybe the brochures don't make the phone ring off the hook.

People are rightfully unhappy with their brochures because most don't accomplish what a good brochure should. A good brochure

- ✔ Gets prospects excited about doing business with you

- ✔ Communicates enough information to support a purchase decision

- ✔ Communicates enough feeling to create a strong, positive impression or image

- ✔ Serves as a simple minicatalog that describes your various products or services

- ✔ Supports *all* your marketing activities by serving as a handout for salespeople, a great mail piece for prospecting, a useful update for existing customers, a giveaway at events or trade shows, the perfect accompaniment to a formal proposal or press kit, and so on

Whenever you present yourself to the public, you can use your brochure to break the ice. Because brochures can be such effective icebreakers and salemakers, you may want to create a line of brochures — one for each purpose, service, or product, plus a general one that presents your company well. Single-purpose brochures are more effective and easier to design well, so I usually recommend creating a separate brochure for each major need or purpose.

Brochure design considerations

Freelance designer Rick Ward, who helped me with this chapter, often advises his clients to collect examples of brochures they like before coming to him to finalize their designs. I recommend keeping a file folder somewhere in your office labeled something like "Brochures I Like." Whenever you see an appealing brochure, toss it in that folder. That way, when you have to think about making your own brochure design, you can empty the file folder and look at lots of appealing approaches. One of them may inspire you to do something new and different — and it may work for you.

Keeping function and purpose in mind

To make sure that you have a brochure that does everything it can to help you sell your product or service, first you need to analyze the possible uses of that brochure. Don't design your own brochure or ask an expert to design it without having a clear list of all its purposes. Otherwise, the brochure won't fit those uses, and you may be disappointed with it.

Before you tackle the project of designing a new brochure, fill in the sample worksheet in Figure 11-1.

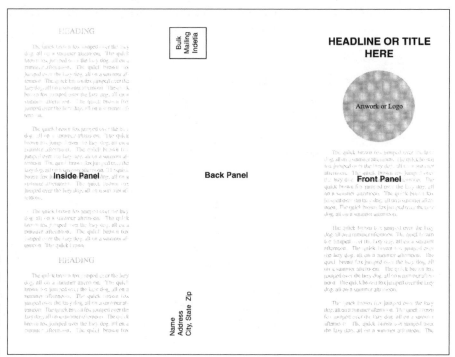

HEADLINE OR TITLE HERE

Artwork or Logo

Bulk Mailing Indetia

Back Panel

Inside Panel

Front Panel

Name
Address
City, State Zip

Figure 11-1:
Fill out a
brochure
design
worksheet.

Figure 11-1:
Fill out a
brochure
design
worksheet.

After you identify all the likely uses for your brochure, think about the design requirements of each intended use — and make sure that your design incorporates them. (If you can't come up with a design that does all the things you need, maybe you're trying to accomplish too much. Single-purpose designs are usually best, so be prepared to print more than one brochure if you have multiple uses for them.)

For example, say that you checked "Include in letters to prospects" in the sample worksheet. Now you have to figure out how you're going to mail your brochure. Will you simply fold it up and have room on the outside for an address and stamp? Or will you enclose it in an envelope, in which case, you need to find out what size and style of envelopes you're going to use. Then, make sure that you design your brochure to fit them. If you plan to use your brochure for mailings, you may want to specify an upper weight limit for it — a factor you don't need to worry about if the brochure is only meant to be handed out.

Infinite materials at your fingertips

Brochures are unusual in the variety of options they present. You're working not just on one piece of paper but on as many as you want to include. And you have the option of folding the paper or using separate sheets, so you can think three-dimensionally about your brochure.

In addition, you have more options for materials than you do for ads or letters. Brochures can be on regular or coated paper, but you can also get creative and use unusual cover stocks or even foil paper, embossed covers, clear or opaque covers, inside sheets, and so on. In fact, if you don't mind assembling brochures by hand, you can even include unusual materials, such as cloth (how about a silk sheet between the cover and the first page?). Nothing's stopping you from using a leather or wood cover either, although I don't recommend using exotic materials unless they tie in to your image or relate to your product line. But brochures give your marketing imagination plenty of scope!

Sizes and shapes

I suggest looking first at simple, inexpensive, standard design options before going crazy. They give plenty of room for creativity but use standard paper sizes. And you can vary these paper sizes by folding them in different ways so you still have plenty of room for creativity. The standard precut paper sizes in many countries are

- ✔ Letter (8½ x 11 inches)
- ✔ Legal (8½ x 14 inches)
- ✔ Tabloid (11 x 17 inches)

Of these three standard sizes, the first two are the most common and the easiest to work with. I recommend working within the possibilities that these two standard sizes present unless you have a good reason not to.

The first option is to use standard 8½-x-11-inch paper, which you can work with horizontally or vertically, as Figure 11-2 shows. With a little imagination, you get five excellent brochure layouts out of this standard paper size: horizontal half fold, accordion fold and tri fold, and the vertical half fold and fold over.

Similarly, you can fold a standard legal-size sheet of paper measuring 8½ x 14 inches in many ways to create different brochure layouts. Figure 11-3 shows the same five options executed with legal-size paper. Because of the longer length, the various folds create completely different brochures from the ones made with letter-size paper. For example, compare the horizontal half-folds in the two figures. The smaller letter-size paper gives a vertically oriented page, whereas the longer legal-sized paper gives a chunkier, magazine-style page with the same horizontal fold.

So among these two standard (and therefore inexpensive) paper sizes and these five different folds, you have ten different brochure options. Each fold makes a unique page size and therefore supports different approaches to page layout and design. In designing your brochure, think like a painter who first decides which size canvas to work on. The choice of canvas size may be as important to the success of the painting as the design and execution of the painting itself.

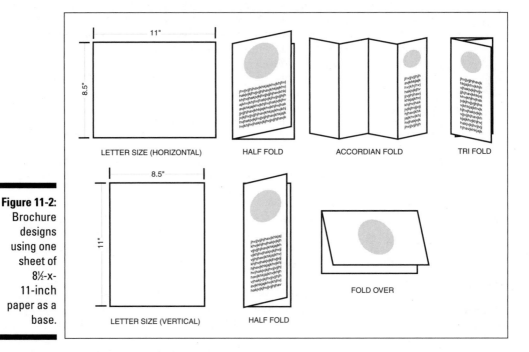

Figure 11-2: Brochure designs using one sheet of 8½-x-11-inch paper as a base.

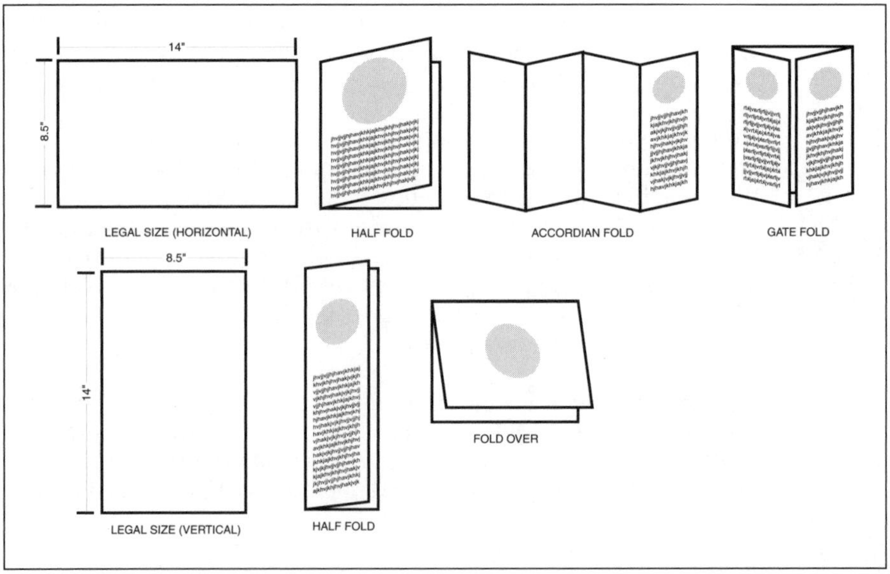

LETTER SIZE (HORIZONTAL)   HALF FOLD   ACCORDIAN FOLD   TRI FOLD

LETTER SIZE (VERTICAL)   HALF FOLD   FOLD OVER

Figure 11-3: Brochure designs using one sheet of 8½-x-14-inch paper as a base.

LEGAL SIZE (HORIZONTAL)   HALF FOLD   ACCORDIAN FOLD   GATE FOLD

LEGAL SIZE (VERTICAL)   HALF FOLD   FOLD OVER

Sometimes you want your brochure to have an unusual shape or size to help it grab attention or make a statement. In this case, the added expense of a nonstandard paper size makes sense. For example, a car dealership may print an oversized, heavy, glossy-coated stock brochure cut in the shape of a car. The cover may show the owner, key salespeople, and key service people as if they're riding inside the "car," viewed through the "windows" of it. Such a brochure costs more than an ordinary one, but this concept is a highly appealing and memorable one.

If you intend to mail your brochure, make sure that it fits within postal regulations and a standard envelope size, otherwise you have to find unusual envelope sizes (and possibly pay extra postage). I recommend starting with a search at the printer for unusual envelope sizes; that way, you don't get stuck with a great design that you can't match with an appropriate envelope.

Paper characteristics

Paper weight, or basis weight, is the weight in pounds of 500 sheets of 17-x-22½-inch paper. Cut-size paper usually comes in bulks of 500 sheets called a ream. Twenty-pound paper (written 20#) is a lighter paper than, say, 24# paper. When you're printing on both sides, use heavier paper because it's more opaque so you don't see the words or images on the reverse side of the page. You also want to choose heavier paper if your piece is going to be handled a lot because it's more durable.

Lighter-weight paper, such as stationery paper, is called *offset paper,* and heavier card stock, such as the paper used for business cards, is called *cover stock.* You can use either type for a brochure. Try folding and handling different types and weights of paper before you decide what to use. But remember that if you intend to do mass mailings of your brochure, the heavier papers cost more for postage. So weigh and price the postage on several options before you make your final decision.

You also want to consider the finish or texture of the paper you use. Paper with a texture or "grain" feels nice but may not be advisable if your brochure has a number of photos because the texture of the paper will break up the ink for the photo, making it look coarse or muddy. If you're reproducing a lot of photos, stick to paper with a solid surface to keep the them sharp and clear.

Layout tips

Printers basically use two programs for page layout: Adobe PageMaker and Quark XPress. Your printer has at least one of these programs. In some cases, these programs can read layouts that were constructed in other programs, but check with your printer beforehand to find out what the shop is capable of.

And increasingly, printers can work from Word files, which is helpful for hack designers (like you and me) who don't want to buy and master a new program. And newer versions of Word incorporate a basic Adobe Acrobat output capability that allows you to convert your Word file to Acrobat's format (Portable Document Format, or pdf) — which printers are also increasingly willing to use. The printing industry is more accommodating to Word users than it used to be, and you may be able to design a serviceable brochure or flier in the basic word processing program that your computer already has and then have a local printer produce them directly from a CD or e-mail attachment. This option is definitely progress for budget-conscious marketers!

When laying out the text and artwork for your brochure, keep in mind that printers need a *gripper margin* — the blank space that's needed on the edges of a document so that the printing press can grab the paper and pull it through the press (see Figure 11-4). Usually, the gripper margin is about ⅜ inch, but it varies, so check with your printer for specific needs. The gripper margin area needs to be totally free from text or images.

Figure 11-4:
Leave a gripper margin when you lay out brochures.

Next, think about how you want your text and artwork to lay out on the paper. You won't find any absolute rules for how many illustrations or pictures you can use in any one brochure, but you can follow these general guidelines:

✔ **Shoot for a balance between text and artwork or photos.** Too much text can be boring, and a well-placed photo or illustration can break it up nicely.

✔ **On the front panel of your brochure, place an image and/or an opening statement or paragraph to catch your reader's attention.** This front panel is very important. It needs to draw readers to the brochure and make them want to check out the information inside. You have to catch many people's attention with this panel, so consider how people will receive it. If it's in a display rack, will the rack hide most of the cover? Maybe you want to design it to compensate for the rack.

✔ **You may hear your printer refer to *serif* and *sans serif* typefaces.** Serif typefaces have little feet-like appendages on their ends, whereas sans serif typefaces don't have those feet. (This paragraph is in a serif typeface.)

✔ **You measure type in point size.** For example, ten-point type is a small point size:

The quick brown fox jumped over the lazy dog.

A large point size is 24 point:

The quick brown . . .

✔ **Make sure that the body type is readable; the size should be no less than 10 to 12 point.** Consider your audience. If the people reading this brochure are elderly, use a bigger type size, such as 14 to 18 point. If folks have a hard time seeing the type, they're not going to bother. Also avoid large areas of *reverse type* (where the type is white or a light color on a dark background) because it's much harder to read.

✔ **Try to stick with one or two families of fonts within a brochure.** Too many font styles can look sloppy and confusing. Each family has many styles (for example, **Bold,** *Italic,* narrow, and <u>Underline</u> in the Helvetica-type family) so you have plenty to work with. And don't forget that you can change the size to add variety. For example, you can use all the following variations in size in a single brochure — the largest for major headers and other sizes for minor headers, the body copy, and the fine-print details.

Helvetica 10 point

Helvetica 12 point

Helvetica 14 point

Helvetica 16 point

Helvetica 24 point

✔ **Mix up straight paragraphs with other ways of laying out text, such as checklists and tables.** The changes of pace you create keep the text appealing. Notice that I tend to work in checklists, bullets, and tables fairly often in this book.

Headline type

Headline type is made for just that: headlines. It's usually bigger, sometimes bolder, and sometimes more ornate than the regular text. Headline type isn't meant for the body of the article — it would be too hard to read. Its purpose is to grab the reader's attention and draw her into the article below. Headline type is usually used on brochure covers and paragraph headings.

Body type

Body type is used for the body of the text. Because it needs to be simple and easy to read, it's usually (but not exclusively) restricted to serif fonts, which are easier on the eyes, especially at smaller type sizes.

Type alignment

The way type lines up on the paper supports an image or conveys a feeling. Formal, conservative images require *justified type* (where both the left and right sides of the type align at the margin). A *ragged right margin* (text not lined up on the right; used in this book) gives a less formal look. You can also center titles, and sometimes you can justify the text on only the right side, like when it floats in open space with a photo or box to the right of it. Figure 11-5 shows you what each of these options looks like and how printers and designers refer to each option.

The quick brown fox jumped over the lazy dog. The quick brown fox jumped over the lazy dog.The quick brown fox jumped over the lazy dog. The quick brown fox jumped over the lazy dog.The quick brown fox jumped over the lazy dog. The quick brown fox jumped over the lazy dog.The quick brown fox jumped over the lazy dog. The quick brown fox jumped over the	The quick brown fox jumped over the lazy dog. The quick brown fox jumped over the lazy dog.The quick brown fox jumped over the lazy dog. The quick brown fox jumped over the lazy dog.The quick brown fox jumped over the lazy dog. The quick brown fox jumped over the lazy dog.The quick brown fox jumped over the lazy dog. The quick brown fox jumped over the	The quick brown fox jumped over the lazy dog. The quick brown fox jumped over the lazy dog.The quick brown fox jumped over the lazy dog. The quick brown fox jumped over the lazy dog.The quick brown fox jumped over the lazy dog. The quick brown fox jumped over the lazy dog.The quick brown fox jumped over the lazy dog. The quick brown fox jumped over the	The quick brown fox jumped over the lazy dog. The quick brown fox jumped over the lazy dog.The quick brown fox jumped over the lazy dog. The quick brown fox jumped over the lazy dog.The quick brown fox jumped over the lazy dog. The quick brown fox jumped over the lazy dog.The quick brown fox jumped over the lazy dog. The quick brown fox jumped over the
JUSTIFIED LEFT (Ragged Right)	**JUSTIFIED RIGHT (Ragged Left)**	**CENTERED**	**JUSTIFIED**

Figure 11-5: Your options for aligning type on the page.

Text wrapping

With *text wrapping,* the lines of text end right where they bump into artwork. Some layout and word processing programs allow you to wrap text around art, which gives you another nice design option. (In Word, go to the View menu. Select Toolbars, Drawing, [if your Drawing toolbar isn't already on screen] and then click on the first icon, an *A* with a cube. This produces a drop-down menu. Select Arrange from it to see the options on how to handle objects, such as clip art or photos. You can choose to have the art bump the text so that the text wraps around or beside the art, or you can make the art float independently. The same basic options exist in any design program.)

Copy or print?

One of the first things you have to decide when creating a brochure is how to produce it. Traditionally, this decision means whether you have it copied or printed, but today you can also consider making it yourself on an ordinary inkjet printer. Some of the factors that determine this include

- Whether or not you have large runs of 1,000 pieces or more; if you have 1,000 pieces or more, having them printed is better than copying them.

- Having small runs (under 1,000 pieces) printed isn't cost effective. The price per unit goes down as quantity goes up. Photocopy instead.

- Printed pieces tend to have better quality, especially when you have a lot of photos in your marketing piece. Photos usually don't reproduce well on a copier.

- Will people look at the brochure once and then throw it away? Or is it something a person will hold onto and possibly refer to from time to time? If it's something that people will use one time, copying may make sense. But copied pieces don't stand up well to continuous handling. In a copier, toner dust heats up and affixes to the paper's surface. This toner dust, after being heated, doesn't fall off easily but eventually may scratch or rub off. Printing, on the other hand, is far more durable because the ink sinks down into the paper, locking it in and making it impossible to remove.

- If you want small numbers (under 30) of a brochure at a time, why not just design it in Word and print it out on brochure paper on your inkjet printer? The print quality can be amazing on homemade brochures, and doing it yourself gives you the ability to adapt the design to your immediate needs.

Figure 11-6 illustrates the differences between copying (which puts toner on the paper) and printing (which works ink into the paper). Whether you print your brochures yourself or do a run on a printing house's large-scale printer, the principle is the same.

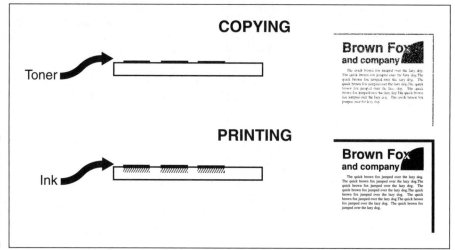

Color

Adding color to your brochure grabs the viewer's attention and makes it more appealing to the eye, but each added color requires an additional print run and thus, adds cost. But you can add color in different ways, such as by using

- ✔ **Pantone Matching System colors:** Printers use a universal ink color system called the Pantone Matching System. This system allows printers to match ink by referring to swatches that show the color along with the exact mixture of inks needed to obtain that color. So if you want to add color to your brochure, you need to ask a printer to let you see a set of PMS color samples so that you can select from it.

- ✔ **Four-color process:** In this process, printers achieve full color by separating the image into four basic colors: cyan, magenta, yellow, and black. Printers shoot film of the image in each of these colors and break the colors down into tiny dots. These dots, when arranged next to each other, create the full color effect, and you can see the arrangement of dots only with the aid of a magnifying glass, or *loupe*. The effect of the four-color process is excellent — it can reproduce fine art or photography quite accurately. But four-color printing is expensive because of the extra film-work involved, as well as the need for four runs through the press.

- ✔ **Alternatives to four-color process printing:** Some alternatives allow you to have a variety of colors but still keep costs down. When using

PMS colors, screen the color(s) at different percentages. For example, your brochure may have only two colors, such as black and blue. In a different area of the brochure where you use the color blue, use the blue screened back to 80 percent, 60 percent, and 20 percent. This technique gives the impression that you're using four different shades of blue when you're actually using blue at 100 percent, 80 percent, 60 percent, and 20 percent. This way the printer can do all the blues on one run through the press. And although the shades of blue plus the black give the feeling of five colors, the brochure needs only two runs — one for black and one for blue.

✔ **Raster Image Processing (RIP):** Another alternative for avoiding the high cost of the four-color process is to have your publication RIPped to a color copier. Some printers have their computers hooked up to color copiers and can RIP your file to the copier and get a similar product to four-color copying. This process is especially good when you need only a few brochures. You pay an initial RIPping cost and then for each page printed at the cost of a color copy.

✔ **Inkjet and color laser printing:** For very small runs, you can use any decent inkjet printer. For example, many of the HP inkjet printers can produce a good quality color brochure using HP brochure paper. You have to print and fold them yourself, so I wouldn't make more than ten or twenty at a time. But for small runs, the inkjet option is great.

Or you can print your marketing materials by using a laser printer. My firm is about to acquire a high-quality, high-volume color laser printer, which will allow us to produce hundreds of color sheets for brochures, fliers, and other printed products. Laser printers cost several thousand dollars, or, for one that can print tabloid (11-x-17-inch) sheets in good color at high speed, $5,000 to s$6,000. But if you think your company will use it enough to justify the cost, why not set up your own print shop in-house? It can save a lot of money in the long run.

My firm is getting one of these laser printers to produce short runs of dozens to hundreds of color catalogs, brochures, and booklets for mailings, trade-show handouts, and color covers for booklets. My company is spending the extra money on a laser printer capable of printing tabloid size materials because then it can create center-folded and stapled publications, such as catalogs that have 8½-x-11-inch pages — half the size of a tabloid sheet.

When laying out a brochure for any of these printing options, avoid large fields of solid color because they add to the cost of a printed piece, and some electronic printers have a hard time keeping the ink consistent throughout the field of color. In some cases, you can screen large solid colors to give them more consistency.

Artwork

Illustrating a brochure adds visual appeal and, if the illustrations are appropriate, makes it more persuasive. "Seeing is believing," as the saying goes! But just as with type design, you need some basic technical knowledge before you're ready to select artwork for your brochure. The catch is that how you want to produce the final output partially determines how you choose and prepare your graphics in the first place.

You have a number of overlapping categories to choose from (and of these, high-resolution postscript output and vector images give you the highest quality). Here are the definitions and technical details of these options:

- ✔ **High-resolution postscript output:** This technical term simply means any digitized artwork (or text) that has a resolution over 800 dots per inch (or dpi); the more dots per inch an art image has, the higher its clarity or resolution is. Computers store high-resolution art files as an encapsulated postscript (EPS) or Tagged Image File Format (TIFF) image.

  Postscript output is done on a Postscript Imagesetter. High-resolution postscript output gives you good results with offset printing (the most common high-quality option for printing 500 or more copies of anything on paper), so whenever you want to print a piece, I recommend Postscript. If you use a graphic designer or artist to help you with your brochure, make sure to ask whether he can provide the printer with high-resolution files in EPS or TIFF format. (*Hint:* The correct answer is "yes." Consider another designer if you don't hear this answer!)

- ✔ **Low-resolution postscript output:** Any digitized artwork that has a resolution in the 300 to 700 dpi range is called a low-resolution postscript output. You use this resolution for "low-end" art pieces that you will copy and for Web site images. The original output comes from a laser printer. If you have a modern computer system in your office, you can probably generate this kind of output easily from your system. But remember this image isn't suitable for printed brochures or catalogs — only for photocopies or Web pages.

- ✔ **Bitmapped images (or "raster images"):** When you bitmap an image, you digitize and store the image, using small squares (pixels) arranged on a grid to represent the image. Bitmapped images are fine, as long as the image stays at the same size or smaller. If you blow it up, though, the small squares grow larger, making them noticeable and giving the image a poor appearance. Figure 11-7 shows a bitmapped picture of a clock, which reproduces well, and then shows what happens when you blow up a section of that clock image. The enlargement looks terrible!

✔ **Vector images:** You can use vector images to get around the problems of blowing up bitmapped images by using mathematical equations to represent the lines and curves in artwork. They stay clean and clear at any level of enlargement because the computer program literally redraws them to the new scale. Most logos are vector images because they're reproduced in many different sizes for different uses. Figure 11-8 shows how a vector image enlarges.

Section of bitmapped image enlarged 400% to show pixels

Figure 11-7:
Don't
enlarge
bitmapped
images.

The examples of bitmapped and vector art, as shown in Figures 11-7 and 11-8 are both examples of line art. *Line art* consists of any black-and-white image with no gray areas or screens. These images can be anything from line drawings to black-and-white logos.

You can also print forms of art other than line art — in other words, art that has grays or shades of color in it. But, wouldn't you know it? Doing so adds more technical issues.

Avoid using anything drawn in pencil, such as drawings or sketches, because these images are very hard to reproduce. If you have to use a pencil drawing, the printer may suggest making a halftone print of the image to save the gray areas from burning out. Follow this advice and don't grumble about the minor added expense. (A halftone print is a high-quality option using screens; your printer will know all about it.)

Figure 11-8:
Vector
images
enlarge
without
losing detail.

Photography

Printers usually like to work from black-and-white photos that you supply (assuming that you want one- or two-color output). Color photos, especially *low-contrast photos* (photos that don't have a lot of difference between dark and light areas), tend to muddy up when you reproduce them in black ink. But sometimes you have to use color photos because that's all you have or because you need to produce a four-color brochure. So make sure that the photos are high-contrast (that is, they have a lot of difference between the dark and light areas). High-contrast photos have more definition and reproduce better.

If you (or a photographer) are planning to take pictures of your products, facilities, or people, make sure you use a high-contrast film (one designed to produce sharp, clear images). In general, slower films (ones with lower American Standards Association, or ASA, numbers) give higher contrast and sharper images. (I often use 200 ASA film in a Nikon camera so I know that I'm shooting through a high-quality lens with good optics and a fairly high-resolution film. If you prefer digital photography, remember that it's still all about light, so light your subject well and use a camera with very high resolution and good optics, such as a Nikon digital camera.)

I admit that I'm old fashioned about photography. I believe that nothing is quite like the rich colors and high resolution you get with a low-speed color film in a high-quality traditional camera. If you're going to photograph in color for your brochure (or catalog, ad, or Web page), I recommend using a slow-speed color film. Kodak and Fuji make good 100 and 200 ASA color films.

Your printer has to break photographs down into a series of dots (halftones) for the shaded areas to be reproduced. Without gray areas, photos would be black and white and become posterized, as Figure 11-9 demonstrates. Ask your printer how to avoid this problem.

Figure 11-9:
The same photograph handled in two different ways for printing.

The halftone version of the balloon photograph in Figure 11-10 is actually a screened image in which the screen breaks up the tones into more or fewer black dots. The eye blends these tones back into a "whole" image, but you can see that the smooth blending of tones is an optical illusion when you blow up a portion of that image, as in Figure 11-10.

Figure 11-10:
When you magnify the halftone photo image of the balloon four times, you can see how the halftone handles the different shades.

Clip art and stock photography

You can use copyright-free images, such as clip art and photos, when budget constraints eliminate the possibility of hiring professional illustrators or photographers. These images are copyright free, so you don't have to pay royalties or get special permissions to reproduce them. They're usually available on disk or CD, and you typically pay a usage fee — but that fee is low compared to the cost of hiring an artist or photographer to create custom artwork.

Many companies sell copyright-free images — try searching the Internet or asking printers or designers for leads. Printers usually have a source for these images, but they may mark up the price. You can also purchase copyright-free images at software supply stores, as well as download them from the Internet. The company Hemera sells sets of CDs with tens of thousands of images on them that you can use for free after you purchase the set of CDs for a modest price. I used quite a few of these images in my firm's brochures, fliers, and PowerPoint presentations, and some of them even found their way onto my company's Web sites as well. I recommend Hemera's products if you're having trouble finding low-cost sources of photographs or illustrations for your marketing materials.

Crop and fold marks

Crop and fold marks tell printers where they need to cut or fold a marketing piece. You need to mark these instructions on your original piece with a *hairline* — the smallest weight printed line possible — to ensure accuracy. In the following list, I briefly review the standard terms and symbols that you need to know to communicate with your printer or binder:

- ✔ **Crop marks:** *Crop marks* are guides that show the printer where to cut a page. If you need to print your brochure on larger paper and then cut it down (like when the ink bleeds all the way to the edge of your page or when you specify a nonstandard size), the printer uses the crop marks to cut in exactly the right place.

- ✔ **Fold marks:** *Fold marks* tell the printer where to fold the paper. But make sure that he understands which *way* to fold the page!

- ✔ **Score marks:** *Score marks* indicate where the printer should *score,* or lightly cut, the paper. When using heavy paper, you sometimes need to score before you fold in order to get a clean, crisp fold. In that case, you need to mark the fold line as a score line, too.

- ✔ **Perforating marks:** You use *perforating marks* when a brochure includes a coupon or postcard that you want people to tear out. Perforating marks show the printer where to make the *perforations* — a series of short cuts in the paper.

Figure 11-11 shows you how to indicate these various marks on the originals you give to the printer.

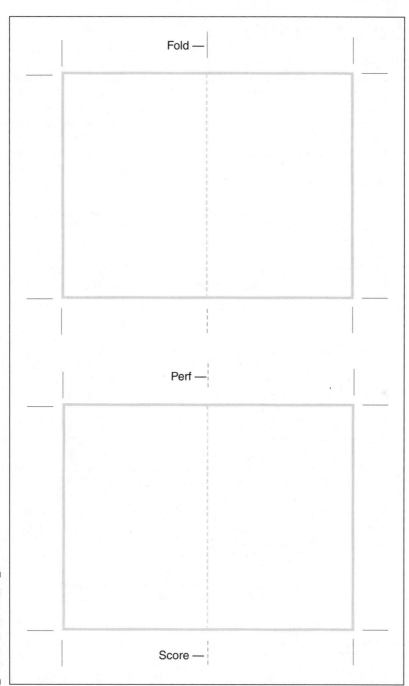

Figure 11-11:
Paper-
handling
instructions
to the
printer.

Digital Brochures

In my firm, we're beginning to include a CD along with the printed materials in some of our mailings and client proposals. I expect to see more and more firms including CDs with their marketing materials in the future because they give you the ability to show more and various kinds of information. A CD can contain lengthy documents in pdf or Word formats, as well as extensive photographs and even streaming video. Or, if you have high-quality video about a product or service, you can use a DVD to distribute a video brochure. It's basically an infomercial on a disc — instead of in the harder-to-handle traditional VHS video format.

When is using the more extensive capabilities of a CD or DVD rather than, or in addition to, a traditional brochure more worthwhile? I recommend using a CD or DVD in either of these situations:

- ✔ If your "story" is complex and detailed, and prospective customers need and want to do extensive background research before buying
- ✔ If you want to make a good impression by using a new medium in a creative way

I use CDs for the first reason, because when I sell a complex service — like management training — I know that people want to see a lot of information, including examples of our instructors in action. And that kind of info is best done using new media rather than a traditional brochure.

If you have trouble visualizing how to set up a CD brochure, think about the design as a Web page. Why? Because you (or any competent Web design firm) can create Web-page style designs, just like any you see on the Web; the only difference is that you launch them off the CD. See how using this media opens up your design options?

If you want to make the CD highly interactive, you can even dedicate an area on your main Web site to support the CD and include links to it. If the CD user has his computer online all the time (more and more people do), he'll hardly notice that the CD brochure morphs into an interactive session on your Web site. And you can keep the Web site up-to-date with new information or promotional offers in a way that no brochure can be updated.

Captivating Catalogs

You can think of a catalog as an elaborate brochure. If you think of it as an elaborate brochure, you'll happily discover that you already know a great deal about how to design and print catalogs, because everything I cover earlier in this chapter about brochures applies. In fact, many simple catalogs are indistinguishable from brochures in their basic design, use of paper, and layout. The only difference is that a catalog focuses on describing a product or service line, which is what makes them catalogs instead of brochures.

But more elaborate catalogs are usually made up of multiple pages stapled together. The most common catalog format uses sheets of tabloid (11-x-17-inch) paper, folded in half. When folded, each tabloid sheet gives you four 8½-x-11-inch pages to work with. When you use just one tabloid sheet, you have a front and a back page (these pages share one side of the sheet before you fold it) and two inside pages (which share the other side of the sheet).

Now imagine adding another tabloid sheet to this catalog design. This sheet nests inside the first sheet when folded, and these sheets are stapled together on the fold. With this two-sheet design, you have eight standard 8½-x-11-inch pages to play with — two for the front and back covers and six more on the inside of your catalog.

Add another sheet and your page count goes up by four to 12 pages. Add another sheet, and your catalog has 16 pages you can work with. Bet you aren't surprised to find that most catalogs have page counts that are multiples of four!

Design considerations

I go into considerable detail about the design of brochures because I believe many marketers can and should roll up their sleeves and get involved in designing their own brochures. By getting involved, you don't feel intimidated by the project and can feel free to create and replace brochures whenever you have a need to. The same is true for simple catalogs prepared in the same style as brochures. You can design one-sheet catalogs with one or more folds and have them printed at the local print shop or photocopied quite easily. But if you want to get into more elaborate, multipage catalogs, you need to work with specialists. Your local printer probably can refer you to larger printers who specialize in catalogs, or you can check for these printers on the Internet or ask businesses that already produce good catalogs who they use.

You can also consider hiring a designer who specializes in catalogs. There's more to creating a catalog than the mechanics of design and layout, although those alone can become quite complex when you have many pages. The biggest challenge, however, is to sell product effectively in the pages of a catalog. How you present each purchase option (in copy and art), what you choose to feature on the covers or inside covers (where you get the most impact), whether you include an index, what sort of look and feel you go for — all of these decisions are really quite sophisticated and difficult, so I recommend spending the extra money for an expert's input. Printing a multipage, four-color catalog costs a great deal and mailing it is expensive, too. You may as well invest enough in the design to give yourself good odds of getting a profitable return on that investment!

Benchmark catalogs for your reference

You can easily find good examples of multipage, full-color catalogs by examining your mail. Clothing retailers like J. Crew and Lands End usually have well-done catalogs that can serve as your benchmarks. Also look at glossy, sophisticated magazines on the newsstands for interesting approaches to graphic design that you may want to earmark for a catalog. Just like with brochures, I recommend keeping a folder of catalogs that appeal to you so you can review their various designs the next time you need ideas.

Notice especially how good catalogs

- ✔ Use their front covers to feature special products or offers or to create appealing moods

- ✔ Organize their contents in intuitive ways so that readers can quickly find sections of interest

- ✔ Vary the page layouts so that each page doesn't look like the last and avoids monotony

- ✔ Give readers plenty of ways to reach the company with questions or orders, including telephone and fax numbers (and perhaps a Web site) on each page as well as a clear, flexible order form

- ✔ Contain clear, accurate, sufficient information about products to support purchase decisions (they answer all the customer's questions well)

- ✔ Are positive in their emotional appeals, using smiling people, enthusiastic language, bright, warm colors, or all three to create an "up" mood in readers

Notice how good catalogs often break up space into smaller blocks by using a column or grid pattern to display multiple products on most of the pages. If you can tighten up the space used for each product without damaging the selling power of your coverage, you can generate more revenues per page. And because design, printing, and mailing costs vary with the number of pages, you discover that hardworking pages make for a more successful catalog.

Also notice that many of the most visually appealing and readable catalogs aren't too cluttered. They have that magic ingredient of great designs — white space. *White space* is the open space that you can see on the page where neither text nor images are. Amateur designers (that's most marketers, by the way) tend to cram too much onto a page, which makes focusing on any one item difficult. Open up your design with a little more white space than people usually use, and your catalog becomes more readable and attractive.

Less is more

Here's an example of the power of white space. A company that sells office supplies wanted to liquidate a lot of inventory by publishing a special sale catalog. At first, the company's catalog had a cover design featuring a photo of a warehouse stacked so high and thick with all sorts of products that it looked like a maze. Across the photo, in big type, ran the title "Everything Must Go!" The design was overpowering, and it hurt the eye to look at this cover, so the company reconsidered.

Finally, the company published a catalog with a cover that was mostly white. This design showed an almost entirely empty, clean, white warehouse interior, cavernous in its emptiness except for one lone box far off in the corner with a man in a dark business suit standing there looking down at it. Across the top of this design ran the headline, "Everything Will Go." This new design was visually appealing and enticed curious shoppers into the interior of the catalog to find out more.

The list factor

So who do you send your catalog or brochure to? This critical question can even override the design question. Even a poorly designed catalog sent to the right people at the right time can still generate a lot of business! So good mailing lists are integral to any catalog program.

A regional business-to-business marketer may be content to send a catalog to only a few thousand names. A national business-to-business catalog usually needs to go to at least 10,000 names, and sometimes four or five times that many. Consumer-oriented catalogs on specialty topics (like model railroading) may go to small numbers of names, but consumer catalogs usually need to go to hundreds of thousands of people to really be successful.

Set your circulation target based on the following factors:

- ✔ **How big the potential market is:** Try to reach at least half your potential market through your mailing.

- ✔ **How much inventory or capacity you have:** Try not to send out so many catalogs that you risk being unable to fill your orders, otherwise customers will become upset and won't respond next time you mail to them.

- ✔ **How big your in-house list of past purchasers is:** If you have a decent size in-house list, your ability to buy similar names from list brokers and to predict their customers' purchase rate is going to be reasonably good. So you can, and should, try to supplement your in-house list. But don't let new names that you purchase dominate your mailing; getting a good response from them is just too hard. So build your list gradually until you have a substantial (for your market) in-house list rather than trying to supplement 1,000 past purchasers with 100,000 names from purchased lists.

✔ **How big your budget is:** In the real world, it doesn't matter that millions of people buy gardening supplies if you only have $3,000 to spend on launching a new catalog of specialty garden tools. Spend cautiously so that you can afford to recover and try another mailing, even if the first one is an abject failure. The path to success is paved with failures, so make sure you can afford to survive a few low-response-rate mailings. Sometimes you may get lucky and discover a mailing design and strategy that really pays off for you — but only if you can afford to stay in the game long enough for luck to strike!

Spectacular Spec Sheets

"Just the facts, ma'am." Too often marketers forget to communicate enough information or to communicate it clearly enough so people can make informed purchase decisions. Marketing communications are often maddeningly vague to serious buyers, who want to know exactly what you do, how your equipment performs, what the specifications are, what the terms are, and so on. What, exactly, *are* the facts?

Enter the specification, or "spec", sheet. A *spec sheet* is a simple, clear, one-page technical description of a product (or, rarely, a service). It contains all facts — or mostly facts; it may also have a testimonial or two and a nice photo or illustration. It often uses a tabular layout to provide consumers with detailed information that they need to make a purchase decision. Spec sheets serve this purpose well, providing the hard-core, informational backup to support more imaginative or persuasive marketing materials. I believe that everyone ought to prepare spec sheets for each product or service they sell. Not all prospects will want one, but those who do will really appreciate it.

Include a spec sheet in the sales collateral for a product if technical specifications are important to buyers or prospective buyers of that product. Include a spec sheet in the collateral materials for a video monitor, fire extinguisher, food processor, outboard motor, golf club, toaster, or remote-control toy car, for example, because buyers of these products may well want or need to know something about the product's specifications.

Formatting your spec sheet

Spec sheets usually are 8½-x-11-inch pieces of paper with printing on only one side. Include your company's name, logo, and contact information on the top or bottom of the sheet. Title it "Specifications for <product name/code>" at the top (or just beneath your company identification). Date it because specifications often change, and you may issue updated sheets in the future.

Use your company letterhead for a simple, quick spec sheet. You can use Word's table option and your office printer to create a simple but professional spec sheet on your letterhead.

Set the spec sheet up in two columns, with the left column listing a category of specifications (size, weight, voltage, pH, and so on) and the right column giving a specific measurement for each category. Use numbered footnotes to define any ambiguous or obscure terms or units. Avoid lengthy descriptions, and don't try to "sell" the product. Spec sheets give specifications; they don't promote. Hopefully the product or service is good and the specifications will do the selling for you!

Here's a simple template for spec sheets:

Specifications for <product>

Date/date/date

Category	Data
Category	Data
Category	Data
Category	Data
Category	Data
Category	Data

Company Name
Address
Phone/Fax
E-mail/Web page

Ensuring that your spec sheet is up to snuff

Spec sheets should be *clear, readable* (don't use type smaller than 11 point, please!), *accurate,* and *sufficient.* Make sure to verify all the data you include on the spec sheet, and include everything needed to describe the product.

To ensure that your specifications are sufficient, have a look at spec sheets of competing products, if possible. Also *ask customers or prospects what information they need.* If you're using units that aren't universal, provide conversions (that is, give the dimensions of a product in inches and centimeters). And verify all specifications with product designers and producers. Ask them if they're *sure* of the specifications. You don't want to be wrong. (If you're in one of those industries where regulations or legal liability are issues, also consider having a qualified lawyer review your spec sheet before printing it.)

If you hire a graphic designer or advertising agency to typeset your spec sheet, leave time so you can thoroughly check its accuracy after the design is finalized but before it's printed. Designers often introduce errors into spec sheets. They may also attempt to "jazz up" the design of your spec sheet. Discourage this urge. Keep spec sheets clean and simple and save the creativity for other marketing materials.

Booklets and Books

Consultants have long used the power of a book to promote their firm and its services. One of the reasons I write books is because they stimulate hundreds of thousands of dollars worth of business opportunities for my consulting and training business. A book can be a powerful demonstration of your expertise, allowing prospective customers to get to know you well enough to decide whether they want to work with you. Of course, the risk is that they decide you don't know what you're talking about, so be sure to approach books with caution. If you aren't a writer yourself, you can find ghostwriters and publicity firms that specialize in writing, designing, printing, and distributing books for business clients. (My firm provides this service for clients, as a matter of fact, but to be evenhanded, I want to refer you to another provider of the service: See www.celiarocks.com for background information from a leading specialist.)

If you aren't a consultant, do you still need a book? Well, anyone whose expertise is important to her customers, including doctors, lawyers, architects, accountants, heating and air conditioning contractors, and so on, may benefit from having a book or booklet of her own. For example, one heating and air conditioning contractor published a short but nicely done booklet titled *How to Increase the Comfort of Your Building* to promote his services. The booklet addressed upgrades and improvements to both residential and commercial structures, with short chapters explaining how and why to install different types of systems. The booklet had nice pictures and diagrams (provided by the suppliers whose equipment this company installed), plus mini-cases of successful projects. The three top people in the company wrote this booklet, and their photos and bios appeared on the back cover. Whenever company employees interacted with new or potential customers, they included this booklet as a handout, and it made a strong, positive impression that helped land the company many good jobs.

How expensive is it to make a book or booklet and use it for marketing? If you keep it short and sweet (64 pages or under, center stapled, makes a good booklet) and provide much of the content yourself, you won't need to pay a lot for ghostwriting. Writing your own material can save you quite a bit of money because the better ghostwriters charge anywhere from a few thousand dollars to a hundred thousand, depending on the project! When the time comes to produce the book or booklet, you can do it in-house using Word — if you're very brave — but working with a photocopy shop that has a Xerox Docutech machine and a perfectbinding machine is your best option. Have the copy shop create a short run of perfectbound photocopied books or booklets from your file.

The last time I made a book for marketing purposes I sent an unformatted Word file by e-mail to a good copy shop in my area and asked to have it laid out in PageMaker and printed using their Docutech. It cost a few hundred dollars for the design work and about $12 per book in copying and binding fees (it was fairly expensive because it had about 150 pages in it). I only needed 50 copies, so this price was fine. But I sent a previous book to an offset printer and binder because I needed 5,000 copies of a 200-page book. (A printer and binder is simply a printing company that specializes in making books.) At high volume, the book cost me less than a dollar per copy, including shipping. A lot of options and price levels are available for printing books, so you can probably find an approach that fits your needs.

Chapter 12

Planning Coupons and Other Sales Promotions

Many marketing experts use the term *sales promotion* to describe the use of coupons, discounts, premium items (special gifts), and other incentives to boost sales. Coupons are probably the best known and most widely used sales promotions, but you can use plenty of other ways to give prospects an incentive to make the purchase. In this chapter, I look at a variety of options, explore some of the best ways (and worst ways) to use them, and end with an analytical approach that helps you figure out whether a specific incentive will prove profitable or not.

The Importance of Profit

Making a sale is easy, if you don't care about profits. Cut the price enough, and almost anything will sell. Witness the junk people buy at yard sales, flea markets, or dollar stores. But you're in business, so you don't want sales if they don't make you money. And sales promotions don't always make money.

In fact, some of the more common examples of sales promotions are hard to accept from a profit perspective. Take the periodic sale and clearance catalogs that London-based Victoria's Secret, a cataloger and retailer specializing in women's lingerie and clothing, distributes. The company usually prints a 7 ½-x-10-inch, full-color catalog with a cover featuring some of the new items. But occasionally, the company sends out a clearance version using some of the items and photos from earlier catalogs, bound in a special sales-promotion-oriented version with a cover advertising all the special prices inside. Here's an example of the offers featured (in bold white print on a dark pink background) on one of its sale covers, a cover that actually had no photos or drawing of products, but simply contained text describing the special deals inside:

"Sale: bras & panties 25% to 50% off!"

"Clearance: discontinued bras $9.99 to $12.99!"

At the bottom of this cover in smaller print, the company added more promotional offers:

"Save up to an additional $75 on a qualifying sale purchase — and defer payment until September when you charge your order of $75 or more to the Victoria's Secret Credit Card. See page 2."

Because the catalog shipped during the spring, deferring payment until September is a fairly appealing incentive. And, obviously, the idea of a quarter to a half off normal prices is an incentive to open up the catalog and do some serious shopping. Women who make occasional purchases from regular-priced catalogs tend to respond more to these sale catalogs and with larger orders.

But is this good marketing or not? The answer depends on what the mailing costs Victoria's Secret and what other objectives the company wants to accomplish. And, most of all, that answer depends on how people react to the special offers.

 ✔ **If Victoria's Secret customers get in the habit of waiting for the special sale catalog before ordering, the marketing won't be profitable.** This marketing simply makes full-price customers migrate to discount-price customers, training them to wait for a special offer. This migration often happens when companies experiment with price-based sales promotions. In fact, recently Victoria's Secret has done fewer sales catalogs in order to reduce this effect.

 ✔ **If Victoria's Secret customers are reminded of how much they like the company's product line by this sale catalog, and not only buy from the catalog but also look more closely at the next few mailings, too, then this marketing is a huge success.** This situation can happen, too, and it does to some extent with these sales catalogs. Many customers use the sales to stock up on some basics but still look forward to seeing new clothes in the next regular catalog. And if each season's new clothes are unique and appealing, many customers will want to purchase them in season and at full price rather than gambling that they'll end up in a sale catalog months later.

In reality, both reactions occur in any sales promotion. You do get customers who simply shop for deals and won't give you more business later on at full price. But you also may remind some customers that they like your products and recruit other customers for the first time, building a habit of shopping with you that carries over to future nonsale purchases. And that result is a great fallout from a sales promotion — one that makes even a break-even promotion worthwhile in terms of future sales and profits.

How Promotions Affect Sales

How does a coupon, discount, or other form of sales promotion work? A sales promotion can basically have one or more of the following four effects on the market:

- ✔ **It takes your competitor's customers.** The promotion encourages the consumer to purchase a new brand or do business with a new vendor.

- ✔ **It attracts brand-new customers.** The promotion may draw in new users who've never bought products like yours before.

- ✔ **It stimulates repeat purchases.** The consumer is more likely to keep buying the product or doing business with the vendor because of the promotion.

- ✔ **It stimulates bigger purchases.** The consumer buys sooner and/or in larger quantities as result of the promotion. (Be careful, though; sometimes a corresponding decline in purchases occurs later on!)

Notice that the net result of all these effects is (hopefully) to generate more sales. That's the bottom line of any coupon or other sales promotion, and it's the reason marketers call these things "sales promotions." Multiple paths can lead to those increased sales, and sometimes the increases are long-term rather than short-term. If you don't see a clear link from your coupon or discount program to increased sales, then forget it. You're wasting your time and your business's money.

Planning Coupon Programs

Boy, have I got a deal for you!

These classic words (or offers to the same effect) are the bread and butter of many marketing initiatives. Offering a discount gives people a reason to buy. It attracts their attention. It converts vague intentions into immediate actions. However, it also costs you money, and that's not so good.

How much will a discount cost your company? Will the increased sales more than offset the cost? Don't know. Better find out. But the result your company gets all depends on what happens. You need to do some careful thinking and forecasting before you offer any discounts or distribute any coupons.

If you print and distribute coupons, any number of things may happen:

- The prospects may ignore them.
- Some prospects may redeem the coupons and become loyal, profitable customers.
- Everyone may ignore the coupons except those people who constantly shop for deals — and these people won't become regular customers unless you *always* offer them a deal.
- Some stores may misredeem the coupons, in which case you end up paying the coupons' face value but not winning new sales.
- Existing customers may use the coupons to buy just as much as they would have without the coupons, in which case, you've just given away a useless discount.
- New sales may flood in, making you very happy — until you realize that the costs of the coupon program are high enough that you've lost money in the process of winning that new business.

In other words, you can't really be sure what will happen, and a number of bad results may occur. Good things may result, too, but those aren't a certainty.

Enter *coupon profitability analysis.* If you do a careful analysis of several possible scenarios upfront and crunch the numbers on each scenario, you have a much better idea of the likely outcomes. Often, when people do a formal analysis, they're horrified at the results. They find that their initial ideas and assumptions have fatal flaws and they realize that they were about to throw away some or all of their profit margins in exchange for very little new business. So I highly recommend doing a careful profitability analysis.

Also, if you did some coupon programs in the past, running the numbers on them is a great idea to see how they worked out. Were they really profitable or not? The answer isn't obvious unless you do a proper analysis. And when you do, you can discover a great deal from these past efforts that can help you design more effective and profitable coupons in the future. Remember that creative experimentation — and learning from your experiments — is at the heart of all great marketing!

The basics of coupon profitability analysis

So how do you perform a coupon profitability analysis? Basically, follow these steps:

1. **Identify all the fixed and variable costs of the coupon program.**

   Fixed costs are costs, such as design expenses, that don't change with quantity of coupons. *Variable costs* are costs that increase with the number of coupons printed and distributed.

2. **Figure out how much product you think you can sell directly to consumers because of the coupon redemption.**

3. **Figure out how much money you make by selling that product.**

4. **Subtract all those expenses from the profits you've earned to see whether the coupon program is profitable or not.**

Now, if you're quick with numbers and accounting, go ahead and make your own analysis. But if you want to cut some serious corners, all you need to do is open the CD1201 file on your CD. I designed the spreadsheet and built in the formulas, so all you have to do is think about your coupon program and enter appropriate numbers into the blank boxes. Then read the bottom-line results. If the program is profitable, you get a nice black-colored number (in U.S. dollars; you can modify the dollar symbol, if necessary, to convert to other currencies). If the program you define is unprofitable, you get a nasty red-colored number in brackets, in which case, try another approach and enter some different figures. Keep fiddling until you get a bottom-line profit based on your projections.

Now, I know I didn't give you a very detailed description of how to use the coupon profitability analysis on the CD, so I recommend following the step-by-step instructions I provide in the next section.

Walking through the process step by step

Please use the CD1201 file from your Marketing Kit CD. This form runs in Excel. To use it, simply fill in the boxed cells with numbers representing your plans for a coupon program. The spreadsheet calculates everything else to figure out your costs and profits.

The general categories of costs are

✔ **Fixed costs:** Fixed costs are the costs of designing your coupon, printer's setup costs, and so on. Be sure to include all fixed costs that are necessary to create the coupon and program.

✔ **Variable costs:** These costs vary with the number of coupons. Note that many such costs are conventionally measured on a cost per 1,000 coupons rather than on a cost per individual coupon. When you get quotes from printers and the companies that handle coupon redemptions, those quotes will probably be in costs per 1,000 coupons.

Filling in the blanks

The following paragraphs go through the coupon profitability analysis line by line, and I show you how to enter appropriate variables so you can see how a coupon program might work. You have to fill in 13 cells in order to complete an analysis of a future scenario or past program. I guide you through each one.

Number of coupons: _____

How many coupons do you plan to distribute? If you're planning on giving them out through a store or other public site, you may not be able to guess accurately how many coupons people will pick up. So just take your best guess, print a specific number, and then test several levels of distribution: Say *(a)* the entire print run, *(b)* ⅔ of it, and *(c)* ⅓ of it. If the program seems like it may be profitable at all these levels, then it's probably a good idea to try. Often, however, companies distribute an offer to a mailing list of a known number or to the subscribers of a publication. In these cases, you can use basic circulation or list data to determine how many coupons you'll be distributing.

Face value of coupons: $_____

What are you planning to offer the users of the coupon? Typically a coupon gives a discount on the purchase of a single product, so that's how I set up this spreadsheet. Enter a dollar value representing the amount the coupon is good for. For instance, if you plan to offer a $20 discount off the next purchase of a carton of your special industrial cleaning fluid, then enter $20 in this cell.

Ah, but how much of a discount do you need to offer to get a good response? I was afraid you'd ask that! A good but vague rule is to offer just enough to get someone's attention. If you offer too much, well, you're just giving the product away. If you offer too little, nobody pays attention. So what discount should you offer? Regular coupon marketers run lots of experiments until they find some formulas that work. If you don't have any idea of what to offer, you need to run some experiments yourself. Start with a nice, safe number. "Safe" means from a bottom-line perspective, which means a number that's considerably less than your profit.

For example, say you make a cool new cat toy that you sell at wholesale to pet stores for $1.75, which they mark up to a retail price of $2.49. When you examine your costs, you find that it costs you approximately $1.20 to make and deliver each unit, so your profit is $0.55 on each cat toy you sell. Now, offering a $0.55 discount would be a costly experiment, wouldn't it? But a $0.25 discount you can readily afford. On the other hand, is that discount enough to get anyone's attention? Maybe not. The redemption rate may be pretty low. So perhaps a $0.35 coupon is better. This discount still leaves a little profit to cover (hopefully) the costs of the coupon program, but offers enough off that it may get a reasonable response rate from cat owners. You may want to start there and see what happens.

Design and consultation fees: $_____

If you hire a graphic designer, marketing consultant, or ad agency to design your coupon, you're going to have to pay her. Enter the cost here.

Setup costs for producing coupons: $_____

If you're having a printer produce your coupons, you'll have some setup costs. Enter those costs here. If you're buying ad space in a newspaper or other publication for your coupons, then you probably don't have to pay setup costs, so just enter a zero.

Other fixed costs: $_____

If you expect to incur any other upfront or other fixed costs, be sure to add them in here. Forgotten costs come back to bite!

Production costs per 1,000 coupons: $_____

If you're having a printer produce the coupons, your printer can give you this number (along with the setup costs, above). Ask him what the costs are at several different volume levels because there may be a sliding scale based on quantity. If you're inserting your coupons into a publication, just enter zero in this blank. Then the next line item is the one for you!

Distribution costs per 1,000 coupons: $_____

What will the newspaper, trade magazine, or coupon booklet publisher charge you for inserting your coupon in its publication? What will stores charge you for placing your coupons at the point of purchase? What will some hot Web site charge you to put your discount offer in a banner ad? If you're using someone else's service to distribute your coupon offer to prospective customers, enter that service's cost per 1,000 coupons here.

Legitimate redemption rate (Percent of coupons properly redeemed): ____%

What percentage of those coupons will people actually use toward the purchase of your product? It could be 100 percent, but I doubt it. Usually a small percentage of coupons are actually redeemed. For under-a-dollar discounts on consumer nondurables, often just a few percent of coupons are redeemed. For larger discounts and/or higher-cost items, the rates may be higher, even over 10 percent. But again, there's no substitute for experience, so if you've done similar coupon programs in the past, use them as your basis for estimating. If not, well, recognize that you're running an experiment and don't do anything on such a large scale that you'll regret the results later!

Misredemption rate (Percent of coupons redeemed wrongly/for the wrong products): ___%

Programs rarely work exactly as you hope. Sometimes the store clerks or order fulfillment staff apply the coupon to the wrong product. Sometimes somebody finds some way to scam you. If there are ways for things to go wrong, they will. So build a little error into your projections and make sure it won't kill you.

The problem with misredemptions, obviously, is that you end up paying the face value of coupons but not getting a product sale in return. So the misredemptions come directly off the bottom line. Fortunately, misredemption rates are generally quite low.

Processing costs per coupon redeemed: $_____

If you're using a totally computerized system in which the coupon is scanned or the discount is applied to a customer code number, then you don't really have any appreciable processing costs. Your system (or some stores' systems) just processes the things automatically. But most coupons actually end up being handled by someone somewhere, and that handling costs you money, whether you use a redemption service or hire someone to do it. When you subcontract coupon processing, the costs are generally in the 5-to-15¢ per coupon range. If you plan to have someone do it by hand, estimate how many he can do per hour and work out what it costs per coupon. Enter your estimated processing cost per coupon in this blank.

Other variable costs per coupon: $_____

If other incremental costs exist that I didn't think to include, put them here. If not, just enter "0" on this line.

Percentage of these sales that would have occurred anyway: ___%

The spreadsheet calculates the number of sales from coupon redemptions. It does this based on the number of coupons and the legitimate redemption rate you entered. If, for example, you plan to distribute 100 coupons and you anticipate a 5 percent redemption rate, the spreadsheet calculates that you will sell five units as a result of the coupon program. Now, many people just chalk up all five of those units as resulting from the coupons. In other words, they give the coupon full credit for all those sales in which customers redeemed a coupon. But is that fair? Maybe not. What if some regular customers would have bought anyway, but at full price rather than at the discount rate? Then your coupon isn't really bringing you their business.

So in this blank, you can account for those regular users who would have purchased anyway. You do so by estimating what percentage of all redemptions they will make up. Make it a high percentage if you think that the distribution method that you're using will reach lots of regular, loyal customers. Make it a low percentage if you think that the distribution method will reach mostly new prospects — such as users of your competitor's products. Make it a zero if you're introducing a new product that doesn't have any regular users.

Profit contribution per sale: $_____

How much do you actually make in profits from each product that you sell? Calculate this number based only on the direct costs of making and selling one unit of the product. That number is the profit contribution per sale, and hopefully it's a positive contribution!

The bottom line is . . .

That's it! When you fill in all those blanks, you get "the answer." In fact, you get a number of answers. The spreadsheet tells you what your fixed costs, variable costs, and total costs should be, assuming that your estimates are correct. The spreadsheet also figures out how many new sales you should get as a result of coupon redemptions. Finally, and most important, the program calculates the total *incremental profit,* that is, the amount of money that your coupon program makes or loses.

Testing multiple scenarios

Because this spreadsheet has built-in formulas, you can and should test many different variables in order to get a feel for the range of possible outcomes. For example, I highly recommend that you test several different redemption rates. Build low-, medium-, and high-redemption-rate scenarios. Make sure that the coupon program appears profitable at all likely redemption rate levels before you run it, because you can never project redemption rates with complete accuracy.

Learning from experience

When the coupon program is done and you have the actual numbers, compare each variable with your upfront forecast for it. Learn from your mistakes — yes, you will make mistakes. You can't forecast any coupon program with complete accuracy. In fact, unless you run very similar programs routinely, forecasting any program with even rough accuracy is hard to do! So the name of the game is to learn from your experiences.

Here are some great questions to use in debriefing yourself and preparing to design even better coupon programs the next time around:

- ✔ Did you do enough coupons to reach your market?

- ✔ Did your method of distribution get enough coupons to your target market?

- ✔ Did you offer enough of an incentive to attract new business (indicated by sufficiently high redemption rates)?

- ✔ Did you offer more than you needed to in order to attract new business (indicated by far higher redemption rates than expected)?

- ✔ Were your fixed costs higher than you expected and, if so, how can you cut them next time?

- ✔ Were your variable costs higher than you expected — and if so, how can you cut them next time?

- ✔ Were too many coupons misredeemed and, if so, how can you reduce errors and/or cheating in the future?

- ✔ Did processing each coupon cost more than you expected and, if so, how can you reduce this handling cost next time?

When you look at these specific questions, you're working on the key variables that drive the profitability of coupon programs. Learning more about each of these variables and how to control them gives you more control over the bottom-line profitability of your program. Like anything you do in marketing, experience helps you refine your formula.

Ah, but did it work?

There's one more question you really need to ask after distributing a coupon or other sales promotion. This final question has little to do with the profitability of the coupon program. The question is: Did the coupon achieve your broader marketing objectives? In other words, did your coupon do one or more of the following:

✔ Attract new customers, some of whom will become regular buyers

✔ Help ward off competition

✔ Boost sales for the period

✔ Introduce customers to a new or improved product or service

✔ Support or enhance other advertising or sales initiatives

✔ Help cushion a price increase

✔ Help cross-sell another product to existing customers

✔ Help motivate the sales force by giving them a new sales incentive or tool

✔ Make your distributors, retailers, or other intermediaries happy and more willing to push your product or service

✔ Help you gain access to greater distribution

✔ Help you migrate customers to direct or Web-based purchasing

✔ Increase repeat purchase rates

✔ Maintain or increase your market share

✔ Attract frequent switchers — those customers who are always looking for a deal

✔ Attract a specific, attractive segment (or group) of customers with an offer designed for and distributed to them

✔ Make a profit

As this lengthy list demonstrates, many reasons exist for distributing coupons or offering special deals. Sometimes marketers are willing to run a coupon program at or below break-even costs in order to accomplish their marketing objectives. The most important objective may not be to make a profit; it may be to give your salespeople an incentive or tool for boosting distribution. In this case, you may be happy to take a hit on the coupon as long as you get greater distribution because you figure it's so valuable that it's worth investing in.

So in some situations, losing money on a coupon program may be just fine. But you need to know how much you'll lose, and you need to think through the likely longer-term returns. If another percentage point of market share is likely to make you tens of thousands of dollars over the next year, who cares if it costs you hundreds or thousands of dollars to win that share? The point is, you just need to know what your objectives are and know what the costs of your coupon program are. If the objectives justify the costs in your mind, go for it!

Or, if you want to play it safe, you can just stick to profitability as your primary goal for each coupon program. Then you'll be happy to pick up small gains on any other objectives. The decision is yours. After you have the information and analyses at your fingertips, you can make good decisions, try them out, benefit from the results, and make even better decisions the next time.

Some Alternative Approaches to Sales Promotions

What if you want to offer some incentive to prospects, but you don't want it to be price based and to cost you directly on your profit margin? Here are some alternatives that usually build sales or loyalty without costing you as much of your profit margin.

Offer free food

Face it: People love to eat, at least if the food is good, the location is pleasant, and the company is tolerable. So put some marketing imagination into ways of using free food as an incentive.

One insurance company in California recruited its agents by offering a free seminar at the most luxurious hotels and restaurants, complete with a free meal of the agents' choice. The company promoted the offer with postcard mailings to purchased lists of agents. Then it followed up with a phone call from its call center. Its turnouts were best when the company held the event at the best possible restaurants. And when the dust settled, giving away a free meal in exchange for the chance to build long-term business relationships was really quite economical. (By the way, my editors thought this example was not relevant to a marketing book, and you may at first glance, too. It is, however, a good example of business-to-business marketing, where the target is an intermediary, an insurance agent. Sign up agents, and they, in turn, will sign up end customers, giving you a potentially huge return on your investment in free food!)

Another good example — this one retail oriented — is JC Penny's occasional practice of giving out chocolate bars at the door. Each is wrapped in a coupon, and the discount offered in these coupons varies, so customers may get lucky and win the rare 50 percent off coupon.

Give gifts

Plenty of other alternatives exist for your sales promotions. Only your imagination limits your options in this, as it does in everything you do in marketing. I recommend collecting examples of clever sales promotions from other marketers — especially marketers who aren't in your industry and don't compete with you. When you look around at all the ideas people try in the world of marketing, you can often find something that adapts well to your business and industry.

Maybe you can try making better use of premium items. Many businesses do. Rocks Communications, a marketing agency that I mention in several earlier chapters, recommends using "lumpy envelopes" with interesting, even funny, gifts inside them. The contents can be simple and useful — or simple and zany — it's up to you. If your envelopes are three dimensional, people open them, and almost 100 percent of them get read — which is way above average for direct mail. Spending between 50¢ and $5 to make an envelope interesting and memorable often pays off well.

I know one executive of a regional moving company who had a bunch of high-quality canvas tote bags embroidered with her company's logo and phone number. She gives these bags out to good customers and prospects, and she reports that the bags are very popular. Also, they tie in nicely with her service, reminding people that her business can help them carry things from one place to another. She has probably gotten more repeat business and referrals from this simple gift item than she would have gotten new business from a series of print ads offering 5 percent discounts on her services. And the premium item is obviously a lot more profitable.

Offer rewards for repeat business

I highly recommend looking at loyalty rewards and programs. Many businesses are exploring this concept. A program can be something as simple as the "coffee card" that collects stamps each time you fill up until you earn a free coffee. Or, a loyalty program can be something as complex as an airline's frequent flier club, with all its rules and benefits and tie-ins to other companies' sales promotions, too. Or maybe you can find a unique formula of your own.

On the CD

Check out the following file on the CD-ROM:

✔ Coupon Profitability Analysis (CD1201)

Chapter 13

Spreading the Word with Newsletters

*Y*ou have both knowledge and news that may be of interest to customers and prospective customers. Use a newsletter to make sure they find out what you have to share with them. Think of newsletters as a great way to "spread the word" about your business, products, and people, as the old expression puts it.

You can also use a newsletter to make connections with people. Let the newsletter share some of your (or your company's) warmth and enthusiasm, along with the facts. You may often hear people talk about *relationship marketing* — a buzzword that generally means building a more genuine, meaningful, lasting business relationship with your customer. In my mind, a newsletter fits in wonderfully with this strategy. A newsletter gives you many opportunities to explain yourself and to present the readers with useful information, entertainment, and other "gifts" on the printed page or via e-mail, CD, or Web site.

Newsletters are a great vehicle to deliver information and bring people up-to-date about your company, product, or organization. Depending on the content, you can publish them monthly, quarterly, or yearly. (I like the idea of sending out a newsletter at the holiday season, even if you don't do one any other time of year.) Like brochures, letterheads, envelopes, and business cards, newsletters reflect your company's personality and should be consistent with the look and feel you have reflected in your other publications. In this chapter, I not only share enough technical information to help you create great newsletters, but I also do my best to convince you to treat newsletters as a very powerful and important marketing medium.

Why You Need a Newsletter

I really like newsletters as a marketing medium, and if you don't currently have a newsletter, I strongly suggest that you consider creating one. (If you do have one, I strongly suggest that you consider improving it.) Why do you need a newsletter? Here are just a few reasons. Newsletters are

- ✔ Relatively cheap to produce (but that's just the beginning of why I like them)
- ✔ A great engagement device that gets people involved and interested
- ✔ One of the best ways to express your personality and values, as well as your offerings
- ✔ Remarkably flexible — you can use them to convey information, promote your own offerings, share customer testimonials, provide interesting or amusing content, share a funny cartoon, and so on
- ✔ A relationship builder that helps retain good customers, as well as attract good prospects

Best of all, most of your competitors don't know how powerful a well-done newsletter can be. So you have a chance to outflank them on this one!

Examining the Elements of a Newsletter

The following sections describe the most important parts of a newsletter. Electronic newsletters don't always have these elements, but in my view, they should because these elements help attract and hold reader attention.

Masthead

The *masthead* is the area that appears at the top of the newsletter. The design of the masthead should remain consistent throughout all your newsletters, changing only the date and volume/issue numbers. Consistency in the masthead brings identification to the publication. If you change the masthead, people won't recognize your newsletter each time they receive it.

Mastheads usually contain the following:

✓ The name of the newsletter — usually done in a headline typeface — that reflects the nature of its contents

✓ The name of the person or organization that publishes the newsletter

✓ Date of issue, as well as issue and volume numbers

In addition, the masthead should grab attention and set a positive tone for the newsletter. Put time and care into the choice of name and the way you display it. Later in the chapter (and on the CD), I show you some exemplary newsletters. Take note of their different approaches to masthead design. Although each design is different, all the approaches reflect care and thought.

Articles

When you decide which articles to include in your newsletter, make sure that you cover a *variety* of topics. You want to have something of interest to everyone.

Keeping it short and sweet

Make sure that your stories contain solid nuggets of useable information, such as when and where events take place, what happened (news is always of interest), what *will* happen (forecasts are always of interest), and how to perform tasks successfully (how-to tips and lists are great). Also, make sure you *tell stories.* Tell who did what, when, and why they did it, how they did it, and what happened. People read the news for stories, and the same is true with newsletters. Include case histories, interviews with people who are telling their stories, or simple news stories describing an event or happening.

Write short, to-the-point, simple articles using any or all of the formats mentioned in the previous paragraph. By short, I mean 100 to 300 words. That is very short, as you'll soon discover when you start writing. Use the Word Count option under Tools in your Microsoft Word program to count and cut if you're over your word limit. Short articles don't have to be brilliantly written because they allow the reader to get the key information quickly, so just bang out three to ten short articles and call it a wrap!

If you're a bad writer, you need to hire a writer to do the newsletter for you. But the problem is, most writers don't know enough about your business to write a really smart, useful newsletter. Consider writing poorly written but functional articles yourself, and then hire someone to edit them. Or, work with a writer or publicist who knows your industry. I've sometimes worked on newsletter projects for clients (I design them and find the right researchers and writers to do a batch of issues in advance). My feeling is that you need to manage the writing aggressively to keep it interesting and useful. Otherwise, the newsletter just becomes another throwaway.

Grabbing and holding the reader's attention

Design is almost as important as writing in making an appealing newsletter and building a following for it. Lay out articles in such a way that they capture the reader's attention and invite them to read further. Break them up with new paragraphs at least once every two or three column inches. Interrupt long flows of text with headers, tables, bullet points, or an illustration.

Try to use interesting sentences, especially at the beginning of each paragraph or section. If the first sentence grabs the reader, you probably keep her attention for the rest of the paragraph. How can you ensure that each paragraph and each major section of a newsletter article has an engaging and attention-grabbing introductory sentence?

The only way to be sure opening sentences are catchy is to go back and write (or rewrite) them *after* you've written the article. Take a half hour or more just to craft good lead sentences that queue up the content of the paragraph or section. Sentences that stimulate the imagination by asking an interesting question or challenge a common assumption are also good. Imagine that you're editing an article for a company newsletter that has the following paragraph in it:

> *The Divisional Quality Improvement Team leaders got together last week for a leadership training event that included classroom study, a self-assessment of their leadership styles, and two hours of "experiential training" on a high ropes course. The training was sponsored by Corporate Headquarters and lasted for six hours. It took place at Sleepy Hollow Retreat Center in Headlesston, Indiana.*

The preceding paragraph is an example of the kind of writing that consigns most corporate newsletters to the recycle bin. If you have time, get some quotes from people about how scary the high ropes course was and how it really taught them what true teamwork is all about. Maybe someone overcame a fear of falling that you could include a personal story about. Content can always be improved when you put on your storyteller's hat. But even if you don't have time to perfect this article, you can do a great deal by simply adding good introductory sentences. For instance, you might amend that boring article as follows:

> *What lengths — and especially heights — will our volunteer team leaders go to in order to improve their own performance? The Divisional Quality Improvement Team leaders got together last week for a leadership training event that included classroom study, a self-assessment of their leadership styles, and two hours of "experimental training" on a high ropes course. The training . . . (and so on).*

By adding a catchy opener, you greatly increase the rate of readership for that article.

Headers (like this one)

Headers (or headings) should be set in a larger and bolder type than the body of the article. A header should not be too wordy, but it must contain enough description to invite the viewer to read on. Instead of my going on at length about how a header should be written, just read a bunch of mine throughout this book, and you can at least see the type of headers I prefer.

You can use headline type for your headers or use bold type from the same family of type used in the body of the article. Figure 13-1 illustrates some of the choices that printers (and some desktop publishing systems) offer for headline type styles.

Kabel BT

Bauhaus BT

Aurora Condensed

METROPOLITAINESD

Figure 13-1: Headline type styles.

You don't want to use too many type styles in a single publication. As a rule, I recommend sticking to one type style for most of your copy. But headers are the exception. You can try a contrasting style for the headers because it sometimes adds an appealing contrast to the design.

Figure 13-2 shows a header added to the paragraph I used as an example earlier in the chapter. The header is set in 14 point Helvetica, and the body copy is in 11 point Times to illustrate the impact of contrasting styles and sizes.

Figure 13-2: Header and body copy.

Team leaders on the ropes

What lengths–and especially heights–will our volunteer team leaders go to in order to improve their own performance? The Divisional Quality Improvement Team leaders got together last week for a leadership training event which included classroom study, a self-assessment of their leadership styles, and two hours of "experimental training" on a high ropes course. . . .

Use plenty of headers. When in doubt, break up a story with more subheads. People have short attention spans, especially if the writing isn't the greatest in the world. So give them many smaller chunks to read, each wrapped up nicely in a good header.

Type

The body of an article should use a readable type set large enough so you can read it easily — which means preferably 12 point and no less than 10 point. A serif font style is more readable than a sans serif style. *Serif fonts* have the little decorations at the ends of the lines of font, as you can see in the serif font this text is written in. Times and Palatino are popular and attractive serif fonts. *Sans serif fonts* have clean edges. Save these fonts for headers because they're easier on the eye. Helvetica is the most popular sans serif font. Figure 13-3 illustrates the difference between serif and sans serif letters.

If the type is too hard to read, you'll lose your readers' attention.

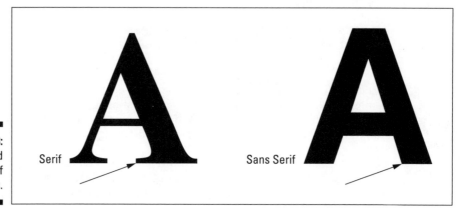

Serif

Sans Serif

Figure 13-3: Serif and sans serif letters.

If you're designing in Word (which can produce two-column, neat-looking newsletters at low cost), avoid using Times. The Times font is designed for viewing on-screen, not for printing, and it's often the default font. Switch to Times New Roman, which is optimized for the printed page rather than the screen.

Never select a font because it has a cool name. Stone is a neat-sounding font, but I don't recommend it for most uses. Apple Chancery looks and sounds interesting, and a majority of preteens like to use it for school papers, but avoid it for business uses because it's hard to read. Also, avoid all fonts designed to look like handwriting, comic book scripts, or old typewriters, unless you have a really, really good reason to use them. You have hundreds of fonts to choose from, but most of them are inferior to the classics I mention earlier in this section.

Columns

Use columns whenever you have a large amount of type. The eye may waver and jump from line to line when it has to follow lines of type that go across an 8½-inch-wide sheet. If you break up the same article into two or three columns, the line is shorter so the eye has to stay focused for a shorter amount of time and doesn't get sidetracked.

Leading and kerning

Leading refers to the space between the lines of type. Layout programs have an automatic setting for adjusting the leading, but you can also adjust it manually. Adjusting the leading manually comes in handy when you're trying to get just one more line to fit in a particular article. By adjusting the leading to a smaller size, you can scrunch up the lines and allow that extra line to fit in. Type size and leading are usually written in this form: 10/12. The type size appears on top of the slash, and the leading size appears on the bottom. Figure 13-4 shows you the type of spacing that leading and kerning control.

Try to be fairly consistent with leading and type size throughout the publication because irregular type and leading sizes look out of place.

Figure 13-4:
Leading and kerning control the spacing of your type.

Leading → The quick brown fox jumped over the lazy dog. Then the lazy black cat crawled under the fence.

The quick
Kerning

Kerning, also known as *character spacing,* refers to the space between characters (letters). Like leading, layout programs adjust the kerning between letters automatically, but you can manually override this command, too.

After you write and lay out your newsletter, check for *widows* and *orphans*. These are words or sections of words (when they're hyphenated) that are awkward to the eye at the end or beginning of a line. You want to make sure that the reader's eye can flow naturally and easily from line to line. Redesign as necessary to eliminate any rough spots where the reader may get hung up or confused. For example, if a line ends on the word "a," you may want to manually insert a *soft carriage return;* in Word, a soft carriage return breaks the line without inserting a paragraph-separating break. Eliminating such disorienting strays takes only a few minutes.

Flow and readability

Make sure that your newsletter flows (see Figure 13-5). If you have to continue articles on another page, don't make finding the continuation difficult for readers. If possible, keep articles together to make reading less frustrating. (And remember to keep articles short. If they're short, you won't need to break up many of them.)

If you publish your newsletter on a tabloid-size sheet (11 x 17 inches), lay out the articles to keep page turning from becoming a problem. Specifically, don't make readers have to flip over the document because the next articles are upside down. Also, minimize the amount of flipping back and forth between pages. You lose readers when you make the reading path too challenging.

Size

You can publish newsletters on virtually any size paper. The main determining factor is the amount of content you have (think smaller if you have a limited budget!). Newsletters can range from both sides of an 8½-x-11-inch sheet to a 11-x-17-inch sheet that's printed on both sides and folded in half. Or you can add more sheets and staple at the fold to make lengthier newsletters. You can also apply the formats and designs for brochures that I cover in Chapter 11 to printed newsletters, which gives you lots of interesting options.

Figure 13-6 shows the two most common and easiest formats for newsletters. Plan to use one of these paper sizes and layout styles unless you have a very good reason (and extra money in your budget) to deviate from them.

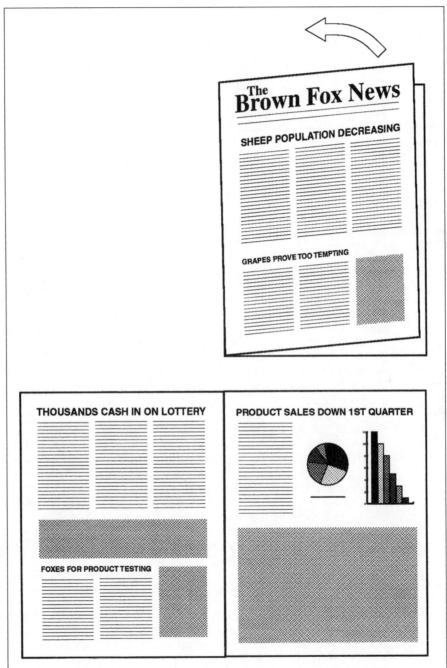

Figure 13-5:
Make sure the layout supports a natural, easy flow through the pages.

Figure 13-6:
The two
most
practical
formats for
newsletters.

LETTER SIZE (8.5" X 11") NEWSLETTER   TABLOID SIZE (11" X 17") NEWSLETTER

Photos and artwork

I cover the use of visuals in many places in this book, especially in my discussions of brochures and print ads (see Chapters 9 and 11). Like with brochures, you can use photos and artwork to make a newsletter article more interesting and to create an appropriate mood or feeling. *Text wrap —* when text wraps around a box containing artwork rather than stopping above the box and continuing below it — can also be an effective strategy in a newsletter.

For technical information about how to handle artwork, what your choices in photocopying and printing are, what screens are, how to handle color, and so on, turn to Chapter 11. I cover all these details in my discussion of how to design brochures, and you can directly apply this knowledge to newsletter design and production, too.

Looking for Inspiration from Top-Notch Newsletters

I keep a file of newsletters that are well written, well designed, or have an innovative approach that may give me good ideas. I suggest you keep a similar file. These newsletters can be your sources of inspiration. Don't copy them directly, but do look to them for ideas. Because good design is timeless, referring to older examples and trying a design idea or approach that hasn't been used lately is helpful. Fashions come and go: Maybe your newsletter can be the originator of a new old fashion.

Whatever style you use, make sure that your newsletter looks clean, professional, and isn't similar to anything your competitors publish. Benchmarks from outside your industry can help you take an original and distinctive approach.

Highlighting strengths and uniqueness

The first newsletter I show you from my own files is one that expresses the unique character of Collective Copies very well. This business is, as its name implies, a worker-owned collective, which gives it some distinguishing values and ensures a high level of commitment and concern from all employees. As a result, the business tends to build long-term relationships with customers based on superior service and a willingness to be flexible and helpful. The newsletter helps communicate the business's uniqueness and serves as an active communication channel between the business and its customers.

Figure 13-7 shows a page from one of Collective Copies' newsletters. The newsletter was given away in the store and also sent to a mailing list of regular customers, so plenty of customers had a chance to find out all about the organization's planning retreat and to see a copy of their mission statement. See what I mean about how newsletters can communicate so much about your unique personality and character?

On your CD, you can find two full newsletters from Collective Copies (filenames CD1301 and CD1302), which exemplify good homemade publishing — clean, appealing design; good use of headers and columns to break up the text into bite-sized chunks; and lots of interesting content, from practical how-to tips to information about new services and interesting stories. And note that the Glossary and Quick Tips sections may contain some useful information for you as you prepare to design your own newsletter.

Also note that these newsletters include an "Erratica" column, which is made up of amusing quotes from famous people. This column is a great way to add a little extra value to your newsletter. Sometimes people keep a newsletter and pass it around because it has a great quote or cartoon in it. See Chapter 9 for details on how to use quotes and cartoons, as well as for sources for reprintable cartoons.

Packing a double punch: Using a newsletter as a press release

You can use your newsletter as a kind of ultimate press release, as Verité, a human rights group that inspects factories in dozens of countries to ensure safe and fair labor conditions, does. Its newsletters are more sophisticated than most, and they look and read like fine magazines. The organization gets many compliments and thank-yous for its newsletters. In addition, its newsletter is a source of revenue and helps support the group's charitable work. Many individuals and organizations pay an annual subscription fee to receive this quarterly publication. If you put enough care and valuable content into a newsletter, it can have a very high perceived value in the wide world of customers and prospects.

Figure 13-8 shows a cover of one of Verité's newsletters. Note that it features a striking photograph and a bold, distinctive graphic design that make the newsletter visually intriguing and have a very professional appearance. The organization displays its name and logo on the masthead along with the newsletter's name (*Monitor*) set in a distinctive type style. And although the cover obviously doesn't contain any of the newsletter's content, it certainly makes the newsletter's subject matter clear. The subtitle, "Exploring the dynamics of the global assembly line," sums up the scope of subject matter. The photo and its caption ("Garment Workers on their way to work in Bangladesh") help set the scene. And the "In this issue . . . " feature gives readers a preview of the issue's contents.

The back cover of the Verité *Monitor* (which you can view on your CD, file-name CD1303) provides a much more detailed listing of contents by page number. The *Monitor* also does what every good marketer should do: It asks for the business it wants! Its "sponsorship and subscription" box asks readers to subscribe at various levels, from a $25 individual subscription to a $150 corporate subscription. It also includes an option for funding the newsletter at higher levels as a sponsor or donor. Because the organization presents these options, every issue yields new subscriptions and donations.

You can also find the interior pages of the *Monitor* on display on your CD (file-name CD1303) if you want to peruse this well-written, excellently designed newsletter. The newsletter is perhaps more ambitious than you are likely to produce — the issue on display here has 28 pages, including front and back covers! But it's designed and written by employees of the organization, demonstrating what is possible if you take your newsletter seriously. (If you do generate a nice newsletter, remember to send it to your media list! Verité gets some coverage from the press each time it mails this newsletter.)

Planning Retreat

During the final weekend in February, with our business still growing, our customers coming to us with ever more novel requests, and technology roaring on into the 21st century, Collective members closed-up shop and headed for the quiet of Delta Organic Farms (see the side-bar) to do some serious thinking about our business over the next five years. What can you look forward to? One of the first things to come out of our efforts is a mission statement. We found it useful to clarify what we're about when we set about visualizing where we're going.

5 Years ago, we set goals that seemed pretty ambitious at the time. We met them all. With that in mind, we once again set the bar high with plans ranging from an improved computer network to just short of world domination. Not all of what we'll be doing will be visible from the other side of the counter, but some of the things that will be include: additional staff, new document-feeders in the self-serve area, wider desktop publishing and scanning capabilities, added equipment for things like booklet-making, a second fax machine, expanded oversize copying, on-line networking, pickup and delivery, mailing services, new carpeting in the customer area and a really cool web site.

We're looking to offer educational workshops and materials to help customers who do it themselves do it right, and to organizations wanting to know more about collectives and our business structure.

Behind the scenes, we'll be scheming away to find more space, restructure the space we have and make our space more enjoyable with a 25 disc CD player. We'll be interviewing prospective collective members and training ourselves on the many new technologies available to us. We'll be upgrading our computer system and organizing our donations procedure. Work on our website is nearing completion and we hope to have it up this Spring!

Mission Statement

We are committed to achieving success in business by...

Serving our customers to the very best of our ability and resources.
In the service of this goal, we apply our knowledge, creativity and experience to communicating effectively, foster an atmosphere of mutual trust, kindness and respect, and continually educate ourselves and our customers.

Fostering a fun, safe, free, creative, trusting and respectful working environment.
We commit ourselves to taking the time to celebrate one anothers' successes, console our losses and promote personal growth.

Minimizing our environmental impact.
To this end, we will continue to seek out alternative fiber papers, recycle, minimize our waste and our use of waste-producing materials and methods, and explore promising alternatives to such materials as they become viable.

Contributing to our community and supporting local business.
We return 10% of our profits to the community that sustains us. We resolve to implement ways beyond this by which we might be of help to the community. We will promote, frequent and assist area businesses how and whenever possible.

We strive to empower all workers and to be a model/resource for positive and profitable worker-ownership.
We create secure, empowering and financially rewarding jobs for our own workers, and strive to facilitate the creation of similar opportunities for all

Delta Organic Farm

We held our retreat at this nearby farm Bed & Breakfast and Conference Center and want to express our thanks and appreciation to owners, Jim and Penny. Our stay was pleasant, the conference room comfortable and sunny. Coffee, tea and fresh fruit apeared throughout each day as if spirited there by elves. And the food! We opted for vegetarian fare and the meals, prepared in the Delta kitchen from their own organic produce, eggs and even maple syrup, were out of this world. We give Delta our enthusiastic recommendation. Delta Organic Farm Bed & Breakfast & Conference Center, E. Hadley Rd., Amherst, MA. 253-1893

How could I possibly overthrow the government when I can't even keep my dog down!

- Dorothy Parker

Figure 13-7:
This newsletter page gives insight into Collective Copies' character and values.

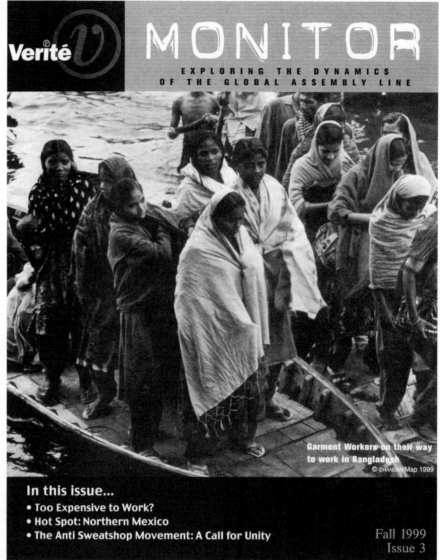

Figure 13-8:
This newsletter from a well-known human rights group presents a sophisticated, magazine-like appearance.

Learning from a Newsletter Case Study

Ira Bryck is the director of the UMass Family Business Center, a nonprofit organization that businesses join in order to participate in educational events, such as presentations and discussion groups. Under Ira's guidance, the majority of the organization's marketing budget goes into a well-written, informative newsletter that includes summaries of the many events that his group puts on.

Figure 13-9 displays the front page of one of Ira's newsletters. Much of it is displayed on your CD (filename CD1304).

A first-person account

Because Ira is such an experienced and enthusiastic newsletter publisher, I thought you'd appreciate his insights and experiences. Here are some comments he provided when I asked him how he produces his newsletter and what it accomplishes for his organization:

> *When I first started this program, Mass Mutual, one of my sponsors interviewed seven directors of family business centers who had more experience than I had, and each said the newsletter was a total waste of time. I looked at their newsletters, and they lacked any real content. Their articles about companies were really shallow and self-serving.*

> *So I decided to do a much better newsletter. A lot of the presenters, who were accustomed to having their three-hour talks boiled down to a thousand words by a professional writer, tell me these articles are the best pieces they've ever seen cover their work, and they want to use them for their own marketing.*

> *When I was in retail (I had a children's wear store), we would put a great deal of energy into our window displays, and they became the silent salesmen. They gave people the ability to see who we were and whether we were a fit for them. I use the newsletter the same way. It shares the work we do and demonstrates that we have a wealth of information. I've basically decided to make my "window dressing" extremely helpful and not just a tease. I mail my newsletter to thousands and thousands of people who have never been to a forum, and a healthy percentage of them end up joining as a result.*

> *On my newsletter, I put the address sticker on the opposite side of the box requesting more information so that when they tear off and mail the postcard asking for information, I get my sticker back with their name and address. A lot of times, I see that people have mailed back a newsletter that I addressed to someone else, so I know that the newsletter is often passed along.*

> *The newsletter often helps me develop new customers. A couple of years ago, I got the employees at a local business into a discussion about the center, and I sent them some literature in the mail. When I called the business back, the person I talked to was very negative. He said I was pestering him — which is a more negative reaction than I usually get. So I said, "I'm really sorry, I don't mean to pester you, but let me just send you the newsletter." He read this newsletter quarterly for 16 issues — each issue full of information that would have cost him a total of $2,200 to receive as a member of my organization. I decided to call back, and the employee on the line said, "You know, it's funny, we've all been reading your newsletter for three years and talking about it, and we were just thinking of calling you and asking to join."*

I also get people telling me that they agreed to take my free offer of the newsletter just to get me off the phone, but after reading it, they realized that the work I'm doing is really great and they want to participate.

Newsletters are also a great giveaway at talks that I give at Chambers, Rotaries, and business groups. A newsletter's a lot better than a pencil! I tell audience members that if they're interested in information about family businesses, they can give me their business cards and I'll send them the newsletter. I've encountered many people who come to Rotary to eat lunch and end up getting involved after reading a few issues of my newsletter.

Don't forget about costs

As long as I was interviewing Ira about his newsletter, I decided to quiz him on the costs involved. His approach (because he really wants to make sure that his articles are good) is to hire a professional writer at 50¢ per word, or about $500 per article. Each newsletter is made up of four articles written by professional writers, in addition to pieces by interesting people Ira bumps into who can contribute a good article. People usually give him articles for free, and his corporate sponsors also give him articles (which he accepts as long as they're educational and noncommercial).

Printing one copy of the newsletter costs about 50¢, and sending it via bulk mail costs about 25¢. Ira sends the newsletter for free — no subscription cost. He also hires a graphic designer to lay out the newsletter, adding a few hundred dollars to his costs. He sends out about 4,000 issues, which he has offset printed (the most common form of printing, offered by most printers).

Ira gets double duty out of his newsletter by posting all the content on his organization's Web site. He points out that posting the newsletter has really helped make the site a valuable and popular one: "My Web site was recently recognized by Yahoo! as the most comprehensive family business Web site, partly because I post all my newsletters on it."

Taking a Simplified Approach

All this talk about offset printing, expensive freelance writers, and bulk mailings may discourage some marketers. If you don't want to put the time and money into a newsletter that the more complex approach requires, consider doing a simpler one that you can print on single or stapled 8½-x-11-inch sheets and distribute by hand.

Alfredo's Photo Gallery is the perfect example of a business that uses a simple newsletter. With a retail storefront featuring a wide range of photographic artwork, a virtual gallery on the Web, and professional services ranging from aerial photography to sports photography, this small business has a big message to communicate. How does Alfredo's Photo Gallery make sure that its customers and prospects are aware of all it has to offer? It publishes a simple, two-page, monthly newsletter, printed on the gallery's color laser printer and designed using standard desktop publishing software. This self-published newsletter serves its purpose well and costs almost nothing. (Figure 13-9 shows the first page of this newsletter, and you can see all of it in more detail on your CD, file-name CD1305.)

Alfredo's
Photo Gallery News
October 1999

Pioneer Valley Photographic Artists
The new organization of world class photographers now has a membership of 40 with diversified portfolios of various types of photography. Projects now underway are a year 2000 calendar, permanent exhibition space at the Arts Alive Gallery at the BayState Medical Center in Springfield, Mass.; an exhibit at Arts Unlimited in Chicopee, Mass.; a cooperative calendar effort with the Pioneer Valley Planning Commission; a professional video of the organization; and initial work toward setting up a web site. It appears that the mission of the organization is well on the way to being met!

Photographic Artist of the Month

Greenhouse Ruin by PVPA Member Ken Kipen

This month's recognition goes to Ken Kipen. Ken specializes in black & white photography using, primarily, a medium format camera system. He does all of his own processing, printing, matting and framing enabling him to control the results to his high quality standards. His work centers on landscape, things of beauty, and interesting subjects such as the "Greenhouse Ruin" shown above. He has a unique capability of capturing composition and lighting to give excellent results. Ken resides in Ashfield, Mass. and samples of his work are regularly on display at Alfredo's.

Alfredo's Sports Corner
Former UMass Stars Receive National (International) Recognition

Former UMass Stars Brian Scurry and Marcus Camby have been in the limelight recently. Briana Scurry with her dramatic goal blocking giving the US Women's Soccer Team the World Cup Championship in an event internationally televised. This exciting event is being called one of the most significant of the past 50 years in sports and has catapulted women's sports to a new level. Marcus Camby's excellent play in the NBA Finals was also given special recognition. Larry Bird called Marcus the MVP of the semi-finals between the New York Knicks and the Indiana Pacers!

An Affectionate Hug, Briana Scurry, UMass Coach Jim Rudy

Game 5 NBA Finals, Marcus Camby, David Robinson

Monthly Supplier Quality Recognition
This month's recognition goes to the **US Postal Service**! They simply have done an excellent job in sending glass framed photographs for Alfredo's around the country. They have been delivered on time with no damaged shipments--100% good quality and service. A special thanks goes to postal workers in Amherst and South Hadley for their help and care.

Figure 13-9: Alfredo's Gallery News is an engaging, self-published newsletter that commu-nicates effectively at minimal cost.

Saving a Tree: Electronic Newsletters

We live in a computerized world, meaning that interesting variations to traditional printed products are extremely popular. In this section, I discuss a few of the most common variations.

For details on how to create electronic newsletters, contact a media designer with marketing experience. If you're interested in a referral, you can find links at www.insightsformarketing.com. You can also check out the growing list of *For Dummies* books about Web page design; I'll keep the latest editions ready on the Web site for your convenience.

E-mailing a Portable Document Format (pdf) attachment

Many organizations have switched their newsletters from print mailings to e-mail documents, which isn't a bad method if your target readers check their e-mails routinely and like to receive news this way. Write and design the newsletter as if it were for one or more 8½-x-11-inch printed pages. Then convert it to a pdf file and attach it to an e-mail addressed to your subscription list. The e-mail subject line simply needs to announce the newest issue of the newsletter so recipients know it isn't spam and don't delete the attachment before opening and reading it.

E-mailing an html page

Another option is to design a simple, half-page-size newsletter in html as if it were for a Web page. Then insert it directly into an e-mail so it appears on-screen for the recipient. With this method, you get the content in front of your recipients without having to depend on their opening an attachment. Some people don't like receiving big, visual e-mails — they think you're hijacking their computers — so you have to decide whether or not your audience will object to this approach.

Sending hybrid e-mails

Hybrid e-mails basically display what looks like a banner ad from a Web page or, even more simply, a one-line link. When the reader clicks on the link, her Web browser opens up and she's taken directly to a Web page.

Of course, now you can deliver your newsletter content on a Web page, which opens up the options for design. For example, in addition to conventional articles, you can include high-quality color photos, animation, and even streaming video. Earlier in this chapter, I present an article describing a company training retreat in which employees went on a ropes course. You may find it hard to make a text-oriented description of this event interesting, but imagine how much more appealing your coverage will be if you show a video of the event on your Web site with a short caption underneath.

Mailing a CD

Remember that you can create and mail a CD rather than a printed newsletter. The CD can contain your newsletter, either in printable form (as a pdf or Word file) or in color designed for on-screen display. Your CD can also contain supporting information and materials — almost anything that you can imagine — because a CD has so much more capacity than a printed newsletter. Use the CD to provide more and better photos to illustrate the newsletter. Or put the latest copy of your full catalog and price sheet on the CD in folders that readers can open when they need this information.

On the CD

Check out the following items on the CD-ROM:

- Collective Copies newsletters (CD1301 and CD1302)
- Verité Newsletter (CD1303)
- The UMass Family Business Center newsletter (CD1304)
- Alfredo's Photo Gallery News (CD1305)

Chapter 14

Taking Advantage of Publicity

. . . .

In This Chapter

▶ Understanding the value of publicity

▶ Generating great publicity

▶ Creating a media kit, press release, and mailing list

▶ Formulating your publicity plan

. . . .

*T*his chapter is probably the one that you, as a small- or medium-size business owner, feel most like skipping over because creating newsworthy stories about your business may seem out of your reach. Don't feel discouraged! Publicity is a very real part of your marketing plan, and it's one that *is achievable* for you. Besides, understanding what publicity can do for your company can save you a bundle in advertising costs.

Publicity is a special, powerful tool. But it doesn't have to be complicated. In this chapter, I discuss what exactly publicity is (and what it isn't), and I show you how to create a workable publicity plan for your business, product, or service.

Publicity in Action

Imagine that you own a midsize tooling company that caters to the furniture market in North Carolina (which is often called the furniture capital of the world). Growing your business has two components:

▸ Producing the best quality products available (satisfied customers keep coming back and refer other customers)

▸ Getting name recognition to attract a whole new customer base

Suppose that you place a story (I discuss how to place a story in the section "Pitching Your Release to the Media" later in this chapter) in the business section of the largest newspaper (by circulation size) in the region. The story is about the fact that your company just received the most sophisticated machine in the world today to produce the kind of tools needed by the furniture industry.

The first result of this positive publicity is that new customers will call you to find out more about what you can do for them. In addition, your existing customers gain more confidence in your products because the newspaper or magazine article validates the fact that your company is progressive. Another positive result is that in a tight labor market, potential employees and current employees become aware of your cutting-edge capabilities and consider you a good company to work for, and employees naturally want to work for the best.

So, with one carefully placed article, you've increased your company's name recognition, reinforced that your company is the best, and highlighted the fact that your company is a great place to work because of the cutting-edge technology it possesses. Not bad, huh?

Another valuable way you can use this article is to post it on your Web site and send a copy of the article (with a cover letter and a product information sheet) to new and potential clients (note that you'll need permission from the publication for both — but permission is routinely granted). You may even do something as simple as placing a reprint of the article in the envelopes that hold your employees' paychecks or your customers' invoices.

Publicity can be merchandised internally and externally. By showing your employees how important the company they work for is, you help retain employees, spread goodwill, and build accountability. Don't forget to post or distribute good press clippings internally so that your employees see that their company is in the news. And, of course, make sure to use news coverage in marketing to customers and prospects, too. Use copies of press clippings as handouts or quote them in a brochure, catalog, or Web page. And, if you anticipate television coverage, e-mail your best customers the day before to let them know.

Story ideas

Your publicity program is a powerful image builder. Not sure what story to tell the world, though? Here are some ideas you can use in a story:

✓ Your cutting-edge technology

✓ Your quality product or service

✓ The many ways your company gives back to the community

✓ The awards your company has won

✓ That your company is growing — renovating, relocating, and updating

✓ How good your people are

✓ What a great leader your CEO is

✓ That your company has started a new advertising campaign

✓ Any other interesting or important news about your business or the people in it

Just What Is Publicity?

Publicity tells the story of a business, executive, or employee within the business. A good publicity campaign results in a positive public image and attracts new customers and makes you a more desirable employer, too.

In short, editorial coverage creates a publicity-marketing umbrella that other forms of marketing cannot compete with. Just think about it: Are you more likely to hear two businesspeople saying, "Hey, did you see DeHart Tooling's new direct-mail piece?" or "Hey, did you see that article in *The Charlotte Observer* about DeHart Tooling getting that new machine?"

Publicity versus advertising

One of the most interesting things about publicity is that people often don't understand the difference between publicity and advertising. Consider advertising that you pay for, such as posters, brochures, newsletters, billboards, direct mail, and advertisements: You write a check to produce them and place them in front of an audience. Advertising involves *paid placement of marketing messages.* Not so for publicity.

Publicity is *not* advertising. You don't pay for an interview on a radio or TV program or for the space a newspaper or magazine uses to write about your company. If a local business program interviews you or a TV station comes to your company and videotapes a special event for the evening news, it doesn't send you a bill. Publicity falls into the editorial side of any media company's business, not the advertising side. This means that not only is publicity free for your company, but it's also inherently more interesting and credible than space or time that you pay for.

Publicity versus public relations

Publicity is not public relations, either. Publicity is a tool of the public relations umbrella. Public relations, as a function, generally includes all sorts of other stuff, such as how you relate to your community — which may or may not generate profitable publicity for you. I'm going to focus on getting you publicity, because that's what you need to promote your business.

Publicity, in short, is obtaining free editorial coverage based on factual, interesting, breakthrough, and newsworthy information about your company, product, or service. Now, the question is, how do you do get publicity? Read on to find out.

How to Generate Great Publicity

Many companies hire a professional public relations firm to help them obtain publicity. In many cases, hiring a good public relations firm is a much better investment of your marketing dollars than advertising is. However, the smallest businesses can probably do it themselves, and even larger businesses can consider doing some of their publicity internally (I tell you how to do this in the section "Pitching Your Release to the Media" later in this chapter).

Be newsworthy

Basically, you should do publicity (or hire an expert to do it for you) if anything about your business lends itself to generating news coverage. How do you know whether your business is newsworthy? Here are some criteria to determine whether your company's story is newsworthy:

- ✔ **Show of progress:** One way to determine whether your company is a good candidate for publicity is to determine, through a focus of your marketing program, whether the information you can share about your company, product, or service shows progress. Progress is always newsworthy.

- ✔ **Local angle:** The closer the story is to a reader's home or business, the more important it is to them. In many cases today, so much generic global information is available through the Internet and syndicated wire services like the Associated Press that the real gem to a reporter is a real person at a real company telling a real story with a real local angle.

  But, to give you the best chance of making it in a paper (or in a magazine or on the radio or on TV), you need to do your homework before you approach the media. Specifically, you need to prepare some thoughts and information, and you need to package your contributions to the media in one or more of the forms that they're used to working with. (The following sections look at what forms the media like their information in and how you should prepare them.)

- ✔ **Unusual:** Your company's story is different — not the same old story recycled over and over again.

- ✔ **Timely:** Of course, you want your story to make sense considering the business conditions or the time of year.

  By the way, *timely* means that your company is doing something before anyone else. If you're the third company to send out a press release about new ideas for holiday gifts, the media is a lot less likely to pick up your story than if you had been the first one to do it.

- ✔ **Needed and important:** Your company provides a needed service or is doing something significant for the local or regional area that's *important right now.*

But isn't much of what we do newsworthy?

The way to generate publicity is to let journalists know about anything that you can point to as having news value because it represents significant progress, has a local angle, is unusual, is timely, and/or is important right now.

Sounds easy, doesn't it? I know what you're thinking:

- ✔ My company is doing lots of great things that are newsworthy.
- ✔ But no one from the media calls the company to ask about it. Why not?
- ✔ How the heck is the media going to know what's important to me and my customers about my business, product, or service?

Well, nobody in the media is going to cover your business unless they know what's newsworthy about it. Media professionals don't read minds, you know. So you simply have to tell them.

It's not newsworthy until journalists know about it

The idea of you calling a business reporter at the largest paper in your region and telling him about a new product or service you offer or about a sales record your company has achieved or about the expansion your company is making within the state isn't so far fetched. But most — really almost all — businesspeople never pick up the phone and call a journalist or editor to share their information. When have you ever initiated such a call? What, *never?* Those editors must be getting the idea that you don't like them. They may think that you don't *want* news coverage.

Any media professional needs information, and most of them need and want some help gathering that information. The days of the reporter with a steno pad, trench coat, and hat, seeking out a great story, are gone for good. Sure, reporters still have beats, but their beats are probably the largest companies in the area. No business reporter today can do his job effectively without the help of others to keep him informed. And under the "others" category are professional publicists who work at public relations firms, seasoned public relations professionals who work internally at companies, and then there's *you.*

By becoming a liaison with the media, you can help your company accomplish one or more of the following:

- ✔ Inform people about how to choose, buy, and use your product or service
- ✔ Persuade consumers to buy your product or service
- ✔ Counteract misconceptions about your product or cause
- ✔ Get customers in your store or on your Web site
- ✔ Get information to the public on issues your organization is concerned about

> ✔ Bring people to an event or a series of events
>
> ✔ Recruit highly qualified employees
>
> ✔ Attract investors

Because reporters need help gathering information that isn't readily available — such as a breaking story about your company — the chances of your company getting coverage for what it's doing is pretty likely. Finding good stories is always a problem for journalists. And their problem is your opportunity.

Take a look at CD1401, which is a copy of a press release sent by one of the leading U.S. furniture makers to a national list of editors and reporters. This release tells a simple but compelling story: Century Furniture joins forces with a famous designer, Oscar de la Renta, to create patio and garden furniture inspired by the antique outdoor furniture from the estate of the Duchess of Devonshire. The company timed the release to come out just before the industry's biggest annual trade show in High Point, North Carolina, and it attracted interest from a wide variety of media, including Sunday supplements of major newspapers, which often run seasonal stories on landscape design.

Developing a media kit

The first step you need to take to generate publicity is to develop a media kit. Some newspaper people and many publicists still call this a "press kit." But, I like to call it a media kit because the press has become more than a newspaper or other printed publication.

A *media kit* usually consists of a folder (with two inside pockets) that includes one or several news releases about your company, photographs that relate to the information in the releases, a background sheet with an overview of interesting facts about your company (such as its history or milestones), bios and photos of your management team, and any other information that compiles a complete overview of your company as it stands today.

The media kit can serve as the basis of your publicity program because media professionals can always refer to it at a moment's notice for factual information about your company. The primary purpose of a media kit is to help news people report your story as thoroughly as possible. It saves the reporter's time and shows that you and your company are competent and serious about providing accurate, up-to-date information. News people won't use everything in a media kit, but it sends the message that you're organized and have very positive and real information about your company.

A side note to the development of a media kit is that it's a great internal exercise to see where your company has been, where it is now, and where it is going. The process of organizing your company on paper, overviewing its history, its products, its executives, its milestones, and its sales accomplishments is a great way to take a look at your company as a whole.

Assembling your kit

To assemble your kit, you can start by purchasing shiny duotang (two-pocket) folders at your local office-supply store or major office-supply store chains. These folders are available in many colors and usually come 25 to a box. You can insert all your information inside the folder and interchange the information as needed. Some companies even print stickers for the cover (with the company name and address on the sticker) because it's a low-cost alternative to printing directly onto a folder. (Place the sticker on the outside of the folder and center it on the front cover.)

But why be cheap? First impressions are the most important, right? I recommend investing a little money in this part of your publicity program and getting two-pocket folders with your company name and logo printed on them. (Remember, you won't be buying advertising for this program, so the money you spend will be on the preparation of the materials and the time you spend doing publicity, which won't really be very much compared to buying ad space or time.)

If you anticipate a move or a new area code coming to your city, you may want to print a smaller quantity or leave off your address and phone number and focus on putting your name and logo or a picture on the cover.

You'll find many additional uses for this printed media kit folder. When you're not using it for publicity, it makes a great folder to give customers. You can use it to interchange price sheets and information easily. You can also use it as your employee handbook to hold information that employees need. You may even find yourself bringing one to the bank when you visit your loan officer or passing them out at the pressroom at a trade show. So consider the many uses a media kit folder can provide your company and design it accordingly.

What about using your Web page as a media kit?

Sometimes a company's Web page is its media kit. Go to several businesses' Web pages and you're likely to see most of the components of a media kit. You can use your site this way, if you like. Some journalists will be happy to visit your site to pull off the background information that they need. But I still recommend producing a written copy of a media kit because even in our wired world, reporters for both electronic and print may want the convenience of a kit that they can refer to, throw in their briefcase, or put in a file.

Many companies are developing pressrooms on their Web sites that list all their press releases, photographs of executives, or products that the media can easily download. I believe that right now things are in a transitional stage, where some media professionals are incredibly techno-savvy and actually prefer getting everything electronically, while others still prefer having the traditional media kits and photographs arrive on their desks via snail mail.

Now is not the time to make a decision about which way your company wants to go. Offer both options and let the reaction to technology dictate the future of how your media kit will look over the next couple of years. Develop a media kit and also have the people who are posting the information on your Web site include the materials from your media kit.

What's the hook?

Now for some bad news. Did you know that most media kits never get more than a passing glance from journalists? In general, media kits don't generate publicity. Not on their own. Not without a *hook;* that is, a current, interesting story to provide a focus for the media's coverage. So your media kit is just a foundation for generating publicity. You still have some more work to do.

The hook is the newsworthy information in your most current press release. How will you create that press release? By figuring out what is really exciting about your executives, staff, products, services, earnings, special event, or milestone. I discuss press releases in detail in the next section.

The Press Release That's Going to Get You Publicity

The best way to decide what the story should be is to ask yourself what's new at your company. So, ask yourself now: Have you launched a new product? Did you add new employees? Did you have outstanding earnings for this quarter? Are you expanding in the region? Will you be merging with a new company? Is it your anniversary? Do you generate more or better marketing for less money than any of your competitors? Do some of your employees run in marathons or volunteer for a local charity? Does your business support a youth soccer team or league? Do you have an unusual employee recognition or reward program or event?

Whatever your story is, whether you received a new contract with a major client or you just received an award, you want to put it on paper in the form of a press release.

Because space and time equal money, keep your press release brief, breakthrough, and newsworthy. How? Imagine that you're writing a short article for the front page of your local paper.

Good versus bad press releases

A good press release is professionally typed and sent out on original letterhead. It includes the name of the contact person, his phone number and e-mail, the date, and the copy: *For Immediate Release.* It also

✔ Has a great headline

✔ Is double-spaced

✔ Is clearly interesting

A bad press release — one that will end up in the garbage can — is

✔ Too long

✔ Missing a much-needed visual, such as a photograph, which can help tell the story

✔ Not newsworthy

✔ Too soft or self-promotional

✔ Poorly written with obvious mistakes

✔ Is incomplete and lacks valuable information that makes the story more interesting

✔ Shows little attention to details

✔ Arrives late or off-season

Getting a reporter to take notice

Try putting yourself in the reporter's seat for a moment. A reporter receives many press releases a week. She may have only an hour to read them, so she has to make quick judgments and scan a paragraph or two of each one. Keep in mind that she also gets e-mails and voice mails every day, too. Your release has to rise to the top of this weighty pile of communications. And the pile is far bigger at larger newspapers, where you may be most eager to get coverage.

Make your press release as professional as possible so a reporter places yours in her credible pile. Make it stand out! Here are some of the tricks. Your press release needs to

✔ Consist of news that's really news, not just promotional material. (Newsworthy means something that represents significant progress, has a local angle, is unusual, is timely, and/or is important right now.)

✔ Contain the name, address, phone number, and Web site of your company in the upper left-hand corner of the first page. Also, give the name, phone number, and e-mail of the person to contact (probably you) for further information.

✔ Be short. Yes, short! (No more than two pages.)

✔ Be word-processed and printed on your company's letterhead on a laser printer. If it's more than one page, use a matching second page and staple your pages together.

✔ Be spell checked and read over by several different people for accuracy and typos.

I'm serious about checking your release for accuracy and professional appearance. In many cases, you're sending it to editors and writers. They will *know* whether or not it is well written and professionally laid out and printed. Have several people at different levels in your company read over your press release. You'll be surprised by what different people may see. The third reader often finds a mistake that the first two missed or adds some insight that nobody else thought of.

If your release must go to a second page, try to end the first page with a completed paragraph or, at least, a completed sentence. Type **-More-** across the bottom of the first page. Then start the second page with a brief heading in the upper-left corner that includes the name of your company and page two.

Mark the end of your release with the digits **-30-** or the number sign, **###**, repeated several times across the page. These symbols are two versions of journalese for "that's all there is for now."

Making sure your press release is "news ready"

A good press release reads like a news story, which is exactly the point. A good release sounds as if it's ready to be inserted in a paper. Here's how to write one that meets this important criterion.

- ✔ **A good release starts with a *headline*.** A short title at the top tells the media what your hook is. "Local business agrees to support youth soccer programs for five years." "Tooling company adds cutting-edge equipment." "Author explains the secrets of generating publicity." Whatever your hook, start right off with it so they "get it" right away.

- ✔ **Next, a good release has a *lead paragraph* that covers the who, what, when, where, and why of the interesting subject that you're sharing with the media.** Then, subsequent paragraphs clearly and cleanly elaborate upon that story by filling in the details or adding interesting tidbits.

Who, what, when, where, and why: That's the journalist's mantra. Let it be yours when you write a release, otherwise they don't have a story fit for print (or air) until they've answered those questions. In a way, you can think of that opening paragraph as providing the *bait* for your hook. And that bait is the who, what, when, where, and why that provides a journalist with all the essentials needed to turn a hook into actual editorial content.

> ✔ **Finally, a good release needs to follow through on the promise of the header and lead paragraph with a few more paragraphs of *supporting text and images*.** Make sure that this supporting text is truly relevant and to the point, not boringly repetitive. Provide some interesting or important background information. Throw in a quote or two from a company representative, if you like. Give some evidence to support your contention that you've actually done something important or unusual or timely. And if at all appropriate, provide a photo or other visual to illustrate the story.

File CD1402 is a press release from Apex Performance Systems, a sales training company. This release meets the three criteria I listed. It starts with a headline that could just as well appear in a business magazine: "Point, Click, Learn and Earn: The Brave New World of Online Sales Training." Its opening two paragraphs tell the whole story of how Apex's new process (which uses the Internet) is an improvement over traditional sales training seminars. Then the rest of the release gives more details that a journalist may need to describe the Apex product in a story.

Whenever you can, let your press release sit overnight before you send it. Check for accuracy and errors, but most of all, make sure that you have an interesting story to tell and that you tell it with all the facts you can.

Pitching Your Release to the Media

When you have your press release (probably about two double-spaced pages) and media kit ready, you need to *make a media pitch*. In other words, you have to sell your story.

Make your first media pitch by selecting one reporter and trying the process once. Select the newspaper that's the main paper in your region and choose the reporter who covers the beat most affiliated with what your company does.

For example, if your company is an art gallery and is opening a new exhibit, you'd obviously contact the art editor at your local paper. If your company just bought a huge piece of land to develop over the next two years and your local paper has a reporter who covers construction and development, the connection is there.

You may also call the section of the paper that best relates to your company and ask who writes about your specific topic. You'll usually find that someone is happy to point you to the correct contact.

Here's a list of some typical specialty areas at a large metropolitan daily:

Art	Entertainment (News)
Movies	Sunday Editor
Books	Events Calendar
Music	Television
Business	Fashion
News	Technology
Real Estate	Features
Editorial	Theater
Science	Food
Education	Travel
Society	Foreign Affairs
Entertainment (Criticism)	Women's Page
Sports	Home and Garden
	Local

Lots of choices, aren't there?

Before you approach the most appropriate person, confirm the reporter's name, business address, and phone number via phone. You have to be sure you know who you want to talk to and how to contact him.

Good work! Now you know who you want to send your press release to, why he would be interested in writing about it, and where to find him. You also have a thorough media kit on your company (in case a simple story turns into a feature article), and you have a press release that tells the breaking story that your focus is on today.

Including a cover letter

Finally, you're prepared to generate some publicity. Well, almost. Your next step is to put together a short, clear cover letter that tells the reporter why you think he should write about your company. It can go something like this example:

Dear Doug Smith:

I enjoy your feature article every week as you overview construction and development in western North Carolina. I particularly enjoyed your article dated June 1, 20XX, regarding the proposed new highway. I think your readers will enjoy hearing about the land my company is purchasing for development. The attached press release specifically outlines our plans.

I have also enclosed a media kit, which gives you background information on our company and a visual rendering of the proposed project. These materials can be e-mailed to you or they can be obtained in the pressroom on our website. I will follow up with you shortly.

Best Regards,

John Builder

Now you're actually ready to make the contact. Put your cover letter, press release, and kit into an envelope (don't fold them!) and send them via first-class mail.

Don't forget to follow up!

You absolutely must make a follow-up call. If you want to be successful with publicity, never send anything that you don't follow up with. Four or five days after you send your package, make a follow-up call and talk to the media person about your potential story. You may get voice mail or you may actually get a live person on the phone. In case you actually talk with the reporter on the phone, be sure to have the media kit and press release right in front of you so that you can quickly discuss key points.

If you get voice mail, which is most common, make sure that you've practiced a solid voice mail message that goes something like this one:

"Hi Doug, this is John Builder. You may not recognize my name, but I'm the Director of Marketing at Build Right Construction Services. I read your articles all the time in the Gotham City Observer and sent you a press release that I think is something you can use and is something that your readers will be interested in. As you know, my company has just purchased a tract of land, and in the package I sent to you, I have overviewed our plans. You can reach me at 555-6666, right here in Gotham City, and I look forward to talking to you soon."

I can't emphasize enough the importance of calling a reporter. Don't be shy and don't think you shouldn't call because you'll be bothering them. If you don't bother reporters just a little bit, they probably won't notice you or your story.

Making that follow-up call is far easier when you have something in mind that's worth saying — and that you know the reporter will find worth listening to. Find some significant detail that wasn't covered in your press release (either on purpose or because it wasn't confirmed yet). Then you can feel good about calling because you have another piece of valuable information to share with the reporter.

Put it in the mail?

Different journalists have preferences about how they like to get their media materials. With today's explosion of information technology, you have quite a choice of distribution methods — mail, overnight service if a deadline is looming, via fax if it's extremely time sensitive, or electronically via e-mail that delivers it right to an editor's computer. Send it snail mail if it's not time sensitive. You can include a note that the release (or entire media kit) is available electronically just for the asking.

When following up on your press release via the phone, remember that *the media needs you* to give them good stories. For all you know, that reporter is trying to figure out what to write about for her next article, and you may provide her a great service by putting together your information, sending it to her, and following up in a timely fashion to answer any questions she may have.

Dealing with rejection

When you pitch a story, you're selling your hook to journalists. I know it's not "real" selling because you aren't asking for money, but it's akin to sales in that you need to select a target, make an approach, find a way to present your information, and ask them to do something that's beneficial for you.

And sometimes they do. But often, the media ignores you and declines to cover your story, in which case, you need to deal with rejection, just as you do in personal selling (see Chapter 17 for helpful advice). Now, remember that rejection means nothing to the journalist and should mean nothing to you, either. Maybe they just don't need your story right now. Or they just don't think the hook is very sharp. Or they don't think the story is very relevant to their area or focus. But because you presented yourself professionally and politely, they're still happy — in fact, more than happy — to see your next release or hear your next voice mail follow-up on a mailing. So rejection doesn't preclude later coverage.

In fact, a journalist who has rejected you in the past is more likely to cover your company than someone who has never heard of you. Even though a journalist declines to cover a specific story, she generally makes a mental note of the source and puts you in a physical, or at least a mental, "possible sources" file. Your well-prepared, professional letter, press release, and media kit earned you the right to be a source of news in the future. So don't let rejection worry you. You're still closer to coverage than you were before you made the contact.

And, just like a salesperson, you can always contact more journalists. Eventually, if you send out enough releases, you'll strike pay dirt. So the next step for you is to compile and maintain a list of media contacts (more about this topic in the next section).

Creating Your Mailing List

In addition to the one targeted reporter at the largest paper in the area — who can probably do more for your company's exposure than all your marketing efforts combined — to really have an effective publicity program, you should have a *comprehensive* list or lists. (Yes, I said lists — more than one — in fact, maybe many.)

Plan your lists intelligently so that you don't waste your time or effort approaching people who are inappropriate for your publicity goals. If you believe that one newspaper can give you enough publicity for your purposes, concentrate on the needs and requirements of that newspaper. But usually, businesses need to contact a broader range of journalists and editors. There is no hard rule, so your only true guideline is how far you want to reach out with your message.

Organizing contacts for easy access

You'll have occasions when you want to make a mailing to a specific type of medium — large metropolitan dailies, smaller daily papers, weekly newspapers, trade magazines, local television, or radio. It's a good idea to begin by keeping them in separate lists so that you can easily extract them for a particular use. Also, if your geographic areas become larger, you can easily expand these more specific lists.

You may need only one or two lists of a very limited nature to begin, but planning for future lists at this time as well pays off. You'll get a good understanding of what your growth potential is and you'll establish a workable pattern for your lists: how you keep them, the type of information you collect — that sort of thing. As you prepare more and more lists, you can shuffle and combine them for temporary or immediate goals. This eliminates the need to build a new list each time you send out a mailing.

The lists you may eventually be building could include:

- Company "hometown" media
- Branch offices' "hometown" media
- Wire services that have a bureau where your company is based
- Daily newspapers (A list: big papers)

- Daily newspapers (B list: smaller papers)
- Weekly newspapers (C list)
- Television and radio stations (those that have business shows that may cover your company; you'll find the appropriate producers in the stations' news production department)
- Trade, professional, and technical journals
- Consumer publications (usually national; look for a reporter who covers your subject and thinks you're unique)

Finding the names for your list

Deciding what sorts of lists you want to compile is one thing, but actually creating those lists is quite another. Where are you going to find the names of the appropriate editors, writers, and other journalists?

Scouring print media

One suggestion is to go to a local newspaper stand in your city and buy all the publications that someone who would use your products or services would read (you probably read many of them anyway). You can find out who's writing about your subject, and you can literally start a print database that way.

If you make business-to-business sales, you also want to compile a list of contacts at trade and industry publications. You can always find at least a few publications read by purchasers in any industry. Put those publications on your list. If you aren't sure what your customers read and what professional associations they belong to, ask them!

Tracking down contacts in local radio and TV

For radio and television programs that may offer opportunities for exposure, you can simply go through a television-programming guide published by your local paper. If you see that Channel 10 in your area offers a business-focused program every Sunday morning, you know that the producer of that program should appear on your media list.

What? You were thinking Oprah, Peter Jennings, Dan Rather, Tom Brokaw, or the front page of *The Wall Street Journal?* Your company may produce products or services that warrant exposure nationally, but for learning the process of publicity, I recommend starting by focusing locally. You can use the experience you gain and the techniques you master on a local basis for regional and national publicity. It's far easier to go to the local media first to gain experience and confidence. And, in truth, most publicity is local and regional. Over the long run, this media is where most businesses get the ongoing exposure they need.

Opting to buy a list instead

A second option is simply to order a list from one of the media list-management companies in the country, such as Bacon's Information in Chicago (call 800-776-3342, or 800-PR-MEDIA, or visit www.bacons.com). This company publishes bound guides to magazines and newspapers, radio, and television. The company can also pull a list for you based on your criteria and charge you only for the records that they pull for you. You can obtain the records on disk along with a printout.

For example, suppose your company offers services to banks in the southeastern United States. As a starting point, you'd ask the researcher at Bacon's to pull a list of all the banking reporters in the Southeast at every daily and weekly newspaper and every business-industry trade magazine that has a banking reporter. After you have that list, you literally could get to know every editor on that list by sending them your press release and media kit. These media contacts are perfect for your company because they fit the criteria of being in the right region and being specialists in the field of banking. To pay a list company to pull the list for you is probably a good starting point and probably worth what it charges.

Remember to check your list for changes each time you use it. No matter how your list originates or how you decide to update it, check your list frequently.

How do you judge the value of publicity?

Advertising firms develop an advertising plan based on an overall budget. For each ad, the firms plug in the price of the ads appearing in each medium or outlet. Publicity firms show their value by telling you how much you would have paid if your free editorial coverage had been paid advertising. For example, Pittsburgh-based Rocks-DeHart Public Relations, a public relations firm that specializes in publicity, recently sent a memo to one of its clients that said:

Congratulations, your product has appeared as a featured product in Computer World Magazine. *Included was a photograph of the product, taken from our media kit, and a description of why it is so interesting. The one-page ad rate for* Computer

World Magazine *is XXX. Your free editorial covered one fourth of the page, and was therefore equal in value to XXX. As you can see, the time it took to develop the media list, write the press release, send it, and pitch it was time well spent.*

I think that this comparison to advertising understates the potential value of publicity. Editorial coverage in *Computer World Magazine* (as long as it isn't negative) will have a far greater impact on purchase intentions than the average ad. Basically, publicity is the form of communications that gives you the most impact. If you spend even half as much on publicity as you do on all your advertising, you'll find that it generates business far in excess of its cost. Give it a try!

Don't oversend to your lists. Make each and every contact with the media count, just as you would want every contact with your customers to count.

Planning Your Publicity Program

Putting your publicity plan on paper is a great idea, and members of any professional publicity firm will prepare a written plan upfront before they do anything for you.

A simple step-by-step planning process

To form a publicity plan, follow these easy steps:

1. **Determine a date when somebody in your company (who has a background in writing and communication skills) will be able to gather all the information needed to put together a media kit.**

   Remember that your company will update and print out the media kit throughout the year and that it's an ever-changing document.

2. **Determine a date when your media list will be in place.**

3. **Determine a date to decide what your first story is.**

   Ask yourself (or others), "What is the good news about our company?" Develop your "hook." Think like a journalist. And do it by a specific date — or you may never get around to it!

4. **Decide when you'll do the first mailing.**

   Pick a date a couple of months out for your first mailing unless an urgent event or breaking news story forces you to rush it. By that date, mail your first press release to your media list.

5. **Schedule people and time for follow-ups.**

   This step is of the utmost importance. Over the couple of weeks following your mailing, make sure that someone from your company personally contacts each reporter on the list with a phone call pitching the press release that has been sent.

This plan is a simple one, involving only those activities that I show you how to do earlier in this chapter. Five simple steps. Do them, and you're in the publicity business.

Utilizing a media contact sheet

Although your media list is most likely in a database form so that you can merge letters and print labels, a media contact sheet placed with a printout of your list in a media binder is a valuable tool for your ongoing publicity program. Figure 14-1 shows what a media contact sheet looks like. You should make up a sheet like this one to suit the needs of your particular campaign.

Timing is everything

Timing is everything. One of the greatest benefits of working with professional publicists is that they really plan ahead. Sometimes up-and-coming publicists get everything right except the timing. But timing is crucial. If you run a gym and have a star bodybuilder coming to your gym on Saturday and you think that you're going to send a press release to the media that week, you've made a fatal error. Always give the media as much time as you can so they have time to put it on their work schedules, do the interviews, write the stories, submit them to their editors for placement, and react to the timing of the event.

Media Contact Sheet

Name of the Reporter:

_____

Name of the Newspaper:

_____

Name of the Column:

_____

Beat:

_____

Reporter's Address and Phone Number:

_____

What Has Been Sent:

_____

Summary of Last Conversation with Reporter:

_____

Figure 14-1:
Media
contact
sheet.

Talking it to the street

I hesitate to mention it, but there is another great way to get out there and generate some great visibility for yourself and your business without buying ads or even creating a media kit and press release. That is to simply be a public speaker at events that attract people who may become customers or may lead you to customers. When you speak at a local business club or group, a convention, or a conference, you're taking your content directly to interested people rather than relying on the media to distribute it for you.

And often, when you know you have a speaking event on the calendar, you can use it as a source of publicity by creating a press release and notifying an appropriate media list that you're making a presentation. Tell them what you'll be speaking about, why it's a new or important approach, and who the sponsor and audience are. Send out your press release a couple of weeks ahead of the event, but not too far ahead, otherwise the media will forget about it by the time it occurs.

Whenever possible, the best policy is to make sure that the media receives your press releases as soon as you can possibly get the information on paper. Remember that you're asking for free space, and the reporter may not have any room at the last minute. Yesterday may have been a slow news day, and the reporter didn't know what to do. If you had gotten your release to him a day earlier, he may have been grateful to have it. Likewise, if you're pitching to weekly or monthly papers, such as industry trade magazines, and if you want to pitch that a famous bodybuilder will be at your gym next month, you better allow the media time to fit it in with their publication schedules — which means you need to be weeks or even months ahead of the event.

Don't worry about sending out your press release too soon because you can always call again and/or send a reminder newsflash as the event date nears. Early releases make doing a more aggressive campaign on your part possible. What I mean by an "aggressive campaign" is that you can follow up with a phone call, a reminder news flash, and perhaps even a last-minute e-mail reminder.

On the CD

Check out the following files on the CD-ROM:

✔ Century Furniture's New Product Announcement Press Release (CD1401)

✔ APEX Performance Systems' New Process Press Release (CD1402)

Part V
Sales and Service Success

The 5th Wave   By Rich Tennant

"Answer the following survey questions about our company's performance with either, 'Excellent', 'Good', 'Fair', or 'I'm Really Incapable of Appreciating Someone Else's Hard Work'."

In this part . . .

*I*t all comes down to sales in the end. Are they up or down? Did you land the new account or not? Did the customer reorder or switch to a competitor? Did the leads from the trade show convert to sales or just end up wasting your time? The answers to these vital questions are often written in the details of how you select, approach, and interact with your prospects. Even the best marketing programs too often founder on the shoals of sales errors and mistakes.

In this part, I share techniques and processes for managing customer interactions and for closing important sales. I also show you how managing your attitudes can and does drive sales success — or lack thereof. Finally, I help you integrate great customer service into your sales and marketing success, because whenever you have an opportunity to serve a customer, you have a hidden opportunity to make the next sale too, and the next, and the next. . . .

Chapter 15

Mastering the Sales Process

*T*he point of marketing is to generate sales. The point of sales is to generate sales. In spite of their differing perspectives, the two fields are aligned in their purpose and often in their practices. Yet each offers a fascinating and unique set of strategies and techniques. Combine these strategies into an integrated approach, and you have a pragmatic, action-oriented set of tools for finding good prospects, converting them to customers, and retaining and growing these customers.

You can generate sales in many ways. With the new options on the Internet, some businesses conduct their sales and marketing without using any of the traditional means. No salespeople. No mailings. No ads. No stores. No service personnel. No brochures. Everything is virtual.

Other businesses emphasize direct mail and use a toll-free number to make sales. Still others advertise their products to consumers and let retailers or distributors worry about getting products out where people can actually see and buy them. The options are endless — only your imagination limits your choices in marketing!

But at its heart, marketing must come down to sales. This chapter looks at how the sales process works and how to maximize its effectiveness in your business.

Walking through the Sales Process

Every expert has a different model of the sales process. Some models are simple. Many are highly elaborate. And, to be honest, few of them really give you much help in improving your sales success because they're rarely realistic or prescriptive. I favor a model that reflects the reality that you need to do some work to figure out what the prospect needs and you present your offerings to meet that need. I also favor a model that suggests what to do and how and when to do it to optimize your sales efficiency. Sometimes, for example, you may have to abandon a sales call and go on another — something few sales models or trainings are willing to promote. The following is the sales process model I generally prefer when I train salespeople or work on the sales and marketing process for consulting clients:

✔ **Step 1: Contact.** This first step involves identifying prospects through lead-generation systems, cold calls, referrals, and any other methods you can think of to recruit potential buyers. As the name of this step implies, the point is to create the context for prolonged contact with prospects so that you can attempt to make the sale. Speak or write (via e-mail or fax) to prospects and ask for a chance to see them. Set up appointments or find a way to drop by and catch them at an available moment. Plan and make that vital contact that opens the door to the sales process.

✔ **Step 2: Need discovery.** This step focuses on gaining a sufficient understanding of the prospect and his situation to be able to propose a purchase that makes sense for him. Use brief interactions or the beginning of a longer sales meeting to ask confirming and exploring questions in order to learn more about the prospect's requirements. The knowledge and insight you gain in this phase helps you present a proposal that's customized to his needs.

✔ **Step 3: Proposal(s).** In this step, present your offerings to your prospect — show what you have to sell. But because you've done some discovery in the previous step, you adapt your presentation to the needs and wants of the prospect. You may describe certain services or products and not others. You may emphasize price to one prospect, quality to another, and speed to a third. And where possible, show specifically how your products and/or services can help the prospect overcome constraints and achieve his goals.

✔ **Step 4: Attempted closes.** In this step, you ask the prospect for business. You initiate the process of making an actual sale and see how he reacts. If the prospect is reluctant, you can cycle back to Step 3 or even to Step 2, based on your judgment of the situation. Then, make another attempt to close the deal later on.

In general, I suggest trying at least three times to close before you conclude that the prospect is truly unwilling to make a purchase at the moment. After that, you need to do a reality check to make sure you have an appropriate prospect. If attempts to close go poorly, you may decide that this is the wrong prospect for you. Maybe he just isn't ready to buy yet, or maybe he wants to but can't afford to. If you discover a problem that prevents the sale from going through, back off gracefully and quickly look for another prospect. No use wasting time on improbabilities when the world is full of new possibilities waiting for you to discover.

✔ **Step 5: Follow-up.** In this step, you contact the prospect after the sales meeting to thank him for his time (and for the order, if you closed), to reinforce any key points, and to prepare the prospect for the next contact. If your attempts to close failed, explore the reasons why and seek a future opportunity to re-contact him and initiate another sales effort. If the close succeeded, confirm the purchase and prepare the prospect for the next step.

✔ **Step 6: Service.** In this step, you build upon the initial sale. You seek future sales, and you continue to explore needs and propose solutions in an ongoing effort to form a consultative selling partnership with the prospect. Excellent customer service and follow-through on all promises are vital now. You may need to monitor the service and keep up good relations for a long time after the initial sales meeting ends.

Figure 15-1 illustrates this sales process, showing several options for moving through it depending on how the prospect reacts. The sales process may not flow smoothly from step to step. Sometimes you need to revisit earlier steps. Other times you need to abandon all hope and write off the prospect, moving onto another prospect and sales attempt, at least for the time being. (Lost causes sap your time and enthusiasm, so please avoid them!)

The sales process flowchart in Figure 15-1 contains considerable insight about when and how to make the sale. I use it in my training business to improve the performance of salespeople in a wide variety of businesses and industries, so it makes a good framework for the next few sections of this chapter.

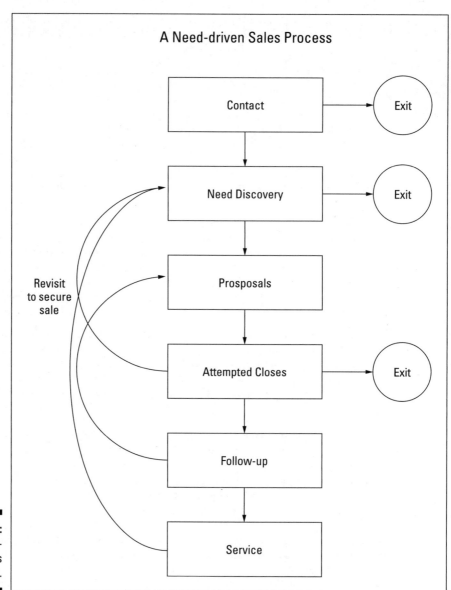

A Need-driven Sales Process

Figure 15-1:
A need-driven sales
process.

Getting the Most out of Your Contacts

You need to identify and then establish contact with any prospect before you can hope to make a sale to her. In this section, I present a few of the strategies you may use to reach out and identify prospects and cue them up for a sales contact. I also present ideas on how to make the most of your call centers. Finally, I explain the importance of need-discovery techniques in building a successful relationship with your contact.

Gaining contacts

Throughout this book, methods for gaining contacts are illustrated over and over, as are details about how to implement many of these methods. Here are some of the ways of generating *leads* (names and contact information of likely prospects):

- ✔ Attend or display at a trade show, convention, or other event that attracts prospects. Make sure that you find ways to interact with prospects and collect information about them for later follow-ups. Although many trade shows have had reduced numbers in the past several years, the numbers are picking up again. And one thing is for sure, if you don't attend, you're surely invisible to potential clients.

- ✔ Buy mailing lists from list compilers, brokers, membership organizations, or subscription-based publications. Send letters, postcards, fliers, or other mail solicitations inviting prospects to return something by mail, visit your Web site, or call if they're interested in more information. Use telephone sales or personal sales calls to follow up with the ones who respond.

- ✔ Buy e-mail or fax lists (until these options are regulated out of existence) and use them just as you would a mailing list (see the preceding paragraph).

- ✔ Network with friends and customers to find new prospects.

- ✔ Speak at industry or community events to let people know the work you do and to share your expertise. Collect leads after the event.

- ✔ Run a small display ad in an appropriate magazine or newspaper and include your telephone number, Web site, and/or address. Use the ad to generate inquiries from interested prospects.

- ✔ Develop a telephone sales script and have an employee, temp worker, or telemarketing firm (for larger lists) make calls to generate leads or to try closing some sales for you.

- ✔ Send an e-mail newsletter to interested prospects, sharing useful information and positioning yourself or your business as a source of expertise. In the newsletter, include marketing messages designed to bring prospects your way, either by phone or through a supporting Web site.

Utilizing your call center

Many businesses list a toll-free number in directories, marketing materials, and ads, and then wait by the phone for calls. When calls come in, they're typically from prospects expecting to talk to someone who may be able to help them make a purchase. So the salesperson answering the phone is in an enviable position She simply needs to help callers figure out what they need and then write up the orders.

But is it that simple?

If you have non-salespeople answering the phones and taking orders, you're missing a great chance to do some selling. Anyone who responds to a marketing communication and makes the effort to call you is a serious prospect and deserves serious sales attention. Whoever handles that call needs to be knowledgeable and skilled in soft-sell sales methods because, in addition to simply writing up the prospect's order, the salesperson can conceivably pursue a number of other marketing objectives, such as:

- Gather useful information about the caller for your database (and for use in future marketing initiatives aimed at the caller)

- Cross-sell other products/services to the caller

- Help the caller make a tough decision

- Diagnose the caller's situation and suggest solutions (involving your products/services if possible, of course!)

- Project a positive, helpful, interested image for your business that will bring the prospect back again and stimulate positive word of mouth

- Handle any complaints or concerns with sensitivity, recovering the caller and preventing him from hanging up with a negative feeling toward your business

- Gather useful suggestions and ideas from the caller for use in refining the marketing program, product offerings, or other elements of your business process

I think these are valuable objectives that you shouldn't ignore. Yet many businesses put people to work at their reception phone or call center without giving them enough training and support to pursue such objectives. In fact, few operators or telephone salespeople are ever given a list to think about. They don't even know they should aim for these objectives, let alone know how to achieve them!

Exploring need-discovery techniques

The better you understand customers' needs and how they prefer fulfilling those needs, the better you can position yourself and your products or services to get a good sale. Large-company marketing programs use extensive marketing research to explore customer needs. In smaller organizations, individual one-on-one discussions with customers and occasional do-it-yourself surveys can work just as well. In all organizations in which individuals interact face to face with prospects and customers, you can gather a great deal of information using need-discovery techniques.

Need-discovery techniques were developed for use in consultative selling, where the salesperson acts as a problem solver for the customer and tries to become part of the customer's business team. Like a business consultant, the salesperson uses a combination of research and exploratory questions (see "Asking exploring questions" later in this section for a definition) to diagnose the client's situation. This need-discovery process puts the salesperson in a position to generate and propose helpful solutions to the customer's problems. Often, those solutions involve the products and services of the salesperson's business.

Over time, the customer comes to trust and rely on the consultative salesperson. The customer shares more details so that the salesperson can discover more needs and offer more solutions. The result of this process is a collaborative business partnership that is beneficial to both parties. Because collaboration provides many intangible benefits, consultative selling often shifts the focus away from price.

Customers value businesses that emphasize consultative selling for their superior service, flexibility, and willingness to help the customer succeed. The customer who enjoys such benefits isn't as quick to give the business to some new competitor just because the competitor offers a minor price reduction or other incentive.

The following sections look closely at some simple but powerful conversational techniques that help you uncover customer needs and concerns.

Planning your questions

Start by reviewing what you know about your prospects. What are their needs? What are their constraints? What sorts of changes or trends in the news may be affecting them? If you're planning to call on a business, seek out information about the business on the Web and in the local newspapers. In addition, review the business's marketing communications and talk to others who work for or do business with the prospect.

From these inquiries, you should find yourself asking questions and generating hypotheses about the prospect. You should be able to come up with some theories about the prospect's needs. If you have trouble clarifying your thoughts about the prospect, fill in the form shown in Figure 15-2 (a template of this form is on the CD with the filename CD0201, so you can print a stack of them and keep them in your customer files).

Prospect Analysis Sheet

Prospect name	
Does prospect make purchase decision? (If not, who does?)	
Who else is involved in the decision?	
Past purchase history	
Known brand preferences	
Suspected priorities	
Any budget constraints?	
Any time constraints?	
Other constraints of relevance?	
What is their most important challenge or goal right now?	

Figure 15-2:
Prospect
analysis
sheet.

You may need ten minutes to fill in this form. If you're eager to see as many prospects as possible, you may be tempted to skip it. Why plan when you can just give a canned presentation and trust to luck? Because the planning phase greatly increases the chances of building a consultative relationship and securing a sale. Most salespeople find that ten minutes of planning is well invested and worthwhile.

Next, you need to preplan some questions for the prospect. Doing so takes another five minutes. Again, you may be tempted to skip this step, but the sales call will go much better if you prepare. To preplan your questions, review your Prospect Analysis Sheet and simply generate confirming or exploring questions.

Asking confirming questions

A *confirming question* is one that checks facts or checks your understanding or interpretation of the situation. You are wise to use confirming questions to check your assumptions and to update your Prospect Profile. You may be amazed how much of the information you think you know about prospects turns out not to be so!

Here are some examples of confirming questions:

- ✔ *I recall that you said you need to make a purchase decision by _____. Is that still the case?*
- ✔ *Is it true that Bob wants to stick with black-and-white labels for now?*
- ✔ *Are you definitely committed to buying only organic produce?*
- ✔ *Is this a good time to go into the details of what you need?*
- ✔ *Am I right that your top priority is service, followed by price?*

Asking exploring questions

Exploring questions probe to find out more about your prospect's situation. Use exploring questions to fill in missing facts, to seek reasons for preferences or unusual requests, and to seek to reveal more about the prospect's preferences and needs. When you ask exploring questions, you often discover something surprising and helpful about the prospect.

Here are some examples of typical exploring questions:

- ✔ *Why is it so important for your organization to get same-day deliveries?*
- ✔ *Are you the one who's in charge of the final purchase decision?*
- ✔ *Does the color have to match your office color scheme?*

> ✔ *Do you have any other problems that we may be able to help you with?*
>
> ✔ *Why do you do it that way?*
>
> ✔ *Why haven't you updated this equipment in recent years?*
>
> ✔ *What goals do you hope to accomplish this season?*
>
> ✔ *Are you experiencing any service problems or frustrations right now?*
>
> ✔ *Are you looking for ways to cut costs?*
>
> ✔ *Are you looking for better quality?*

Figure 15-3 shows a form you can use to preplan your questions.

Question Preplanning Form

Prospect: _____

Confirming Questions:	Exploring Questions:
1.	1.
2.	2.
3.	3.
4.	4.
5.	5.

Other comments or notes:

Figure 15-3:
Question
preplanning
form.

Now that you've done all this planning, you're bound to have some good insights and questions as you approach the prospect. Basically, the idea is to use your insights from the need-discovery stage to make your presentation interactive and consultative instead of just forcing your information down the prospect's throat.

Making the Presentation

The next goal of the sales process is to present your offer. Otherwise, you wouldn't have gone to the trouble of finding a prospect and setting up an opportunity for contact. You probably already know what you want to say then. Or do you?

Before you present your products or services to the prospect, ask yourself what you found out about the prospect during the need-discovery process. Then focus on how you can help meet your prospect's needs. The idea is to adapt your presentation to fit the specific needs and wants of each prospect. Be flexible. Emphasize different ideas. Offer different approaches or select different items to present.

If you've used the sales process and asked enough questions to understand the prospect's position, taking a flexible approach to presenting your offerings should feel natural. All you need to do is translate your extensive knowledge of the product or service into a clear, compelling presentation. You did say you were an expert in the ins and outs of your product, didn't you? If not, you'd better work on it.

Don't forget: *In the end, everything and anything you do or show is part of your presentation.* You need to have impeccable manners, clean and attractive clothing, a nice smile, and a firm handshake. You also need to have good, attractive reference materials about the product at your fingertips. The chapters on writing and designing good marketing materials come to bear here in the presentation phase of the sales process. Sometimes (like when you send a sales letter) you or another salesperson won't be in front of the prospect; so all the work presenting your offering and asking for business is left up to your marketing materials. Please make sure that you present yourself and your marketing materials in a highly effective manner.

Asking for the Business

You contacted the prospect, explored her needs, and presented your offerings as the most natural and appropriate solution. You think she likes you and your product or service, and you believe the timing is right. Now what?

You have to ask her to do business with you. You have to try closing the sale. Sure, some customers may volunteer their orders and make the sale easy for you. In retail stores, especially, you can easily fall into a passive role and wait for people to step up with a desired purchase. But this technique is always a mistake. You need to manage the close, whether subtly or overtly. And in my mind, nothing's as challenging and interesting in sales as the close. (That's why I cover closing in more detail in Chapter 16.)

Think about what you'll say to ask for the business. The best salespeople know the art of closing by finding a polite way to ask the prospect for the sale. Here are a few ways to ask for the business (see Chapter 16 for more options):

> ✔ *If I have answered all your questions, may I put together an agreement?*
>
> ✔ *Based on everything we've discussed, are you ready to go forward in our partnership?*
>
> ✔ *I'll call you in the morning between 9:00 a.m. and 9:15 a.m. to answer any remaining questions that you may think about tonight, and then I'll send over an agreement so we can go forward. Does that time work for you?*

In the right context, an assertive effort to close can get the prospect past the natural indecisiveness many people feel before making a purchase. Practice closes and make a note of any that seem to work well for you and your customers.

On the CD

Check out the following items on the CD-ROM:

> ✔ Prospect Analysis Sheet (CD1501)
>
> ✔ Question Preplanning Form (CD1502)

Chapter 16

How to Close the Sale

*Y*ou have your foot in the door. The prospect agreed to meet with you. You presented your products or services. You even answered some questions. The prospect seems interested, and you think you have something he needs. Now what? How do you turn that interest into immediate action? Can you actually secure an order before you leave?

To find out, you have to ask for the business by trying to close the deal. In fact, in many cases, you may have to try to close it more than once. Some salespeople say you can't accept a "No" until you've tried to close the deal at least three times. Others say you never accept a "No" when you sense an opportunity for a "Yes." I think the truth lies somewhere in between. I also think that if you make a careful study of closing techniques, you'll have to accept far fewer rejections because *how* you ask for the business often determines whether you get the business and how much business you get. In this chapter, I discuss some strategies for closing the deal.

Realizing That Closes Aren't Only for Salespeople

Few people realize that the challenges of personal selling and marketing are very much the same. Marketing simply sells from a distance. Its ultimate goal is to make the sale, just as in personal selling, so every marketing program needs to have some good closes built into it, whether salespeople deliver them or not.

Sometimes, at the point of purchase, your marketing program "asks for the business" by presenting a tempting product with a price tag, warranty information, usage instructions, shipping options, or other indications that you expect the prospect to purchase it. And sometimes, the marketing materials themselves must incorporate the close. Many calls, letters, faxes, and e-mails to prospects are nothing but long-distance sales calls. And less personal forms of marketing communication, like a direct-mail piece or catalog, also need to incorporate multiple efforts to close the deal.

Because every marketing program needs to include multiple efforts to close, you can often improve the effectiveness of marketing materials by using classic sales closing techniques in the materials rather than in a personal presentation. For instance, in a direct-mail letter or mailed catalog, you can incorporate a number of trial closes that say something like

> *You'll find that our order form is detachable in case you want to check off possible purchases on it as you read the catalog.*

> *If you are serious about solving your problems, you'll no doubt be making regular use of our service, which means you'll want to have our contact information handy. So why not get a head start by popping out the perforated Rolodex card on the bottom of this page and filing it under "O" for our name right now?*

By presenting hypothetical situations relating to future use of your product or service, such *trial closes* help move the reader toward a real close and a big fat order for your business. Trial closes can be incorporated into any and all marketing materials with a little imagination and some basic knowledge of the salesperson's catalog of closing techniques. (See the upcoming section "Mastering a Few Closing Techniques" for more information.)

Mastering a Few Closing Techniques

I've collected a variety of closing techniques from super salespeople who I've met and interviewed over the years and from the sales training programs of a variety of companies. Based on these various sources and the sales trainings that my firm, INSIGHTS, teaches in its workshops, I've compiled a master list of superior closes that you can try out in your own sales and marketing efforts. In this section, I discuss each of the items on this list.

The direct close

The *direct close* simply involves asking prospects to place an order or to sign a contract now. You generally want to ask for the business in a specific manner by saying what you'd like them to do, how much you'd like them to buy, or when you'd like them to start accepting deliveries. The direct close is the most basic technique, so I always start with it. If you're lucky, it works, and you don't have to try anything harder.

The idea behind the direct close is to propose a business relationship and see what the prospect says. He may just say, "Fine, let's get started. Can you draw up a contract?" or "Do you need a purchase order from me?" More often, he begins to negotiate the specifics of doing business, which is also a positive result because it means you're probably going to close the deal after a little haggling. For instance, the prospect may say, "Not so fast, my friend. I'd like to hire you, but we'll need to find a way to do this project for less money than what you suggested, and I need to have some guarantees of performance." Great! The direct-close approach has opened the door to a serious business discussion. If you negotiate in good faith, you should be able to walk away with a deal.

When you're selling products, the direct close should generally include the suggestion that the prospect purchases whatever amount of product is usual or appropriate. You can't expect a store buyer to commit to six months' inventory of your product. Asking her to put in a two-week supply may be just about right, if that's conventional in the category or industry in question.

If you're designing a brochure, catalog, or ad, make sure you incorporate direct-close requests. For example, include an order form or a message such as, "To place your order, call. . . ." On your Web site, ask for business by including a "Proceed to Checkout" prompt or having a section or tab labeled "To Place an Order" or "To Request a Quote."

Here are some examples of direct-close scripts:

- *Shall I write up an order for XYZ product now?*

- *Would an order for x amount be appropriate right now?*

- *It sounds like it might make sense for us to try working together. Would you be willing to sign a contract for, let's say x units, if I get one prepared for you and fax it over later today?*

- *I sent you a detailed proposal for the consulting work we discussed. Did you receive it? Okay, good. I'm calling to see whether you have any questions about it and if you want to move ahead with the project.*

- *Based on what you've told me, it sounds like you really could use the XYZ product right now. I can start processing your order tomorrow, if you want to give me a purchase order number for it before I go.*

Sometimes the direct-close technique just doesn't work. The prospect ducks the question, refusing to give you an immediate yes or no. Often, people avoid responding to a direct close by raising questions or objections that require your detailed response. Respond to their questions fully. Don't be put off by their unwillingness to close a deal. They aren't going to say yes until they're ready. Customers don't care if you're ready. Bide your time, keep the conversation going, if possible, and try another type of close in a few minutes or the next time they give you a chance to talk to them.

The trial close

The *trial close* is a good technique to use casually throughout a sales presentation or discussion as a way of seeing how close the prospect really is to buying. It does *not* directly ask for business, but it does test the waters by asking the prospect hypothetical questions.

To come up with appropriate hypothetical questions, ask yourself what the prospect would know or do if he were really going to order from you. Then ask him questions about those topics. If the prospect's answers are specific and thoughtful, the prospect is thinking the same way you are and may be ready for you to escalate to a real close by using the direct-close technique (discussed in the previous section).

For example, imagine you're selling leases on office equipment and you've just given an impressive presentation of a new copier that includes some desktop publishing features. To test the waters with a trial close, you may ask hypothetical questions such as, "If you lease this machine, would you get rid of one or more of your older machines?" or "Do you think this machine would permit you to do some things in-house that you currently have to pay to have done by graphic artists or printers?"

If the prospect answers these questions with ease, you know that she's thinking in a detailed manner about what leasing your equipment would be like. Your trial close tells you the time is right to work toward a real closing effort. You may go on to say something like, "Well, it sounds like you've thought this through pretty carefully already. Are you ready to sign a contract right now?"

Here are some sample trial close scripts:

- *If you start carrying our brand, will you drop another brand to make room for it?*
- *If you decide to use our delivery service, what sort of volume would we need to be able to handle for you on a weekly basis?*
- *If you decide to switch to us, when do you think would be a good time to make the transition?*
- *Do you have a date in mind for when this consulting project would start?*
- *Do you have a specific project in mind so we can develop a proposal for you?*
- *How much have you budgeted for this purchase, and what kind of payment schedule are you thinking of?*

You can also use trial closes in sales letters, Web sites, brochures, or other arms-length marketing communications. Incorporate questions such as, "Are you in need of specific supplies right now?" When prospects read these questions, some may be spurred to action.

Your attempt at a trial close may not generate the response you hoped for. If that happens, no harm been done. The prospect who answers a trial-close question with an "I don't know" or "I haven't really had time to think about it" isn't ready for a close yet. Go back to probing for insights into his needs and wants and to communicating information about your offerings. Then try another trial close later on. Sometimes you have to try three or four times before you get a positive response. Using trial closes often is okay, as long as you read the body language and verbal responses of your prospect and avoid irritating him.

The wrap-up close

The *wrap-up close,* also called the *summary close* or the *scripted close* by some salespeople, signals to the prospects that the time has come to make a decision. This technique works especially well if you've given some kind of presentation or reviewed information about your offering and their needs and wants.

You perform the wrap-up close by summarizing the main points of the meeting or presentation. Try to recap not only the main points you made, but also the points that the prospect made. In many cases, you can ask the prospect to clarify any information you didn't understand or to ask you any final questions. When you sense that the wrap-up is close to completion, you can naturally move on to the question of whether and how much the prospect wants to buy. Your closing technique at the end of the wrap-up should generally involve a direct close.

Here are some sample wrap-up close scripts:

- ✔ *If I may just take a minute to summarize the main concerns I think you've raised . . .*

- ✔ *To wrap up my presentation, I'd like to reiterate our commitment to meeting or exceeding all your specifications. Specifically, we can . . . and . . . and . . .*

- ✔ *I appreciate all the time you've made for me today, but I'm sure you have other appointments, too. Would this be a good time to wrap up our discussion and see where we stand?*

- ✔ *Well, I think I'm beginning to get a clear picture of what you're looking for. As I understand it, you need . . . Does that sound about right?*

In a wrap-up close, use language signaling that you've reached a natural ending point and that you're ready to move on to the next stage. Also, use body language to signal that you're attempting to wrap up the proceedings. For instance, if you're sitting, sit up straight, put your hands on your knees, and look the prospect in the eye. These body movements traditionally signal an intention to stand up and leave in many cultures, so they help set the stage for a wrap-up.

If you're standing during the presentation, move away from the podium or screen (if there is one), and toward the prospects. Face the decision maker (the prospect with the most seniority or power) directly, as you deliver your wrap-up close. Then pause and let him have an opportunity to reply with a question or with a decision to order.

If you're communicating in a brochure or letter, use a heading, such as "In Conclusion" or "Now It's Your Turn," to signal the start of a wrap-up close. On a Web site, use a summary of the order or a check-the-numbers form that allows the prospect to see what an order would cost — with an option of converting the data into a real order.

The process close

If you use a *process close*, also called an *action close*, a *contract close*, or an *order-form close*, you simply start a closing process and see how far into it the prospect will go. I recommend this technique when it seems reasonably certain that the prospect intends to order. For example, the process close usually works when writing a reorder. The process close is also appropriate when a new prospect asks for an appointment or otherwise indicates interest in making a purchase.

To make a process close work, you need to have a multi-step purchase process in which the prospect is likely to go along with the first few steps. For example, you may start prospects off by completing a spec sheet with them. Or you may enter them into your database of national accounts so they qualify for a discount. After you get them to take an initial step, move on to the next step of the close. That step may be to write down detailed information about their order or project and then read it back to them as if you were checking a formal order.

Here are some sample process close scripts:

✔ *Okay, let's get started on this order form. Do you use the same billing and shipping addresses?*

✔ *To qualify for credit terms, we need to make sure that your company is in our customer database. Can I go through what we've got in the computer right now and make sure that it's complete?*

> ✔ *Assuming you do end up making this purchase, we'll need to have a completed order form. I can get that process started now. What kind of quantities are you thinking about?*
>
> ✔ *The next step is usually for us to prepare a detailed proposal. To do that, I need to clarify a few points. Can we go over those now so I can send you a proposal in the next day or two?*

In some businesses, the deal closes when money changes hands. In others, the deal closes when prospects sign a contract or initial an order form. Whatever that last step is for you, your process close should move you and the buyer inexorably nearer to it. And the nearer you get, the more committed the buyer must be to stick with your process. The process usually ends with a direct request to "sign the order form," "provide your credit card number," or otherwise to complete the process and formalize the sale.

In addition to securing business quite quickly, the process close also weeds out prospects who are just shopping around and aren't ready to close the deal. These prospects will get more and more resistant and uncomfortable as you try to move them through the process. They may bail out by saying something like, "I'm just not ready to sign anything right now" or "I don't think we need to go into all this right now." If they don't appear ready to close, keep them alive as prospects, continue trying to find out more about their needs and wants, tell them more about your offerings, and then try a different close next time.

Weeding out the unwilling

In most businesses where I've worked with salespeople, I've found that they spend a lot of their time (15 to 50 percent, depending on the industry) talking with prospects who seem interested but who drag their heels and then don't make a purchase. Shopping is a lot easier than buying, so I'm not surprised that a lot of apparently interested prospects end up dropping out before the purchase stage of the sales process. But they sure do waste your time! What can you do to reclaim some of this wasted time?

Don't be afraid to ask for the business. Try to close as soon as possible. If the prospect balks, work with her a little more and then try again. After a few tries, you'll have a better idea of how serious she is. If she's just shopping around, she'll pull back as soon as you begin talking about closing a deal, and she'll continue backing off when you probe for objections and try to close again. Your testing of her indicates that she just isn't ready to buy right now. You can ask her whether she's ready. If she's not, thank her for her interest, explain that you're ready to talk later if she decides she wants to buy, and then get the heck out of there. A new prospect awaits, so don't waste time on one who won't close.

If walking away from a potential sale sounds counter-intuitive to you, think about it this way: While you're trying to convince someone to buy who doesn't really want to, can't afford it, or is just fishing for free information, your competitor is probably with a customer who needs what you have and is ready to buy.

The analytical close

The *analytical close* is a guided decision-making process in which you help the prospect compare options and weigh alternatives. You can frame the analysis however you think best fits the situation. Sometimes the key question in the prospect's mind is whether or not to buy. Other times, the question is which of the competing alternatives should the prospect try. More rarely, the prospect may be wrestling over which of your offerings to purchase or how much to buy. The analytical close helps the prospect think through his decision, because until he assesses the decision from all angles, he won't be ready to close.

The analytical close works well for fairly complicated purchase decisions, especially when the prospects are careful, thoughtful, and highly involved in the purchase decision. Use the analytical close when selling an expensive new car to someone who's shopping around to compare models. Use it when someone's deciding what sort of new camera to buy or which insurance policy makes the most sense. Also use it in many business-to-business sales situations, because when people make purchases on behalf of their businesses, they generally take a fairly analytical approach.

Here are some sample analytical close scripts:

✔ *It sounds like you're having a little bit of trouble thinking this decision through in all its complexity. Why don't we analyze your options and see what really makes the most sense?*

✔ *We've explored quite a few different issues as we discussed the idea of a possible purchase. In fact, I'm feeling a little confused by all the details. Would you mind if I did a simple pro/con analysis of the decision you're facing right now so that I can see the issues more clearly?*

✔ *I gather you're seriously considering several alternatives right now. I'd like to help you analyze each of these alternatives, because it will help me see whether my offering makes sense. And it should help you make a better decision, too. Do you mind if we spend a few minutes thinking each of these options through to see how they'd affect you in the long run?*

Presenting the pros and cons

Perhaps the easiest way to conduct an analytical close is to help someone think through the options and reach a comfortable decision by presenting the pros and cons of each alternative. You can present verbally or on paper, depending on the physical environment and the prospect's openness to various alternatives.

To present the pros and cons of making a purchase right now, you can divide a sheet of paper or flip chart into two columns. Label the left column "Pros" and the right column "Cons." But don't feel like you have to complete the table in that order. You don't want to end your analysis with the cons of the purchase. So start by skipping over the pros column and asking the prospect to help you identify cons — anything that he may think is negative about the purchase. For example, you may suggest that the purchase will, of course, cost some money. Then go on to the pros side, listing as many good qualities about the purchase as you can. Frame the qualities in terms of their effect on the buyer. Keep the list personal and specific. You'll find that the pros column naturally grows considerably longer than the cons column because you can more easily list benefits of a purchase than negative consequences.

When you finish the analysis, you can ask the prospect how it balances out in his mind. Say something like, "So, what do you think? Do the benefits outweigh the costs in your eyes?" Hopefully, your offer is good enough and is targeted to someone who really would benefit from it so that the analysis clearly favors a decision to purchase. But if not, don't give up. Just keep the lines of communication open and try another close later on.

Offering multiple scenarios

Another way to approach the analytical close is to offer multiple scenarios and work out in some detail how each impacts the prospect. One scenario may be for the prospect to do nothing right now. Another may be for him to purchase from some alternative vendor that the prospect is obviously considering. And, of course, you have to include at least one alternative in which the prospect buys from you. Then you try to engage him as you analyze each of his alternatives. Your goal is to show the prospect what happens over time and how each scenario affects him. Hopefully, the prospect finds the scenario you construct around the purchase of your product or service most appealing, and your analysis helps him make the decision to buy.

Printed marketing materials also lend themselves to analytical closes. Use tables, charts, diagrams, or statistics to prove the value of your offering.

The sales promotion close

The *sales promotion close* uses an incentive to encourage prospects to take immediate action. The incentive may be a special discount offer that expires soon, an offer to bundle additional products or services into the sale, or any promotion you can dream up, as long as it's likely to interest the prospect and not wipe out your entire profit margin.

Giving new customers a gift is often a great device for securing an immediate close. *Sports Illustrated* has used this technique for many years. It buys large numbers of inexpensive but reasonably nice gifts — a bag with its logo, a portable radio, and so on — and offers to send you a gift for free if you subscribe by a certain deadline.

Gifts can work especially well for business-to-business sales, where the margins are often large enough that you can afford something nice. But remember not to make the gift overly expensive, otherwise you're entering the realm of bribery. A good rule is that you don't want to offer buyers any gift so lavish that they'd be embarrassed to openly display it in their office or home. And remember that some companies restrict employees from accepting any personal gift (to avoid the risk of bribery), so your offer has to be for the benefit of the company, not the individual employee.

If you're uncomfortable with personal gifts when selling to businesses, consider making a modest donation in the individual's name to a charity of his choice. You can call it your "Sales for Society Program" or whatever you like. The prospect may find it quite exciting to select a charity and fill out a donor form (have some nice cards made up for this purpose). This novel inducement feels good, not only because it does some good for society, but also because it helps you accomplish your goal of getting the prospect in the right frame of mind to close the deal now rather than next week.

I used to prefer direct closes because I believe my firm's products and services are good and "speak for themselves." But in the last few years, I've come around to favoring sales promotion closes, and our response rates on mailings, sales calls, and our Web sites have gone up. When my firm sends out a catalog or letter, it often includes a special deal, such as a deep discount or a free sample, if the prospect places an order within the month. And our Web site often features a giveaway, such as a free copy of a book, as an incentive to place an order right away. I like the sales promotion close because it encourages prospects to get serious about their purchase decisions, instead of procrastinating. Many people mean to make a purchase selection but are too busy or lazy to decide right away. A good sales promotion close can get these prospects to take action.

Something Stinks! Passing the Prospect's Smell Test

No matter what you sell, and no matter when, where, or how customers buy your product, you risk losing customers at the last moment unless everything you do seems professional and appropriate. All customers use what I call the "smell test" when they buy — although they often use it quite unconsciously.

When did a person, product, or business last flunk your smell test? Here's a recent example from my own shopping experience: I was all set to hire a company I'd done business with before to do a major upgrading on the heating and air conditioning systems in a building I'd bought and was planning to move my office into. But when the company sent a junior person out to give me a quote and he didn't seem to know enough to answer my questions, I got nervous and delayed the project so I could get competing quotes from other vendors. In the end, I hired another firm that sent a senior person out and prepared a more professional quote.

I bet you can think of plenty of similar experiences. Do you want to buy a product from the grocery store if the package looks dirty or dented? Do you want to do business at a bank where the tellers are sloppily dressed and seem disorganized or confused? Of course not!

At the last moment before purchase, even a small problem can spook your buyers and cause them to hesitate and look for alternatives. So make sure your presentation is professional — all the way through the close. Don't let any minor problems derail a good sale. Dress well. Spell check your proposals, e-mails, and letters. Spell the prospect's name and company correctly. (Yes, misspellings are one of the most common errors salespeople make, and they can lose you the sale.) And (in personal selling), avoid body odor, overly strong colognes or perfumes, and bad breath; it's amazing how sensitive some people are to these smells, so avoid flunking their literal smell tests, too. Professionalism is ten times as important at the close as at any other time during a sale, so give the close ten times as much care and attention.

On the CD

Check out the following item on the CD-ROM:

- ✔ Closing Scripts (CD1601)

Chapter 17

The Sales Success Workshop

*W*hat are the secrets of superior performance in selling? Three things:

- ✔ Quality leads
- ✔ A good impression
- ✔ A positive attitude toward success and failure

Improving the Flow of High-Quality Leads

Who's the best lead? When you ask yourself this question, you're on the road to figuring out what sort of leads you want most, which in turn should help you generate those leads. After all, you can more easily find something when you know what you're looking for! When many people ask themselves what kind of leads they want most, the answer sounds something like

> *I want leads who are actively considering a purchase and who want to talk to me to find out more about my offerings.*

Leads who are ready to explore purchase options and approach you for information are ideal. You know the timing is right. They want to hear your information. And if they approach you instead of the other way around, the situation is much more efficient and easier for you! So how do you generate these ideal leads?

Beefing up your marketing program

To generate great leads, make sure that you have an active, multi-faceted marketing program working to bring you good leads. Here are some ways to bring in good leads, which you should consider doing if you don't already.

- ✔ **Obtain and publicize a toll-free telephone number with someone polite, friendly, knowledgeable, and always available to answer it.** More leads come in over toll-free phone lines than from any other source, according to most studies.

- ✔ **Make your Web site work for you.** For most businesses, the Web is the second-biggest source of leads after the phone. Give your site lots of appeal and rich information for comparison shoppers to use. Make sure your Web site includes multiple ways to contact you — from e-mail, to phone, to chat-room options and e-commerce purchasing capabilities, if appropriate for your business.

- ✔ **Advertise in magazines and use their reader-service card options (postcards included in many magazines for requesting more information from advertisers).** This technique works well for many business-to-business marketers.

- ✔ **Advertise an offer for a free catalog.** You can choose to advertise in print, on the Web, or in postcards or letters sent to mailing lists. If you want to increase the response rate a bit, add a one-time discount or deal that readers can redeem if they order from the catalog. Or just mail out your catalog or a brochure version of it (a smaller highlights catalog is good for testing new lists inexpensively).

- ✔ **Offer free, trial-size samples (or the service equivalent) in ads, e-mails, or letters.** Often, people come forward and identify themselves as good leads when you give them a chance to try something for free. Car dealerships utilize this technique by offering test drives — a great way to attract interested leads.

At my corporate training business, we use this technique by sending out letters to our past customers, offering them a free copy of our newest publication. Those who take us up on the offer often turn into regular buyers within the next six months.

In many businesses, a toll-free telephone number is the best way to bring in leads. Even in the modern Internet era, more prospects prefer talking to someone by phone than contacting someone in any other way. So make sure that you publicize your phone number widely by including it in and on every communication you send out — from ads to bills. And please make sure that you have well-trained, polite people (not machines!) ready to answer those calls. Give them a good form or a computerized database to record information about each caller, and train them in how to use it.

I recently called my local Taylor Rental, and even though I hadn't been in the store for a couple of years, the employee who took my call quickly sourced my records using my phone number and was ready to do business without my having to spell my name five times for him. The telephone should be a cornerstone of your sales and marketing program!

Getting creative when you still need more

If you aren't getting enough high-quality leads, the following fixes often help:

- ✔ Offer free samples or consultations in exchange for contact information at your industry's regional or national trade shows.

- ✔ Put a special offer on your Web site, such as a free month of service or a free special product, for the customer who purchases or makes an appointment with a salesperson within the month.

- ✔ Mail, call, or e-mail the people on your customer list from the past three years to ask whether they need anything else and to let them know about all the products you sell. (They may not realize that you can provide additional products and services beyond what they already purchased.)

- ✔ Run a direct-response ad in an appropriate magazine or newspaper (see Chapters 6 and 9 for design tips).

- ✔ Buy a list of 1,000 names of people who fit the profile of your better customers (for example, people who own homes with gardens in high-income counties or managers of businesses with 50 or more employees). Send an introductory letter inviting them to find out more about your products or services by setting up an appointment, visiting your Web site, or calling for more information. Follow the mailing with a telephone call to see if you can set up an appointment.

- ✔ Send out a press release and generate positive publicity about an interesting product or service you offer. Sometimes media coverage produces a flood of leads (find out how in Chapter 14).

Computer programmers invented the saying, "Garbage in, garbage out," but in sales, this statement applies in spades. Make sure that your leads are high quality. If you don't have enough leads to chuck the poor ones and solely focus on eager-to-buy prospects, then work on your lead-generation methods until you do. Everything else in the field of marketing can and should work to support sales by producing a rich flow of leads!

One of the most-productive activities salespeople and sales managers do in my workshops is to reverse engineer (study and map out) the lead-generation systems and methods of their top competitors. I ask them if they're generating leads as well or better than their competitors. If they answer "no," I instruct them to go back to the drawing board. Good leads are the first secret of sales success.

Using Sales Collateral to Help Win 'Em Over

One secret of superior selling performance is to make a good impression. You can impress your customer by using *sales collateral* — an umbrella term that covers anything designed and supplied to help salespeople achieve success. I'm using a broad definition because I want you to turn your marketing imagination loose and see whether you can come up with better sales collateral.

Sticking with good collateral

Make a dream list of everything you may need throughout the sales process. Good support ensures success! Here are some ideas to get you started:

- ✔ **Impressive stationery and fax forms:** Order your company's paper in multiple sizes for advance letters and other correspondence.

- ✔ **Matching business cards, preferably with information about the company/product and all the correct contact options:** Consider special paper, unusual designs, or even oversized or fold-out cards. If they're noticeably special and interesting, they'll generate calls.

- ✔ **Clear, appealing specification sheets:** Your spec sheets need to describe the facts of each and every product or service accurately so that all your prospects' possible factual questions are answered.

- ✔ **Samples, demos, and/or catalogs:** These marketing materials make showing and telling your prospects about your products and services much easier.

- ✔ **Cases, stories, testimonials, and other evidence from happy customers:** Only a few percent of salespeople have any collateral of this type. Yet, it's the most powerful form of sales collateral! See Chapter 5 for more details and examples.

- ✔ **Attractive, valuable, premium items:** Such premium items include a pen, mug, cap, or box of candies, marked subtly with your company's name and contact information. Prospects appreciate these leave-behinds when they're good quality. These tokens remind prospects that your company exists and that you value their business. Your leave-behinds don't need to be expensive, but prospects should see them as valuable enough to keep.

Avoiding bad collateral

Don't use collateral that hurts sales. Any materials, such as brochures or product literature, that don't look professional and appealing hurt sales. The sales collateral is a vital part of the "packaging" of the salesperson. If the sales collateral doesn't look really good, the salesperson looks bad. The effects of poor collateral on the prospect are subtle and often unconscious, but they're *extremely* powerful. So make sure everything your salespeople carry and/or distribute is polished and impressive. Sales collateral is a very good place to spend your design and printing budget!

In choosing your sales collateral, avoid

- **Plastic:** Cheap plastic folders, clear plastic page protectors, or big, ugly plastic sample cases all say tacky and cheap to prospects. Use high-quality papers and favor cloth or leather cases and bindings, if at all possible.

- **Amateur designs and layouts:** Sure, anyone can design sales and marketing materials in this era of high-quality laser printers, but most people shouldn't. Amateurs often create poor-looking, confusing layouts. Their work just doesn't have that special look that characterizes fine design — and the better prospects notice.

- **Errors:** An amazing number of factual and spelling errors exist in sales collateral. Salespeople perpetually have to make corrections or explain errors in front of prospects, which is like saying, "Please use our business. Of course, we can't even type a spec sheet accurately, but I'm sure we can muddle through your order somehow." Right.

- **Omissions:** Most salespeople go on calls without all the collateral materials and information they need to do a great job. They don't have a good brochure. Their business cards don't have the current address or the company's fax number and Web site. The price list is out of date. Their order form is a cheap pad bought at the local stationery store.

Perception is reality

What's the difference between a nice premium item and a cheap one? A box of truffles in gold foil, stamped with your company name and "We appreciate your business," is nice. A plastic mug stamped with your company logo, filled with hard candies, and wrapped in cellophane and a ribbon is tacky. The items probably cost the same, but customers perceive them quite differently. It makes sense to match the promotion gift to what you do; if your company fixes computers, offer a mouse pad or laser mouse with your name and emergency number. If you're a dentist, maybe offer a toothbrush with your name and phone on it. But whatever you choose, make sure customers think it's valuable, not tacky.

Overcoming Sales Setbacks

Consider this startling statistic: The best way to predict how much a salesperson will sell is to measure her, no — not I.Q., not product knowledge, not connections or experience, but yes — her *level of optimism*. Psychology has shown that how you manage your own attitude really does have a powerful effect on how you sell. It's not a myth; the link between attitude to performance is real and powerful, especially in sales, where the high amount of negative feedback can cause attitudes to easily deteriorate.

Sometimes people refuse your sales pitch. Sometimes they aren't ready, don't like the product, or just aren't in a good mood. In sales and marketing, rejections and failures always exist. How well do you handle them?

A good sales or marketing program is more efficient and suffers fewer wasted calls than a poor program. Although you can improve your success rates and reduce your rejection rates significantly, you can *never* achieve perfection. Marketing is not a precise science. In fact, finding yourself dealing with prospects that always say "yes" is a sign that you need to push your program a bit. Try asking more people or raising your prices. Unless some people say "no," you're not really stretching yourself. So, failures are a natural and important part of healthy sales and marketing.

The bounce-back factor

How successful you are has a great deal to do with how well you handle failures:

- ✔ If you bounce back from each rejection with an optimistic outlook, failure can't hold you back. You keep trying instead of giving up. In fact, you may even try harder.

- ✔ If you gain insight from each rejection, you can reduce the failure rate in the future and improve your odds of success over time.

Both points are closely related. Your ability to bounce back — to stay positive and motivated — has everything to do with how you explain each failure to yourself. If you maintain a positive attitude, attributing failures to appropriate, accurate causes that you can exercise some control over, then you will be resilient. Failures won't upset you or slow you down. In fact, they'll give you renewed energy because you discover something from each failure that should help you with the next try. So, listen to how you talk to yourself when you're trying to make a sale or grow a business. Normally, people don't attend carefully to their internal explanations, but to achieve higher-than-average success, you need to begin to manage normally unconscious or automatic self-talk.

To be a successful marketer or salesperson — or to be successful at achieving your goals in general — you need to take credit for success and avoid blaming yourself for failure.

Generalizing success

Attribute successes to aspects of your own personality, talents, and behavior. Giving yourself at least a share of the credit for each success builds the essential positive attitude needed to maintain motivation and build momentum. People who explain away their successes as simply good luck are encouraging a feeling of helplessness.

Generalizing from a success is helpful, too. Avoid narrow, meaningless ways of giving yourself credit. Don't say something demeaning to yourself like, "Oh, I guess I was responsible for closing that sale, but it was only because I happened to know that prospect personally." It's more productive to explain such a success as follows: "I closed that sale easily with an old acquaintance, which proves that I am able to present this product effectively. I should be able to close sales with other people, too." Generalizing from one accomplishment that you have an ability to achieve others is important as you build the attitudes needed to pursue success.

Getting specific about failure

Attributing failures to factors outside your own personality and abilities is very important. Many people question themselves when they receive a rejection or "no" answer. Instead, you should consider many other external factors that are within your control and are easy to adjust. These factors include the wrong list of prospects, the wrong closing technique, the wrong timing, the wrong way of presenting the product, or even the wrong product. When you look at specific, controllable factors, you can take a philosophical attitude toward failure.

Notice that when you blame specific, controllable factors for your failures, you avoid generalizations. You can easily make sweeping generalizations when you encounter a sales rejection or marketing failure. Big mistake. Big, big mistake. When you allow yourself to generalize about failures, you come to see them as unavoidable. The cards appear to be stacked against you, which discourages you from playing in the future. I've heard many managers and marketers say things like

> *We don't advertise. We tried it once or twice, and it just doesn't work for our business.*

> *We can't do direct mail. Our products don't have high enough prices to work, given the typical low response rates for mailings.*

> *Web sites are fine for communicating information about our business, but it doesn't work to try to close actual sales on the Web. We take a low-key approach to our site. It's really just an online brochure.*

I can't sell. I'm just no good at it. Believe me, I've tried! That's why I sub all our sales out to independent sales reps.

I recorded these actual direct quotes from otherwise intelligent, clear-thinking people I know in the business world. Each quote reflects a belief that prevents the speaker from ever trying something again. And each quote is a broad, absolute conclusion based on a very narrow set of unsuccessful experiences. For instance, the person who said, "We can't do direct mail," works for a business that can certainly profit from direct mail. I know that several of the company's direct competitors use mailings quite effectively. But the man's defeatist attitude, based on a few early failures, prevents his business from profiting in this arena. And the person who told me that the Web can't sell her services is creating a self-fulfilling prophecy by failing to develop a Web site good enough to support e-commerce.

So you can see that allowing yourself to make broad, pessimistic generalizations from failures is very dangerous. It narrows your view of the future and shortens your strategic horizons. It turns off your marketing imagination and drains you of motivation and self-confidence. How you think about and explain those failures has everything to do with whether you bounce back from them, wiser and more motivated than before, or whether you curl up in a ball and refuse to try again.

Retrained for success

Only the few people who instinctively take to sales or who have a natural flair for entrepreneurship truly have healthy, positive explanatory styles. That's bad news because my hunch is that you, like me, were not born with the positive attitude toward success and failure that you need to be a sales and marketing high achiever.

Now for the good news: You can easily change your style and adopt more positive approaches to success and failure. When you retrain those old, unhelpful mental habits, you find yourself coping with failures far more productively and positively. And you find that your new, healthier attitudes naturally lead to greater success in sales and marketing, as well as in life in general.

So how do you train yourself to ensure that you have the most helpful attitudes toward success and failure? Glad you asked:

- ✔ First, you need to develop a profile of your own attitudes by using the Attitudes of Success Profile I include on the CD (file CD1701).

- ✔ Second, you simply need to follow the instructions for interpreting your profile. Where your profile deviates from the profile associated with the highest levels of success in sales and marketing, you find pointers to simple, easy exercises and tips to help you shift your attitudes.

REAL WORLD

Top salespeople manage themselves well

If you know someone who's a master marketer or salesperson, I recommend taking him out for a cup of coffee and quizzing him on his approach. Often, you'll be surprised by what he tells you. Allow me to tell you about a certain acquaintance of mine.

John is affiliated with a big life insurance underwriter but is basically an entrepreneur and must take full responsibility for earning his own commission. As you may know, many people try their hand at this work, but only very few manage to turn it into a lucrative and successful career. John is very disciplined about his work and has managed to write an amazing number of insurance policies over the years, including several for my family and me.

Once, when he was visiting my office, I happened to look over his shoulder at his appointment book, and some funny little tick marks at the bottom of each day caught my eye. Obviously, John was keeping count of something on a daily basis. I asked him about the ticks, and he laughed and said, "Oh, those are just my tallies. I use a code so people won't bug me about it, but really, all I do is keep count of the number of prospects I phone each morning and the number of sales calls I actually go on in the course of the day. See, yesterday, for example, I made 12 prospecting calls, and I went on 5 sales visits."

I asked him why he kept those tallies, and he explained that he had found that the easiest way to get more business was simply to go on more sales calls, and the easiest way to do that was to make more phone calls each morning. The more people he called, the more meetings he was able to set up. So, by tracking the number of prospecting calls, he reminded himself of his goal of calling a certain number each

week. And by tracking the number of meetings, he could see the positive results of his efforts.

Then he laughed and explained that he had a story behind his system. Back in his early business days, he and another salesman had been complaining and saying that they wished they could double their income by making twice as many sales. John pointed out that all they needed to do was make twice as many sales calls, but sitting at the phone trying to set up appointments wasn't much fun, which is why they'd usually quit phoning and go out and start selling as soon as they had a few calls lined up. So John challenged his friend: They both agreed to keep an accurate tally of how many prospecting calls they made by phone each day. And they each agreed to pay the other man $500 at the end of the month if he didn't make twice as many calls as usual. John met his friend at the end of the month, and they both opened their books and counted up their phone calls. John had made his quota of calls, but his friend was just a tad under. So, the friend wrote a check for $500 on the spot.

You may think the story ends there, but not so. Even though he was $500 poorer, John's friend said he wanted to try the challenge again next month. Apparently, he had made enough extra calls that his income almost doubled, and the $500 loss was trivial compared to his gain. After several months of making twice as many calls and reaching their goals, the practice became a habit for both men. In fact, they never quit using this technique because they were both so pleased to find that they were bringing in twice as much revenue as before. And although John doesn't need the kicker of a contest any longer to make those calls, he still keeps up with his simple information system. It serves to remind him of his goal, and with it, he always makes his targets.

On the CD

Check out the following item included on the CD-ROM:

- ✔ Attitudes of Success Profile (CD1701)

Chapter 18

Dealing with Difficult Customers

In This Chapter

▶ Adapting to the customer's style

▶ Assessing style discrepancies between you and your difficult customers

▶ Determining the style of your marketing communications

The world is full of difficult customers. People who complain loudly and make unreasonable demands. People who walk away and take their business with them just because they don't think they can communicate with you. And people who are difficult to sell to because they're hard to get along with or don't seem to like you.

You can't eliminate the occasional crazy customers determined to make not only their own lives miserable, but also yours as well. These few worst cases should be cut from your customer list as soon as possible. But, with the right treatment on your part, the remaining 90 percent of so-called difficult customers can become some of your best and most loyal customers.

So what makes customers difficult? Sometimes a critical incident upsets or angers a customer or prospect and you need to deal with the situation carefully. Most problems, however, arise because of communication issues. So, the best overall strategy for dealing with difficult customers is to focus on how to better communicate with them.

In this chapter, I show you how to figure out which communication style works better than the one you're currently using. I give you a simple but powerful tool for diagnosing style-related communication problems that can help you figure out how to adapt your communication style so as to please the customer or prospect.

Flexing Your Style to Be Customer Oriented

Most organizations know that to be customer-oriented, they have to offer the products and services that customers need and want. By adapting their offerings to the customer's needs, organizations can focus on the *substance* of what the customer needs. But good salespeople know they must also focus on the *style* the customer prefers. They adapt their communication techniques because different customers have different interpersonal styles.

Experienced salespeople, service providers, and marketers already accept the fact that style is as important as substance. Yet they're still likely to encounter some customers who are difficult because of style conflicts. Style is often far harder to get right than substance because human personalities are subtle and difficult to diagnose. As a result

- ✔ The majority of salespeople sell to people who are most like them in terms of personality profiles and communication styles. They don't close many sales with people who have different interpersonal styles, which means they may run into problems with 50 to 60 percent of prospects.

- ✔ Even the most experienced and skilled salespeople encounter some customers with interpersonal style needs they can't meet, and therefore have trouble with 10 to 15 percent of customers.

- ✔ Top-performing salespeople are very good at flexing their interpersonal styles; therefore they encounter even fewer people whose style needs they cannot meet. They may have style problems with 1 to 5 percent of prospects and customers.

No matter where you, your associates, or your employees fall in this spectrum of experience and interpersonal skills, there is still some "business left on the table" that you're unable to obtain because you lack additional interpersonal skills. The purpose of this chapter is to give you the advanced skills you need to understand and adapt to any and all style needs. By focusing the activity on a specific relationship that you identify as troubling or difficult, you can make the results relevant and important in your daily working life.

Sorry, Sinatra, I did it their way . . .

Flexing your style means temporarily changing to the most comfortable style for the other person or, in other words, doing it their way.

In order to flex your style, you must make small changes in your behavior. The sorts of changes you need to make depend on the style differences between you and your customer. For example, if you're dealing with a very private person who may be put off by your more extroverted style, you need to

- ✔ Respect her preference for peace and quiet by giving her more privacy than you need.

- ✔ Ask for her permission to talk with her about her purchase decision instead of assuming she wants to talk about it.

- ✔ Schedule meetings and telephone conversations at her convenience, giving her control over when she talks with you.

- ✔ Use arm's-length channels of communication more fully. Write her notes and send e-mails and faxes. Prepare a written report to present your suggested solution to her problem rather than presenting it in person.

In general, your understanding of her need for privacy helps you make sure that she's comfortable around you. You give her more personal space, you're careful not to overstay your welcome, and you make a point of listening more and leaving more gaps in the conversation to let her think about what you've said. You can solve most of your communication problems just by realizing that her greater preference for privacy is at the root of these problems.

By flexing your own style, you — the public, extroverted salesperson — cool down your style significantly. The personal, introverted customer will feel more comfortable and at ease in future interactions. The customer is less likely to form a negative opinion of you and, in fact, probably will grow to like you. You seem more respectful and polite, and you appear to be a better listener who's more interested in and aware of her preferences and feelings.

Web communication with style

Even when people communicate over the Internet, they want custom treatment in order to feel like their communication needs are being met. But ever try to get help from company employees over the Internet? E-mailing them from their Web site is usually a disaster. Most companies send the same canned message to every query. And that message is rarely helpful.

Here's a simple way to handle e-mail and Web site inquiries from customers: Ask competent sales or service staff to read every e-mail received from a legitimate customer or prospect. Instruct them to e-mail back immediately with a full reply or a request for more information. Also instruct them to ask how the person would like to proceed. Switch to phone? Stick with e-mail? Get detailed information in the mail? See a salesperson? Visit a location of the business? In other words, get the communication going, and give customers choices so you can find out what their style preferences are.

What exactly *is* their way?

Now I want to take a look at your style and compare it to a difficult customer's style (or you may substitute a difficult distributor, associate, or anyone else you want to work better with in the future). Profiling your own style is critical to understanding how your style compares to your customer's.

To complete a style profile, you answer some simple disagree-agree questions, which you can find in the Customer Service Diagnostic (see the next section). These questions give you eight separate scores, which you can plot on a simple graph in order to draw your own style profile and compare it with your customer's. The first four sets of questions address thinking style. The next four sets of questions address interpersonal style. Together, they determine how you work with customers and how your customers prefer you to work with them.

When you look at all this information about yourself and a difficult customer, you almost always find that you and the customer have some significant points of difference. When you adjust your style to accommodate the customer's profile, you overcome those points of difference.

The method I explain is very simple, but it works only when you have the information needed to analyze profiles correctly. Most of the time, people are unable to realize these key style differences until they use a formal diagnostic tool and gain some experience with it. So I suggest that you fill in the Difficult Customer Diagnostic form, which the next section shows. Or you can print clean copies of this and the next form from your CD. The filenames are CD1801 and CD1802.

Utilizing the Difficult Customer Diagnostic

The Difficult Customer Diagnostic is based on an activity I first used with a group of sales managers from a General Motors division. I brought along copies of an inventory of personal style and used them to find out why these salespeople had difficulty communicating with certain customers. In theory, I reasoned that interpersonal style differences could be quite important. And I knew that such assessments were great tools for diagnosing and fixing style problems in interpersonal communications because I had already used them to help work teams learn how to function together more effectively. But would the method work as well in the sales context? I asked the sales managers in my workshop to bear with me and give the idea a try.

The results were overwhelming. The assessment was by far the most effective and popular activity I'd ever conducted in a sales or marketing workshop. Every participant was truly excited about the results. The assessment was simple and easy to run, and it produced results that pleased and informed the participants. At the end of the day, they crowded around me, wanting to talk about this particular activity rather than anything else I'd covered that day (and I'd presented a great deal of material on marketing-related topics). They also cleaned me out of extra copies of the assessment that I'd brought along. Everyone wanted to take the activity back to her office to share with associates and to use on other customers.

In short, I knew I'd stumbled onto something big. But at that point, I was using forms designed for other applications. I had to edit them with a magic marker to make them work. And I didn't have the well-developed learning points and how-tos of a good training. So I passed the idea over to my training materials company, and we went to work developing a tool and method designed specifically for use in the sales and marketing context.

The training activity we produced was the *Difficult Customer Diagnostic,* which gives salespeople (or customer service representatives) the chance to find out what the style issues are behind the difficulties.

Premise of the method

Some customers are more difficult than others. When salespeople or account representatives have difficulties dealing with a particular customer or prospect, in spite of multiple efforts to get along or close the sale, the problem is often one of style, not substance. Many instances occur in which a salesperson has something of legitimate value to offer the customer but can't make the sale because of a mismatch in their styles. Many instances also occur in which an ongoing sales or service relationship seems to be less productive and more difficult than it should be. Again, style issues may be at fault.

In the modern workplace, employees now commonly receive training in how to flex their styles in order to cooperate more effectively with team members or other co-workers. But this simple principle is rarely applied to sales relationships. In the training activity I provide later in this section, salespeople (or customer service representatives) have the chance to

- ✔ Discover that they have significantly different style profiles than most of their difficult customers
- ✔ Pick out some simple prescriptions about how to communicate more effectively with a difficult customer
- ✔ Find out how to improve their ability to communicate with difficult customers in general by adapting their style to suit the customer's preferences

By knowing how to communicate in the customer's preferred style, the salesperson truly becomes customer oriented. Now try your hand at the Difficult Customer Diagnostic, which I present in the next section.

Answering the questions

Rate each of the following statements based on how well they fit your own style and the style of a specific customer you have in mind. If a statement fits very well, circle "5." If it doesn't fit at all, circle "1." Or circle a number between these two extremes. Here's the scale (this scale is also available on the CD as filename CD1801):

1 = Not at all

2 = Not really

3 = Maybe, maybe not

4 = Usually

5 = Definitely

When you finish answering the questions, calculate your scores by adding each set of five questions and entering the totals in the "Total = ___" sections. You get eight scores for yourself and eight scores for your customer. Each score should be somewhere between 5 and 25.

1. Ra Scores

You	How Well Does Statement Fit?	Customer
1 2 3 4 5	Throws self into project without a plan	1 2 3 4 5
1 2 3 4 5	Takes unstructured approach	1 2 3 4 5
1 2 3 4 5	Does not like to follow instructions	1 2 3 4 5
1 2 3 4 5	Likes to work on many things at once	1 2 3 4 5
1 2 3 4 5	Does things out of order	1 2 3 4 5
Total = ___	<- yours **"Ra" scores** customer's ->	Total = ___

2. Se Scores

You	How Well Does Statement Fit?	Customer
1 2 3 4 5	Likes detailed plans	1 2 3 4 5
1 2 3 4 5	Stays focused on a single goal	1 2 3 4 5
1 2 3 4 5	Does things in proper order	1 2 3 4 5
1 2 3 4 5	Follows instructions	1 2 3 4 5
1 2 3 4 5	Is analytical, not intuitive	1 2 3 4 5
Total = ___	<- yours **"Se" scores** customer's ->	Total = ___

3. Di Scores

You	How Well Does Statement Fit?	Customer
1 2 3 4 5	Seeks options and alternatives	1 2 3 4 5
1 2 3 4 5	Seeks new combinations	1 2 3 4 5
1 2 3 4 5	Has many ideas	1 2 3 4 5
1 2 3 4 5	Gets excited about each new thing	1 2 3 4 5
1 2 3 4 5	Asks unusual questions	1 2 3 4 5
Total = ___	<- yours **"Di" scores** customer's ->	Total = ___

4. Co Scores

You	How Well Does Statement Fit?	Customer
1 2 3 4 5	Narrows down the choices	1 2 3 4 5
1 2 3 4 5	Organizes projects well	1 2 3 4 5
1 2 3 4 5	Combines projects to get them done	1 2 3 4 5
1 2 3 4 5	Good at finishing things	1 2 3 4 5
1 2 3 4 5	Finds common ground in arguments	1 2 3 4 5
Total = ___	<- yours **"Co" scores** customer's ->	Total = ___

5. Pr Scores

You	How Well Does Statement Fit?	Customer
1 2 3 4 5	Likes to work alone	1 2 3 4 5
1 2 3 4 5	Not very social	1 2 3 4 5
1 2 3 4 5	Finds collaboration difficult	1 2 3 4 5
1 2 3 4 5	Distracted by too many people	1 2 3 4 5
1 2 3 4 5	Keeps thoughts to self	1 2 3 4 5
Total = ___	<- yours **"Pr" scores** customer's ->	Total = ___

6. Pu Scores

You	How Well Does Statement Fit?	Customer
1 2 3 4 5	Enjoys working with others	1 2 3 4 5
1 2 3 4 5	Very social	1 2 3 4 5
1 2 3 4 5	Contributes to groups with confidence	1 2 3 4 5
1 2 3 4 5	Stimulated by other people	1 2 3 4 5
1 2 3 4 5	Likes to share ideas with others	1 2 3 4 5
Total = ___	<- yours **"Pu" scores** customer's ->	Total = ___

7. Re Scores

You	How Well Does Statement Fit?	Customer
1 2 3 4 5	Attracts people who want to talk	1 2 3 4 5
1 2 3 4 5	Good at sensing how others feel	1 2 3 4 5
1 2 3 4 5	Open-minded	1 2 3 4 5
1 2 3 4 5	Asks lots of questions	1 2 3 4 5
1 2 3 4 5	Appreciates advice and suggestions	1 2 3 4 5
Total = ___	<- yours **"Re" scores** customer's ->	Total = ___

8. Ex Scores

You	How Well Does Statement Fit?	Customer
1 2 3 4 5	Shares ideas with others	1 2 3 4 5
1 2 3 4 5	Expresses feelings well	1 2 3 4 5
1 2 3 4 5	Has strong opinions	1 2 3 4 5
1 2 3 4 5	Not afraid to disagree	1 2 3 4 5
1 2 3 4 5	Champions own ideas	1 2 3 4 5
Total = ___	<- yours **"Ex" scores** customer's ->	Total = ___

Interpreting your scores

Transfer your scores to each bar of the scoring sheet by circling the appropriate numbers on each side of the black square on the first half of the profile sheet. Then, on each bar, darken the area between your two scores to see what your style looks like. Is the bar centered or biased toward one side? (Usually, people have a clear bias.) And is the bar short, indicating a lack of flexibility, or is it long, indicating that you can use both styles? (Usually, bars are fairly short.)

Next, transfer your customer's scores to the second half of the profile sheet. Darken the areas between scores to draw the customer's bars, just as you did for your own. (You can print out CD1802 and CD1803 for easier use.)

Your profile

Random   Sequential

25 23 21 19 15 13 11 9 7 5 ■ 5 7 9 11 13 15 19 21 23 25

How do you think?

Divergent   Convergent

25 23 21 19 15 13 11 9 7 5 ■ 5 7 9 11 13 15 19 21 23 25

What do you think about?

Private   Public

25 23 21 19 15 13 11 9 7 5 ■ 5 7 9 11 13 15 19 21 23 25

Do others use up or give you energy?

Receptive   Expressive

25 23 21 19 15 13 11 9 7 5 ■ 5 7 9 11 13 15 19 21 23 25

Do you tend to listen or talk more?

Your customer's profile

Random   Sequential

25 23 21 19 15 13 11 9 7 5 ■ 5 7 9 11 13 15 19 21 23 25

How does customer think?

Divergent   Convergent

25 23 21 19 15 13 11 9 7 5 ■ 5 7 9 11 13 15 19 21 23 25

What does customer think about?

Private   Public

25 23 21 19 15 13 11 9 7 5 ■ 5 7 9 11 13 15 19 21 23 25

Do others use up or give customer energy?

Receptive   Expressive

25 23 21 19 15 13 11 9 7 5 ■ 5 7 9 11 13 15 19 21 23 25

Does customer tend to listen or talk more?

The scoring sheet appears on the CD-ROM with the filename CD1803.

Comparing your profile to your customer's

Now that you've plotted your own profile and your difficult customer's profile, you simply need to compare the two and see where the biggest difference lies. On one or more of the bars, your score is probably quite different from the customer's. Your shaded area is centered toward one side, while hers is centered toward the other side. Right?

I knew it. Otherwise, she probably wouldn't be a difficult customer! Make a note of which dimensions you differ on so you can use the prescriptions I give you in the next section. For instance, are you more of a divergent thinker, whereas she's a strongly convergent thinker? (The second line of the profiles shows this dimension.)

Make a note of the one or more dimensions in which your profile is clearly different from your customer's profile. These differences are most likely the root of your difficulties.

If you want to know more about what each of the scores in your Difficult Customer Diagnostic means, check out the CD under the file named CD1803. The file includes an interpretation key that gives you detailed descriptions and examples illustrating what each of the style names means. See whether your style profile rings true when you look up the styles that dominate your profile.

Prescribing the cure

Now you need to figure out how to adapt your style to your customer's style. For instance, if you're more of a divergent thinker and your customer is strongly convergent, then you need to adapt the way you think and talk about business with this customer to accommodate her need for a convergent style. For example, convergent thinkers like to focus narrowly and want to move toward closure. They don't want to keep hearing about more complexities or choices. They want a neat, orderly, directional process that gets them to their end goal efficiently. And you can give them that. You can easily accommodate this style need when you understand it.

The preceding example is only one of thousands. To find out how to deal with your difficult customer, simply locate the appropriate section in the table that appears on the CD with the filename CD1804.

If you plan to flex your sales style to work well with a difficult customer, you need to prepare by reviewing the appropriate cell(s) of the table before you interact with the customer. If you fear that you may have difficulty sticking to the guidelines in a meeting or telephone conversation, you should make some notes to use during the interaction so you don't forget your game plan for taming the difficult customer.

Adjusting your service style

Customer service is integral to good marketing because it builds profitable long-term relationships. Just as in sales, the Difficult Customer Diagnostic works well in handling customer service problems and complaints when you have trouble soothing the customer. Some customers just don't like your style. They get increasingly irritated when you try to calm them down. Or they demand to speak to someone else. Some customers become chronic complainers who never seem satisfied. Often the roots of these service difficulties are the differences in your cognitive or interpersonal styles, which the Difficult Customer Diagnostic measures.

When you flex your service style to make sure you communicate well with all your customers, everything goes much more smoothly. You acquire loyal customers who like your style and feel that they have good, open communication with you. You're also more likely to hear about any problems early on so you can move to fix them.

CD1805 on the CD, the Difficult Customer Diagnostic, is interpreted for use in ongoing service interactions or in coping with an escalating customer problem. The principles are the same as in the sales interactions in CD1804, but the application is a little different, so the more service-oriented table is useful to have, too.

Making Sure Your Ads Are Stylin'

A really cool extension of the profiling exercise is to profile the style of your marketing communications. In other words, use an ad, brochure, or Web site (or several of them) to fill in the "you" side of the Difficult Customer Diagnostic. Here are some tips:

✔ Ask yourself how well each statement describes the style that your marketing communications use.

✔ Then ask yourself how well the statements describe your customers in general.

Or, if you have the time and resources, turn the diagnostic into a customer survey (just block out the right-hand answer column) and collect data from 50 or more customers about their own styles.

Does a pattern exist? Which style profile is most common among customers? Does it clash with the style of your ad or Web site? If so, rework your marketing communications to match the dominant customer-style needs so you don't turn customers off with incompatible marketing materials.

Most copywriters and designers who develop marketing materials have unusual style profiles that clash with the average customer. Designers are more random and divergent, and their work is sometimes more public or "in-your-face" than customers want. You can use the prescriptions of the Difficult Customer Diagnostic to help shift designers' styles to be more compatible with customers' preferences — making it easier for your marketing pieces to connect with customers.

You can profit from your knowledge of your own style profile by seeking out customers who particularly like your style and sharing your profile with them. After all, doing business with people like you is always easier. You can use an ad, Web site, sales letter, or newsletter to "call for" people with profiles like your own. Make sure that the piece is an extreme example of your profile. For instance, if you're sequential, make the copy follow a 1-2-3 outline format. Those who share your sequential style are going to enjoy reading it and are going to love your style!

On the CD

Check out the following items on the CD-ROM:

- ✔ Difficult Customer Diagnostic (CD1801)
- ✔ Interpreting Your Score (how to analyze the numbers) (CD1802)
- ✔ Interpretation Keys for the Difficult Customer Diagnostic (CD1803)
- ✔ How to Adapt Your Sales Style for a Difficult Customer (CD1804)
- ✔ How to Adapt Your Service Style for a Difficult Customer (CD1805)

Part VI
The Part of Tens

The 5th Wave   By Rich Tennant

ADVERTISIN' DEPT.

"Snappy ad copy. And it really got my attention."

In this part . . .

1 give you more than 30 quick tips and suggestions for boosting your sales and making your marketing more effective and profitable. Look for ideas that will save you money, maximize your marketing impact, boost results from your Web site, and stimulate new and creative ways of landing new business. And if these ideas aren't enough, feel free to steal as many more ideas as you want from the Web site that supports this book, www.insightsformarketing.com. I'll keep updating this site with more ways for you to make your marketing pay off in profitable sales growth!

Chapter 19

Ten Great Marketing Strategies

· ·

*I*n this chapter, I review an assortment of clever marketing strategies from my files of great marketing benchmarks. (I should add that some of these stories come from Professor Charles D. Schewe, my coauthor on *The Portable MBA in Marketing* (Wiley), who's a big believer in the value of marketing cases and has collected them for many years.) If you don't collect great examples to inspire you, start your collection now. It's an excellent way to keep your thinking fresh and to profit from the insights of others.

Sponsoring a Community Event

PeoplesBank is a New England regional bank that's making a push to open branches in new communities. In my town, the folks at PeoplesBank are promoting their new branch by sponsoring a summer art festival run by our chamber of commerce. The festival, which takes place twice a month from June through September, showcases 30 to 40 artists in outdoor tents scattered up and down the main street of town. The tents are attractive, high-roofed blue structures, and the name PeoplesBank and its logo are emblazoned on one side of each tent.

Suffice it to say that PeoplesBank is the single-most visible brand name in the entire town when the show is going on. And because the show draws visitors from throughout the bank's regional market, it gets a lot of bang for its marketing buck.

Finding the Right Trade Show

Molly Cantor is a successful potter who runs her own studio where she produces an assortment of attractive handmade mugs, plates, bowls, teapots, and so on. Unlike many small-scale studios, Molly's studio distributes products all over the United States. Stores in many states buy her work, and she's usually booked with orders as much as one year in advance.

How does Molly manage to be so effectively "on the map" as a supplier to upscale gift stores? She simply attends one trade show each year where she rents a booth, shows her work, and collects orders. The show attracts buyers from gift stores and galleries far and wide, and they place their orders at the show and then reorder by phone during the year if the products sell well. Picking the right trade show — and focusing all your resources on getting there and presenting you and your products well — is often the best way to build a wholesale business.

Remembering What Your Customers Like

Another great marketing strategy is to keep a record of likes and dislikes in a customer's file or database entry. This technique enables you and your company to cater to each customer's preferences.

Ritz-Carlton hotel services (my inspiration for this idea) maintains a computerized database of past preferences so that returning guests receive customized service. For example, if you ordered a Kendall-Jackson Chardonnay from room service in a Ritz-Carlton hotel last year, you may get a complimentary glass of the same wine the next time you check in to any of its hotels or resorts around the world — a simple, inexpensive customer perk, but one that never fails to wow customers.

Rewarding Large Purchasers

One Christmas shopping season, retailer Toys "R" Us gave away a free Tickle Me Elmo doll to any customer who made a purchase of more than $100, which is significantly more than the average purchase at the store. This inspired me to begin offering free products to customers of my firm's Web site when they placed an order above a certain size — a strategy that we still use today because it's so effective in boosting the number and size of our orders. Too often marketers offer deals that aren't linked to the size of purchase. Thus, businesses tend to reward many small customers. But in most businesses, the fewer big customers are the most valuable. Why not target your promotions to them? Here's one way to go about it:

1. **Calculate your average purchase size.**

2. **Multiply it by 1.5.**

3. **Offer an incentive (discount, free product, special gift, reward, or extra service) to anyone who buys more than that amount.**

Sending Interesting Mailings

Computer supplier CDW sent out an unusual mailing: a red-and-white checked pizza box that said "The right ingredients . . ." on top. When prospects opened it, they discovered those "ingredients" in a list of the company's services and a copy of the latest catalog. Potential customers also found an amusing Velcro dartboard in the shape of a pizza to hang on their walls. And, yes, CDW imprinted its logo and contact information on the dartboard.

Any mailing to customer or prospect lists has a dramatically higher response rate when it's a box or envelope with something bumpy inside. People stop to wonder what's in bulky mailings, and they take the time to open them. They give those odd mailings their attention, which gives you the opening you need to communicate with prospective customers.

Allowing Customers to Access You Easily

At Motorola, key customers receive telephone numbers that link them to top executives at any hour of the day. The idea is to make sure that customers can get in touch immediately, whenever they feel the urge. No leaving phone messages. No busy signals or voice mail. No waiting — ever!

Inspired by this example, I started giving my personal cellphone number to my best customers. They don't use it very often, but when they do, it's because they have an important question. And I'm always glad I'm available to take their calls.

Sharing the Customer's Pain

Service problems aren't very real for the average employee who thinks that these problems are the customer's, not the employee's. To bring service issues to life, try scheduling a weekly "Hour of Horror." Call an all-employees meeting to get everyone into the action. Use this time to share customer complaints, lost customers, and other service nightmares. Ask for suggestions about how to fix specific problems or avoid similar problems in the future.

Turn a negative situation into a positive one. When one of my colleagues received extra Time Life Music CDs even though she'd already canceled (with a payment due), she called and the company told her to keep them free of charge for her trouble.

Letting Prospects Test You Out

Do you think that your product is superior? Let prospects find out by offering them a free trial. Apple used this technique successfully with its "test drive a Macintosh" promotion, and it's a traditional practice among high-end rug dealers. They know that if prospects put a beautiful Oriental rug in their living room for just a few days, the odds of their buying it increase dramatically.

Getting Everyone Talking about You

With a little creativity, any business or salesperson can take advantage of the outrageousness strategy. One children's bookstore called Wild Rumpus (Minneapolis, Minnesota) lets roosters and cats roam freely through the aisles. Birds, lizards, and tarantulas peer out of cages, and a family of rats lives beneath a glass floor. A special children's entrance features a 4-foot-high purple doorway. Anyone who visits this store tells everyone else to go there, too.

In another example, a building materials distributor made sales visits with his favorite prop — a cinder block sitting on an elaborate velvet cushion. He entered the prospect's office bearing his cinder block like the crown jewels of England. Placing the jewel gingerly on the desk, he'd launch into his sales pitch before the prospect had fully recovered from amazement.

Working for Your Customer

Companies that sell to other businesses seldom understand their customers as well as they should. Weyerhaeuser (a forest products company) is an exception to this rule. This company lends many of its employees to customer companies where they work for a week as volunteers. They return with lots of insight and leave behind a reservoir of goodwill and friendship. And they often return with value-adding ideas that make customers happier.

Chapter 20

Ten Ways to Make Marketing Pay

In This Chapter

▶ Ways to cut your marketing costs

▶ How to get more customers

Marketing needs to be bottom-line oriented. It's not a black hole that you toss money into after you pay for the payroll and healthcare; it's a vital part of a growing, successful business and you must approach it professionally at all times. Here are some tips to help you make your marketing a productive and financially-sound part of your business.

Print It Yourself

Traditionally, marketers have been heavy users of printing and photocopying services, and the printing bills tend to get out of control in a hurry. Today you can purchase color laser printers that handle tabloid sheets of paper (up to 11 x 17 inches) and even print long banners. For example, my office uses an Oki C9300 to crank out color catalog pages, covers for pamphlets and booklets, color fliers and product sheets, color covers for binders, and many other marketing materials. The cost per sheet ranges between 1¢ and 10¢, depending on the size and amount of color. With this printer, my company can produce a high-quality color catalog and mail it to 1,000 people without using any printing services. The savings is substantial — we estimated that we paid back the printer's $2,500 purchase cost in the first month!

Do More PR

If anything you do or say might be newsworthy, make sure that you tell the media about it early and often. You need to send out a press release at least every season, if not every month. Publicity is free advertising, and it ought to be a bigger part of your marketing than it probably is.

Use More Distributors

I haven't seen any business that can't sell through other businesses in one way or another. Creatively using distributors (call them sales partners, if you like) is a great way to expand your marketing footprint on someone else's nickel. For example, in my business, someone has the responsibility of seeking and courting distributors, and the goal is to try to add a new one each month. Our sales through distributors have grown from zero a few years ago, to about 20 percent of our total sales now. That's a lot of business we wouldn't have found on our own!

Give More Product Away

It's a paradox: The more you give away, the more you make and the more economical your marketing program is. This paradox is true because, in general, the best advertisement for a product is the product itself (and I'm using the word "product" broadly here, to include services or whatever it is you may want to sell).

So please, find more ways to give prospects an opportunity to sample your wares or experience your service. Doing so cuts out a lot of expensive marketing by giving your prospects the real thing instead of having to spend your time and money trying to tell them about it. Some of the best consulting jobs I've ever done in marketing involved simply figuring out how to get the client's free samples, test drives, or other giveaways to good prospects, so that the product could sell itself. Nothing is more powerful in all of marketing.

And nothing beats a great product, so always work at improving the quality of your products and services. Today's consumers are very informed and you can't fool them more than once!

Edit

As a writer as well as a marketer, I often notice that marketing materials, Web sites, and so forth are out of control. Sometimes my company helps a client save money and produce better results by simply cutting down and cleaning up all its written materials. I guarantee that you can punch up the impact and cut costs if you edit all your own materials with the goal of cutting the total number of marketing pages in half. Give it a try.

Eat Out More

In many businesses, there is the formal marketing program, and then there is the real program — where the good customers actually come from. More often than not, customers really come from word of mouth — from the personal contacts and networks of key people in the business. If this is true for your business, then consider cutting the formal marketing stuff (ads, catalogs, and so on) back by 15 percent and putting that money into networking instead. Go to more events and conferences. Take more customers and industry experts out for lunch. If your personal contacts can produce good leads, then you ought to be eating out every day. Become the best entertainer in your industry.

Slash Unproductive Programs

Every business has a few marketing activities or expenses that don't pull their weight. Usually they exist because they're traditional, and nobody thinks to question having them. Well, I think it's time to sacrifice these sacred cows. If you never seem to get any sales from those expensive ads in your industry's premiere trade magazine, try cutting them out of the budget and see whether anything bad happens.

Invest More in Your Stars

The 80:20 rule usually applies to marketing: 80 percent of the results come from 20 percent of the marketing activities. So figure out what your best marketing activities are and shift funding toward them. For example, in many businesses today, the return on investment for Web-based marketing is considerably higher than for print advertising, yet print still gets a bigger share of the budget. Increasing your return on investment from marketing is easy — you simply shifting your spending into the highest-return activities that you have.

Stage Events

Events like industry breakfasts and how-to seminars for customers and prospects are a powerful way to make a connection and establish your identity as a leading expert in your field. But events take advance planning and organization, so many marketers are intimidated by them and never use them.

Your business should stage at least one high-profile event each quarter. They're surprisingly economical ways to build visibility and attract or retain top customers (see *Marketing For Dummies,* written by Yours Truly and published by Wiley, for how-to information). Oh, but keep those events modest in scope, make sure to invite only those prospects who fit your profile for good customers. You don't want to waste time and money entertaining people who won't ever make a big purchase.

Control Product Costs

The cost of purchasing or producing your product is a hidden driver of your marketing and sales efficiency. Given a big enough margin, you can afford to market anything. Too often, however, I find that my clients expected a poor marketing program to sell something on a razor-thin margin. With a budget like that, nothing is left to spend on sales and marketing, and this situation gives the illusion that the marketing program is to blame when profits are poor.

Rather than blaming the marketing, try cutting costs and improving the margin on the product. The general rule in my business is that we want at least a five-fold difference between our basic production or purchase cost and the list price that we sell the product at. We spend a lot of time and imagination seeking ways to reduce our product costs so that we can market with a big margin. Then we can afford to do good marketing and build a following for the product.

Chapter 21

Ten-Plus Ways to Market on the Web

*T*he Internet is obviously the hottest new marketing medium and is here to stay, so most businesses are at least experimenting with it. Whether you decide to go whole hog and launch an e-commerce business or you just dabble in Internet marketing, you need to be aware of its many valuable contributions to marketing. Here are a few options that are working well for many businesses:

✔ Create interactive, interesting, and/or informational *virtual brochures* on Web sites for customers and prospects. Sites often generate good leads.

✔ Go fishing for prospects by sending e-mails or buying banner ads.

✔ Build relationships with prospects by creating e-mail newsletters.

✔ Create a *virtual store* or *virtual catalog* where people can go to examine your wares and place orders.

✔ Create a site that fulfills the service needs of your customers — for example, by giving them up-to-date information about their orders.

And here are other winning ideas for marketing on the Web.

Have a Well-Defined Objective

No matter how you choose to use your Web site, you must have a clear marketing objective. When you have a marketing objective, you can see what each Web-marketing option is supposed to do for you and why it may appeal to prospects. The basic rule to marketing on the Internet is: *Always design your Web marketing with a specific, well-defined, marketing objective in mind.*

You'll never make money by picking up a hammer and banging things with it, nor will you help your business by spending time or money "creating a presence" on the Web. Know what you're accomplishing. Know why the Web is a good way to accomplish it. Then, and only then, are you ready to discover how to take advantage of this complex tool's many possibilities.

One of the best objectives is to use the Web to generate leads. Another good objective is to try switching your customers from person-to-person to Web-based ordering. Whatever your objective, be clear about it and design your Web site to achieve it.

Use a Power Name

Now that you've figured out what you want your Web site to accomplish, you can pick and register a name for it. Check with your Internet Service Provider (ISP) or any number of registration services that advertise on the Web to find out how to register the name of your choice. And don't be disappointed if the first name you try is already taken. Just try a variant of it.

The best names meet three simple criteria:

✔ They're relevant to the site's purpose.

✔ They're easy to remember and spell.

✔ They're unique — and not easily confused with competitors.

So, for example, www.airtravel.com would be a great name for a site that brokers airplane tickets and vacations involving an airplane flight. It's relevant. It's easy. Nobody is likely to spell it wrong. People tend to remember it because it's obvious and intuitive. Names like that have real marketing power, and you should keep thinking until you have a power name for your business, too. (In fact, I see that a business is using that name to broker Caribbean vacations. More power to them!)

Be outrageous

An interesting alternative is to choose an outrageous name that sticks in everyone's minds like Krazy Glue.

Bookseller Amazon.com is a good example of the effectiveness of this strategy. The name sounds like the company has something to do with travel in Brazil or the preservation of rain forests. But that's not really a problem for Amazon.com because it spent so much money on advertising and got so much press coverage that it taught us all to associate its name with its products. Maybe you should use this strategy, too. For instance, if you market quality cuts of beef on the Web, you could see whether karatechop.com is available and create a high-powered site that uses lots of exciting martial arts images to promote your product.

Be clear

When choosing a domain name, avoid words that can be spelled more than one way. Often people give out Web addresses verbally over the phone, in conversation, or on the radio in an interview or ad. You don't want to have to spell a name or explain that the user has to type an underline to separate two words.

For example, if you're a sail maker, you might choose the address sail.com. But this address is ambiguous because people may think that you're saying *sale* rather than *sail*. Better to lengthen it enough to make the name unambiguous. Sailmakers.com works better.

Be polymorphic

If you're marketing in a non-English-speaking country, consider creating more than one domain name: one in the local language and one in English. English seems to be emerging as the dominant language of the Web, at least for businesses. And your ISP can easily route visitors from more than one address to the same site.

Give Away Great Content

People don't surf the Internet to read sales pitches and lengthy brag-a-logues about how great a company is. The number-one reason people return to a site is content. To attract and retain high-quality visitors, you need to create and post valuable content. That task is a challenge. Are you up to it? If not, consider hiring a writer to create some good content. Also see whether you can give away some technical information or advice that people will value. Your site needs to be a modern-day encyclopedia, a place where prospective customers go for help. The more information you give away, the more you'll sell. Take a look at the site I created (with the able help of my associates Angela and Eric — thanks guys!) to support this book, `www.insightsformarketing.com`. It has dozens of pages of serious, hard-core information that we give away for free.

Check Your Files

What information do you have that you can give away on your site? Most businesses have lots of raw content just gathering dust. Search your file cabinets and hard drives for how-to lists, old press releases, catalogs, brochures, and even old customer proposals or reports. You can create lots of useful pages by editing these source materials.

Minimize Your Load Time

When people have to wait for a table, their interest in a restaurant declines. The same is true for a Web site. No matter how much cool information you give away or how many great products you sell at incredible prices, your site may not be appealing unless people can get to it in a hurry.

What's a hurry? One way to think about it is to compare your site's load time to the load times of some of the most popular e-commerce sites:

Site	Average Load Time (Seconds)
Amazon.com	2.6
bn.com	4.7
Cdnow.com	5.1
jcpenney.com	2.8

I wonder whether or not it's a coincidence that Amazon.com does a lot more business than competitor bn.com (the Barnes and Noble Web site) and that it happens to have a 45 percent shorter load time, too?

Anyway, you get the idea. If your load time isn't measured in a very small number of seconds, you're going to lose a lot of potential visitors. Those big, expensive sites are investing a lot in fast load times, and they're setting the pace for anyone who wants to market on the Web.

Create a Sense of Community

Encourage interaction among visitors, for example, through the use of bulletin boards, discussion forums, and chat rooms (the latter only works well if you have high traffic). When people make meaningful connections on your site, traffic grows and you generate more interest, leads, and sales.

Hold Contests

Stimulate interest through the use of contests for visitors. Pick something that's participatory (visitors submit something of their own) and give prizes or announce winners fairly frequently — for example, every Friday. Post submissions, if possible, to encourage people to spend time examining them. (For instance, a florist may invite people to submit photos of floral arrangements and pick the best arrangement every two weeks.) You may have to do some publicity to let people know about your contest, but the ongoing results can be well be worth the time!

Add a Weekly News Feature

Provide new content regularly. You can do so in a "What's New" section or page or in a regularly updated "News and Views" section, a guest column, or a "Headline News" section summarizing the news in your industry.

Links

Use links to create lots of easy paths back to your site. Often people don't return to a Web site because they simply don't recall it. But if they run into a link and remember that your site was great, then they'll probably come back. How do you create links? The general strategy is to ask other people with Web sites. Usually they'll want a reciprocal agreement, which is fine. Also, try adding a "Link to Us" page on your site with linking images that other site managers can copy and use on their sites.

Appendix

About the CD

- ▶ System requirements
- ▶ What you find on the CD
- ▶ Troubleshooting

System Requirements

Make sure that your computer meets the minimum system requirements listed in this section. If your computer doesn't have the following features, you may encounter problems when using the CD.

- ✔ A PC with a Pentium processor or a faster processor; or, a Mac OS computer with a 68040 processor or a faster processor

- ✔ Microsoft Windows 98 or later; or, Mac OS system software 8.1 or later

- ✔ At least 16 MB of total RAM; for best performance, I recommend having at least 32 MB of RAM

- ✔ A CD-ROM drive

- ✔ A monitor capable of displaying at least 256 colors or grayscale

If you need more information on the basics, check out these books published by Wiley: *PCs For Dummies*, 9th Edition, by Dan Gookin; *Macs For Dummies*, 8th Edition, by David Pogue; *iMac For Dummies*, 3rd Edition, by David Pogue; *Mac OS X For Dummies*, 3rd Edition, by Bob LeVitus; or *Windows 98 For Dummies, Windows 2000 Professional For Dummies,* or *Windows XP For Dummies,* all by Andy Rathbone.

Using the CD with Windows

To install the items from the CD to your hard drive, follow these steps:

1. **Insert the CD into your computer's CD-ROM drive.**

2. **The CD-ROM interface will appear. The interface provides a simple point-and-click way so you can easily explore the contents of the CD.**

If the CD-ROM interface doesn't appear, follow these steps to access the CD:

1. **Click the Start button on the left end of the taskbar, and then choose Run from the menu that pops up.**

2. **In the dialog box that appears, type D:\SETUP.EXE. (If your CD-ROM drive isn't drive D, fill in the appropriate letter in place of *D*.)**

   The CD Interface described in the preceding set of steps will appear.

How to Use the CD with the Mac OS

To install the items from the CD to your hard drive, follow these steps:

1. **Insert the CD into your computer's CD-ROM drive.**

   In a moment, an icon representing the CD you just inserted will appear on your Mac desktop. Chances are, the icon will look like a CD-ROM.

2. **Double click the CD icon to show the CD's contents.**

3. **Double click the file called License.txt.**

   This file contains the end-user license that you agree to by using the CD. When you're done reading the license, you can close the window that displayed the file.

4. **Double click the Read Me First icon.**

   This text file contains information about the CD's programs and any last-minute instructions you need to know about installing the programs on the CD that I don't cover in this appendix.

5. **Most programs come with installers. To use an installer, simply open the program's folder on the CD and double click the icon with the words Install, Installer, or Sea (for self-extracting archive).**

6. **If you don't find an installer, drag the program's folder from the CD window and drop it onto your hard drive icon.**

What You'll Find on the CD

In this section, I tell you what software and files you'll find on your CD.

Software

You'll find the following software on your CD:

- ✔ **Excel Viewer:** Excel Viewer is a freeware program that allows you to view but not edit most Microsoft Excel spreadsheets. Certain features of Microsoft Excel documents may not work as expected from within Excel Viewer.

- ✔ **Adobe Reader:** Adobe Reader is a freeware program that allows you to view but not edit Adobe Portable Document Files (pdf).

- ✔ **OpenOffice.org:** OpenOffice.org is a free multi-platform office productivity suite. It's similar to Microsoft Office or Lotus SmartSuite, but OpenOffice.org is absolutely free. It includes word processing, spreadsheet, presentation, and drawing applications that enable you to create professional documents, newsletters, reports, and presentations. It supports most file formats of other office software. You should be able to edit and view any files created with other office software.

Shareware programs are fully functional, free trial versions of copyrighted programs. If you like particular programs, register with their authors for a nominal fee and receive licenses, enhanced versions, and technical support. *Freeware programs* are free, copyrighted games, applications, and utilities. You can copy them to as many PCs as you like — for free — but they have no technical support. *GNU software* is governed by its own license, which is included inside the folder of the GNU software. There are no restrictions on distribution of this software. See the GNU license for more details. Trial, demo, or evaluation versions are usually limited either by time or functionality (such as being unable to save projects).

Chapter files

The chapter files on the CD all fall into one of the following categories:

- ✔ **Word documents:** You can work with these forms to fit your own marketing needs.

- ✔ **Excel spreadsheets:** Many of the book's worksheets are in this format. Simply fill in the blanks, and you're on your way.

✔ **Adobe Acrobat (pdf) files:** These files illustrate various examples, such as a sample brochure or newsletter. You can't change these files, but you can print them out, if you like.

The following list summarizes all the chapter files on the CD:

CD0101	Customer Commitment Worksheet
CD0102	Customer Survey
CD0103	Know Your Customer Worksheet
CD0104	Know Yourself Worksheet
CD0105	Detailed Customer Commitment Worksheet
CD0106	Five-Minute Marketing Plan
CD0201	Hiam's Marketing Audit
CD0202	Hiam's Marketing Audit Score Form
CD0203	Analyzing and Interpreting Your Marketing Audit
CD0204	Marketing Agenda: Actions Suggested by the Marketing Audit
CD0301	Marketing Plan Template
CD0302	Marketing Budget Worksheet
CD0303	Sales Projection Worksheet
CD0401	Marketing Research Process Diagram
CD0402	Seven Questions to Ask When Reviewing a Survey
CD0403	Customer Debriefing Form (template)
CD0404	7 x 7 Customer Satisfaction Survey
CD0405	Customer Service Audit (template)
CD0501	Creative Roles Analysis
CD0601	Evaluation Form 1
CD0602	Two Dimensions of Your Appeal
CD0603	Evaluation Form 2
CD0701	Modern Memoirs Brochure
CD0702	Script for Soliciting a Testimonial
CD0703	Testimonial Response Script
CD0704	Letter Script for Testimonials
CD0705	Catalog Page from Human Resource Development Press

CD0801	Advertising Objective Worksheet
CD0802	Advertising Budget Template
CD0901	An Image Ad Template
CD0902, 0903	Informative Ad Templates
CD0904, 0905	Call-to-Action Ad Templates
CD0906	Tall Ad or Brochure Cover
CD1001	Sample Business Cards
CD1002	Sample Letterhead, Envelope, and Brochure
CD1201	Coupon Profitability Analysis
CD1301, 1302	Collective Copies newsletters
CD1303	Verité Newsletter
CD1304	The Umass Family Business Center Newsletter
CD1305	Alfredo's Photo Gallery News
CD1401	Century Furniture's New Product Announcement Press Release
CD1402	APEX Performance Systems' New Process Press Release
CD1501	Prospect Analysis Sheet
CD1502	Question Preplanning Form
CD1601	Closing Scripts
CD1701	Attitudes of Success Profile
CD1801	Difficult Customer Diagnostic
CD1802	Interpreting Your Score (how to analyze the numbers)
CD1803	Interpretation Keys for the Difficult Customer Diagnostic
CD1804	How to Adapt Your Sales Style for a Difficult Customer
CD1805	How to Adapt Your Service Style for a Difficult Customer

If You Have Problems (of the CD Kind)

I tried to compile programs that work on most computers with the minimum number of system requirements. Alas, your computer may differ, and for some reason, some programs may not work properly.

The two likeliest problems are that your computer doesn't have enough memory (RAM) for the programs you want to use or your computer has other programs running that are affecting the installation or running of a program. If you get error messages like `Not enough memory` or `Setup cannot continue`, try one or more of the following methods and then try using the software again:

- ✔ **Turn off any anti-virus software that you have on your computer.** Installers sometimes mimic virus activity and make your computer incorrectly think that a virus is infecting it.

- ✔ **Close all running programs.** The more programs you're running, the less memory is available to other programs. Installers also typically update files and programs, so if you keep other programs running, a program's installation may not work properly.

- ✔ **Have your local computer store add more RAM to your computer.** This solution is, admittedly, a drastic and somewhat expensive step. However, if you have a Windows 95 or later PC or a Mac OS computer with a PowerPC chip, adding more memory can really help your computer's speed and allow more programs to run at the same time.

If you still have trouble with the CD-ROM, please call the Wiley Product Technical Support phone number: 800-762-2974. Outside the United States, call 317-572-3994. You can also contact Wiley Product Technical Support through the Internet at `http://www.wiley.com/techsupport`. Wiley Publishing provides technical support only for installation and other general quality control items; for technical support on the applications themselves, consult the program's vendor or author.

To place additional orders or to request information about other Wiley products, please call 877-762-2974.

Index

• *D* •

• *E* •

• F •

• G •

• Q •

Notes

FOR DUMMIES®

The easy way to get more done and have more fun

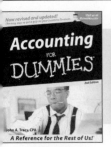

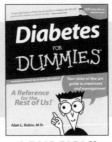

FOR DUMMIES®

A world of resources to help you grow

HOME, GARDEN & HOBBIES

Feng Shui For Dummies
0-7645-5295-3

Gardening For Dummies
0-7645-5130-2

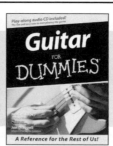

Guitar For Dummies
0-7645-5106-X

Also available:

Auto Repair For Dummies
(0-7645-5089-6)

Chess For Dummies
(0-7645-5003-9)

Home Maintenance For
Dummies
(0-7645-5215-5)

Organizing For Dummies
(0-7645-5300-3)

Piano For Dummies
(0-7645-5105-1)

Poker For Dummies
(0-7645-5232-5)

Quilting For Dummies
(0-7645-5118-3)

Rock Guitar For Dummies
(0-7645-5356-9)

Roses For Dummies
(0-7645-5202-3)

Sewing For Dummies
(0-7645-5137-X)

FOOD & WINE

Cooking For Dummies
0-7645-5250-3

Cookies For Dummies
0-7645-5390-9

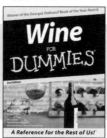

Wine For Dummies
0-7645-5114-0

Also available:

Bartending For Dummies
(0-7645-5051-9)

Chinese Cooking For
Dummies
(0-7645-5247-3)

Christmas Cooking For
Dummies
(0-7645-5407-7)

Diabetes Cookbook For
Dummies
(0-7645-5230-9)

Grilling For Dummies
(0-7645-5076-4)

Low-Fat Cooking For
Dummies
(0-7645-5035-7)

Slow Cookers For Dummies
(0-7645-5240-6)

TRAVEL

Italy For Dummies
0-7645-5453-0

Hawaii For Dummies
0-7645-5438-7

Las Vegas For Dummies
0-7645-5448-4

Also available:

America's National Parks For
Dummies
(0-7645-6204-5)

Caribbean For Dummies
(0-7645-5445-X)

Cruise Vacations For
Dummies 2003
(0-7645-5459-X)

Europe For Dummies
(0-7645-5456-5)

Ireland For Dummies
(0-7645-6199-5)

France For Dummies
(0-7645-6292-4)

London For Dummies
(0-7645-5416-6)

Mexico's Beach Resorts For
Dummies
(0-7645-6262-2)

Paris For Dummies
(0-7645-5494-8)

RV Vacations For Dummies
(0-7645-5443-3)

Walt Disney World & Orlando
For Dummies
(0-7645-5444-1)

Available wherever books are sold. Go to www.dummies.com or call 1-877-762-2974 to order direct.

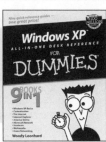

FOR DUMMIES®

Helping you expand your horizons and realize your potential

FOR DUMMIES®

The advice and explanations you need to succeed

SELF-HELP, SPIRITUALITY & RELIGION

0-7645-5302-X

0-7645-5418-2

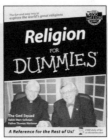
0-7645-5264-3

Also available:

The Bible For Dummies
(0-7645-5296-1)

Buddhism For Dummies
(0-7645-5359-3)

Christian Prayer For Dummies
(0-7645-5500-6)

Dating For Dummies
(0-7645-5072-1)

Judaism For Dummies
(0-7645-5299-6)

Potty Training For Dummies
(0-7645-5417-4)

Pregnancy For Dummies
(0-7645-5074-8)

Rekindling Romance For Dummies
(0-7645-5303-8)

Spirituality For Dummies
(0-7645-5298-8)

Weddings For Dummies
(0-7645-5055-1)

PETS

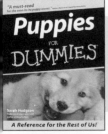
0-7645-5255-4

0-7645-5286-4

0-7645-5275-9

Also available:

Labrador Retrievers For Dummies
(0-7645-5281-3)

Aquariums For Dummies
(0-7645-5156-6)

Birds For Dummies
(0-7645-5139-6)

Dogs For Dummies
(0-7645-5274-0)

Ferrets For Dummies
(0-7645-5259-7)

German Shepherds For Dummies
(0-7645-5280-5)

Golden Retrievers For Dummies
(0-7645-5267-8)

Horses For Dummies
(0-7645-5138-8)

Jack Russell Terriers For Dummies
(0-7645-5268-6)

Puppies Raising & Training Diary For Dummies
(0-7645-0876-8)

EDUCATION & TEST PREPARATION

0-7645-5194-9

0-7645-5325-9

0-7645-5210-4

Also available:

Chemistry For Dummies
(0-7645-5430-1)

English Grammar For Dummies
(0-7645-5322-4)

French For Dummies
(0-7645-5193-0)

The GMAT For Dummies
(0-7645-5251-1)

Inglés Para Dummies
(0-7645-5427-1)

Italian For Dummies
(0-7645-5196-5)

Research Papers For Dummies
(0-7645-5426-3)

The SAT I For Dummies
(0-7645-5472-7)

U.S. History For Dummies
(0-7645-5249-X)

World History For Dummies
(0-7645-5242-2)

Available wherever books are sold. Go to www.dummies.com or call 1-877-762-2974 to order direct.

Wiley Publishing, Inc.
End-User License Agreement